THE BIG
LIE

THE BIG

LIE

SPYING, SCANDAL, AND ETHICAL
COLLAPSE AT HEWLETT-PACKARD

PUBLICAFFAIRS

New York

PublicAffairs books are available at special discounts for bulk purchases in the U.S.
by corporations, institutions, and other organizations. For more information, please
contact the Special Markets Department at the Perseus Books Group, 2300 Chestnut
Street, Suite 200, Philadelphia, PA 19103, call (800) 810-4145, ext. 5000, or e-mail
special.markets@perseusbooks.com.

Book Design by Pauline Brown

Library of Congress Cataloging-in-Publication Data

Bianco, Anthony.

The big lie : spying, scandal, and ethical collapse at Hewlett-Packard / Anthony
Bianco.—1st ed.

p. cm.

Includes bibliographical references and index.

ISBN 978-1-58648-803-1 (hardcover)

1. Hewlett-Packard Company—Management. 2. Hewlett-Packard Company—
Corrupt practices. 3. Business intelligence—United States. I. Title.

HD9696.A3U527 2010

338.7'610040973—dc22

2010002567

First Edition

10 9 8 7 6 5 4 3 2 1

For Dick, Chris, Ann,
Peter, Amy, and Andy

CONTENTS

A NOTE ON SOURCES

This book is based on interviews with many of the central players in the events it describes, as well as on thousands of internal Hewlett-Packard emails and other documents that were made public as part of an investigation of HP conducted by the House Committee on Energy and Commerce in 2006. In addition, I have obtained numerous other documents from private sources.

Hewlett-Packard refused at the outset to grant my request to interview CEO Mark Hurd and certain members of the company's board of directors. Before publication, I sent a letter to HP detailing the book's key observations about the part that Mr. Hurd had played in the events described. In response, an HP representative asserted that my letter contained "many inaccuracies and errant conclusions," but declined to specify them. "We do not believe it would be productive to provide a point-by-point response," he stated.

—ANTHONY BIANCO

CHAPTER ONE

HP SPYGATE

THE BIG LIE is the story of one of the most insidious corporate scandals in the history of Silicon Valley or of U.S. business, for that matter. Although it was called "Spygate" by much of the media that first reported it—and I have used the term to refer to the surveillance that unquestionably took place—it actually was two scandals melded into one: a bone-headed covert operation to find out who was spilling corporate secrets to the press and a cover-up that exacerbated and in some ways outdid the original misdeed. Spygate was exposed to public view; the full story of the cover-up never was. To this day, the tale of what really went on inside Hewlett-Packard's Palo Alto puzzle palace in 2005 and 2006—and who was ultimately responsible for Spygate's transgressions—has been obscured by a campaign of misdirection triumphantly based on the premise that there is no lie as effective as The Big Lie.

In this case "the big lie" was the successful conspiracy to load ultimate responsibility for the spying scheme onto former Hewlett-Packard chairman Patricia Dunn, who was booted from HP's board, vilified in the court of public opinion, pilloried by a Congressional committee, and indicted by the state of California

1

on four felony counts. Dunn, who was battling terminal cancer throughout her ordeal, was not blameless by any means. But this book makes a case for assigning the lion's share of the responsibility for what went wrong inside HP to the executive who took the lead in ousting Dunn and who replaced her as chair: Mark Hurd, the company's chief executive officer.

HP Spygate occurred roughly midway through a decade defined by audacious deceptions in every aspect of American life, from the spurious accounting practiced by the likes of Enron and Worldcom to the Bush Administration's politically motivated warnings about the imminent threat posed by Saddam Hussein's bulging arsenal of weapons of mass destruction and the artfully contrived façades of Bernie Madoff as investment genius and of Tiger Woods as straight-arrow family man. By decade's end, the investment banks of Wall Street had very nearly pulled down the global economy by creating a couple trillion dollars of recklessly risky securities done up to look like gilt-edged, AAA-rated investment merchandise, while regulators either looked the other way or cheered them on.

As measured by its financial consequences, the magnitude of HP's Spygate deceit pales in comparison to Wall Street's trillion-dollar meltdown or Madoff's thievery. In fact, the value of HP's stock has significantly appreciated over the last five years after a long stretch of poor performance. It's no wonder that Hurd, who took charge in 2005, has been hailed as one of corporate America's most effective and operationally astute CEOs. But if there is a universal lesson that can be drawn from the multitudinous scandals of the last decade it is this: Character matters in the end, if not always in the beginning. The point is not merely that moral character is as important to long-run success in business, government, or even professional sports as competency, but that it is an essential component of competency. By this standard, Hurd falls short as a corporate leader.

A great deal is riding on Hewlett-Packard's ability to properly govern itself, for it is a uniquely important, iconic American company. HP may not match Apple and Google for technological cool—as is only to be expected of a company founded in 1939—but today's HP is heir to a gilded corporate legacy that transcends the transitory nature of cool and, for that matter, exceeds the boundaries of Silicon Valley. "Innovative, enlightened, adaptive and fair, Hewlett-Packard under Bill [Hewlett] and Dave [Packard] overshadowed every company of its time, even those much better known and many times larger," observed Michael Malone in *Bill and Dave*, his dual biography of HP's co-founders. "The HP of those years"—essentially the 1960s and 1970s—"still haunts the business world today, as the gold standard few enterprises can ever hope to approach."[1]

Over the last decade, HP has reinvented itself to an extent that few old-line companies ever have, spinning off the scientific instruments business that was its founding glory in the process. Today, HP is a global industrial colossus that is the Valley's largest employer, with 320,000 workers, about the same number in General Electric's employ. It ranks not only as the world's largest computer and printer maker but also as the largest information technology company of any sort, as measured by sales and most every other yardstick that matters. Unhip as it is, HP is one of America's best hopes in a treacherous competitive global economy.

All scandals are sui generis in a sense; the vivid particularities of personality and circumstance are their woof and warp. This certainly was true of Spygate, rooted as it was in the idiosyncrasies of an exceptionally cantankerous and willful board of directors. But the HP saga also reflects universal truths about the nature of corporate life, notably the tendency for ambitious, laudable goals to be undercut by the petty and very personal politics of the boardroom and executive suite. The flaws of human nature are at least as prevalent at the pinnacle of the business world as at its entry level.

HP Spygate also evoked a distinctive set of other, more topical issues, among them the post-9/11 assault on privacy. For agencies of government to secrete security cameras in public places and to intercept personal telephone calls and email messages in the name of fighting terrorism is unnerving enough for many of us. But for a business enterprise to use the same sort of covert techniques in pursuit of a private, self-serving agenda is more objectionable to the average citizen, even when the company believes it is acting in self-defense, as Hewlett-Packard did.

Terrorism is the lesser part of the threat that inspired most large U.S. corporations to continue to build costly, sophisticated security operations right through the last recession. Their overriding fear is the misuse or theft of confidential information, which advances in digital technology have tended to make both more abundant and less secure. In a recent pitch to corporate clients touting its abilities to counter the growing global menace of "electronic espionage," the major consulting firm Deloitte listed these prospective perpetrators: "Hackers, pressure groups, foreign intelligence services, terrorists, disaffected/dishonest employees, investigative journalists, organised crime groups, fraudsters, competitors, contractors (e.g. cleaners), executives on overseas travel (hotels, bars, clubs, airports), or graduates from emerging markets."[2] It's no wonder that many of the biggest U.S. corporations are following the lead of Wal-Mart Stores and reinforcing their internal security divisions with new hires from the Central Intelligence Agency and the Federal Bureau of Investigation.

Corporate spying scandals have been numerous worldwide. Deutsche Bank, Germany's biggest bank, recently admitted that its security department resorted to improperly invasive methods in four separate investigations from 2001 to 2007. In the most egregious of them, the bank targeted a dissident shareholder who'd gotten under the skin of the bank's new chairman with his public criticisms, dispatching agents all the way to his vacation home on the Spanish island of Ibiza. Another charter member of the German business establishment, Deutsche Telekom, confessed in 2009 to a "severe and far-reaching" surveillance scheme that closely paralleled events at HP.[3] Among other things, Deutsche Telekom's security department monitored hundreds of thousands of phone connections in an attempt to uncover which of its board members were routinely leaking news of impending layoffs and other confidential matters to reporters. "Telekom was as full of holes as Swiss cheese," its CEO later complained.[4]

The Big Lie also is a tragicomic case study of corporate board dysfunction—a pervasive failing of the American way of big business that was an important contributor to the great financial crisis of 2008–2009. The boards of Lehman, Bank of America, Fannie Mae, Countrywide, and the rest were throwbacks to the bad old days when, as a recent Yale University study observed, "directors were, in practice, no more than decorative figures beholden to the imperial CEO."[5] For most of the last century, CEOs bred docility into boards by populating them with corporate subordinates, hired-gun lawyers and bankers, close relatives, miscellaneous dignitaries, and golf buddies, many of whom ran other companies. For as long as Bill Hewlett and Dave Packard were around (and they both lived into their eighties) the HP board was old-school incompetence epitomized, though it was only in their dotage that the co-founders packed the panel with assorted sons, daughters, and sons-in-law, many of whom were business neophytes. The clueless passivity of boards made them an obvious target of reform. "In the aftermath of each corporate scandal or crisis," the Yale report noted, "the same question emerged: *Where was the board?*"[6]

In some ways, the so-called corporate-governance movement that started to coalesce in the 1970s around big activist investors like the California Public Employees Retirement System (CalPERS) has been hugely effective. No one (outside executive suites anyway) argues any more that a board's essential role is to support a CEO in all things and offer advice if asked. The new consensus is that directors are supposed to train a gimlet eye on CEOs, to boss them as circumstances require, and to fire them when need be. To this end, a host of new laws and regulations have drastically altered the composition of big company boards, which today are far more demographically and professionally diverse than ever before. Cronyism is now the exception, not the rule, on U.S. boards; more than 80 percent of directors are nominally independent of management, compared with less than 20 percent in 1950.

And yet the fact is that most boards still don't work—or not nearly as well as they should after three decades of shareholder agitation and reform. "There is something wrong with the culture of boards," says George "Jay" Keyworth II, who was an HP director for twenty years and one of the central figures of the Spygate story. "People don't know what their responsibility is. I just don't think most boards do a good job of asking, What is our job? How well is this company doing? How well is it going to be doing a year from now? What are its points of vulnerability and is the

CEO doing a good job?" As Keyworth sees it, "Corporate boards are the last bastion of unexamined corruption in America."[7]

The typical board does indeed seem to be dozing at the wheel, incapable of acting decisively, much less courageously, until crisis is upon them and the value of the company's stock has already been eviscerated. A colossal case in point is General Motors, which has been a prime target of CalPERS and other activist shareholders since the early 1990s. After the federal government finally assumed control of General Motors in 2009, it lost no time in booting seven of the automaker's twelve directors, including CEO Rick Waggoner.

Hewlett-Packard's board proved spectacularly dysfunctional in the end, but passive it was not. In fact, before the HP board was overwhelmed by the ignominy of Spygate, it appeared to have ascended into the vanguard of governance progressivism by sacking the ultra-imperious Carly Fiorina and restraining the power of her successor by splitting her offices of CEO and chairman, and appointing one of the first female non-executive chairs in business. Were HP's achievements illusory? More broadly, has the governance movement mistaken the form of improvement for the actual substance of it? Or has genuine reform been thwarted and even subverted intentionally?

What follows is a corporate tragedy in four acts. Act One revolves around an improbable alliance of two directors with diametrically opposed philosophies. Act Two culminates in as contentious and high-profile a corporate firing as U.S. business has ever seen. Act Three is dominated by the fecklessness of the board's oldest member and his loose-lipped ally. The fourth and final act involves the coopting of a new CEO who is not all that he seems to be.

* * *

LIKE ALL GREAT dramas, Spygate had a larger-than-life pro-
tagonist, a character whose colossal impact for better or worse
defied the limits of his peers and whose visions, dreams, and pas-
sions existed on a scale that overwhelmed most of those who
encountered him, let alone those he felt had crossed him. Tom
Perkins is the Grand Old Man of Silicon Valley—or he would
be if he were not temperamentally unsuited to dignitary status.
Born in 1932, the brilliant but emotionally combustible Perkins
helped invent a lucrative new wealth-making vehicle for the elite:
the high-tech venture capital partnership. Kleiner & Perkins, the
firm that he founded in 1972 with the late Eugene Kleiner, turned
millions into billions of dollars by putting up seed capital for
some five hundred companies, among them world changers like
Genentech, Amazon, and Google.

The quality that set Perkins and his partners apart definitively from lesser rivals in Silicon Valley wasn't brainpower
but willpower. Before Perkins, start-up investing was an altogether more passive enterprise. Most venture capitalists spent
their days crunching numbers from the business plans brought
to them by entrepreneurs seeking funding or the financial reports submitted by companies already in their portfolios. They
did not dirty their hands on the corporate machinery. But
Perkins was himself a technologist and business operator, not
a financier, and he was as incapable of passivity as of breathing
underwater.

Perkins enfolded his entrepreneurial collaborators in a bear
hug of attentiveness that, as a rule, he relaxed only slightly as
Kleiner & Perkins's start-ups grew and prospered. "We were the
masters of meddling," Perkins declared. "We were famous about
calling the entrepreneurs weekly if not daily. . . . We were part
of a team—whether they wanted us to be or not."[8]

Perkins embroidered his VC legend with a strenuously macho style of extra-large living. He assembled one of the world's great collections of exotic sports cars and raced sailing ships of ever increasing size and value in competitions around the world. Most other yacht owners were content to let professionals captain their boats, but not Perkins, who was "recognized as a bellicose but brilliant tactician."[9] In 1996, a court in France convicted Perkins and others of involuntary manslaughter after his yacht collided with a much smaller boat during a race in Saint-Tropez, drowning a French sailor. He paid a $10,000 fine and went back to racing to win. Starting in 2000, Perkins spent six years and $130 million building *The Maltese Falcon*, a sleekly futuristic yacht as long as a football field. When Perkins wasn't aboard the *Falcon*, he divided his time between a Marin County mansion with a spectacular view of San Francisco Bay from nearly every window, and a moated Elizabethan manor house in England purchased from Led Zeppelin guitarist Jimmy Page.

Perkins had begun gradually winding down his involvement in venture capital investing in the mid-1980s. He was fifty-four years old when he stepped down as managing partner of Kleiner Perkins Caufield & Byers and began distributing his part of the firm's equity among his colleagues. Co-founder Kleiner had done the same a few years earlier. (Kleiner died in 2003.) As a partner emeritus, Perkins still keeps an office in KPC&B's branch in San Francisco.

It was there, high atop an Embarcadero Center tower, that I first met Tom Perkins, one bright afternoon in May 2009. What might well be the country's most spectacular urban vista practically screamed for attention through the floor-to-ceiling glass walls of his office: San Francisco Bay laid out in its full cerulean glory. Perkins allowed me only a fleeting glimpse before directing my attention elsewhere. All seven of the other offices in KPC&B's thirty-sixth-floor suite were unoccupied. Perkins seemed less than enthralled to have the place to himself, rattling around its empty spaces like a deposed monarch exiled to a lonely outpost of the kingdom. "It's the high-rent district," he harrumphed as he showed me around. "When the lease runs out I'm not going to renew it."[10]

Perkins was polite, not at all unfriendly but clearly restless. He had even grown tired of *The Maltese Falcon*, having just put his nautical pride and joy up for sale a mere two years after its maiden voyage. "When I'm on it by myself I'm rattling around, and if I invite friends, which I do, I'm working all the time entertaining," he said. "I've been there, done that for years and years—all kinds of boats, all kinds of places. There are no places I particularly want to visit anymore and no friends I haven't already entertained. It's just time for something else."[11]

I'd come to see Perkins with a long list of questions about his involvement with Hewlett-Packard Co., which for him is a company of unique personal significance. He first went to work for HP in 1957, fresh from Harvard Business School and the Massachusetts Institute of Technology, when it was still a smallish company very much under the sway of its founders. Young Perkins grabbed hold of Dave Packard like a human lifeline. "Dave Packard was my mentor, an inspiration, and, I am sure, the father I so desperately needed," Perkins wrote in his autobiography, "the most important influence in my life."[12] In the fourteen tumultuous years that Perkins spent in HP's employ he contributed greatly to its evolution, even though he never smoothly fit into a company that was far more cautious and buttoned-down than he was.

Even after Perkins left HP to start Kleiner & Perkins, the fledgling venture capitalist took pains to maintain a relationship with Packard for years. Perkins's happiness would have been complete if only his mentor had seen fit to reciprocate by making a place for him on HP's board. That happened only in 2002, long after Packard had died, as Perkins's career came agreeably full circle thanks to a circuitous twist of fate.

If Perkins's life had followed a Hollywood trajectory, he would have served his board term with dignity and distinction. Perkins being Perkins, though, the story of his tenure as an HP director turned into the boardroom equivalent of *King Lear*. Perkins could not have held HP any dearer if it had been his own kingdom, yet he abandoned HP on four different occasions—resigning twice as an executive and twice as a director. When he quit for the final time in May 1, 2006, he was, by his own description, "incandescent with anger." And so, curtain up.

CHAPTER TWO

TUMULT'S APPRENTICE

EXTREME AMBITION IS not always fueled by deprivation, but in Tom Perkins's case it definitely was. Born in 1932, he was an only child reared amid the Great Depression. His parents, Harry and Elizabeth Perkins, often struggled to make ends meet and had to move in with better-off relatives for a time. As Perkins tells it, though, his youthful suffering was more emotional than economic. "I arrived late in my parents' lives and they let me know that, all things considered, it would have been better if I hadn't been born," he wrote in *Valley Boy*, a memoir in which he never mentions either his mother or father by name.[1] Harry, a strapping ex-jock, was indifferent to young Tom's academic successes and mocked his nerdish son's futile attempts at athletic endeavor. Mom was much gentler, but alarmingly erratic. "I'll always picture her standing in our little kitchen with a butcher's knife pressed against her wrist," Perkins recalled. "As a kid, I found these scenes absolutely terrifying."[2]

Only in the last few years has it dawned on Perkins that he styled his bold, risk-intensive career in complete opposition to the ultra-cautious approach of his father, who endured a long, scarring stretch of unemployment during the 1930s. A first-rate golfer, Harry could well have had the talent to play professionally but never dared give it a try. He also was an intellectually curious autodidact who read widely, built an enormous vocabulary, and yet spent his entire work life as a fire-risk assessor drone for a big insurance company that saw fit to move him around the country without ever promoting him. "He hated his work, basically," Perkins said, acknowledging sympathetically that his father was a man of "unfulfilled capabilities."[3]

Perkins, who grew up mainly in the New York City suburb of White Plains, won a scholarship to MIT, where he majored in electrical engineering after realizing that he was incapable of excelling at "his first and truest love": theoretical physics.[4] At Harvard Business School, he studied under the legendary George Doriot, who moonlighted as the chairman of the country's first full-time venture capital company. Perkins first met Dave Packard and Bill Hewlett at an electronics trade show in New York City a few months before he was awarded his master's in business administration. Hewlett-Packard was a thriving but still obscure company, unknown on the East Coast except to the scientists and engineers to whom it catered as customers. Perkins's HP job interview took the form of chatting up its co-founders while helping them set up their booth at the trade show. In 1957, Perkins climbed into his beat-up Jaguar XK120 coupe and drove cross-country all the way from Boston to Silicon Valley, which still consisted mostly of apricot orchards, to go to work full-time for Bill and Dave.

Perkins, who had just celebrated his twenty-fourth birthday, descended on Palo Alto with all the subtlety of a boulder dropped into a pond from 20,000 feet. "I expected to be running the place in no time," he recalled.[5] Was Perkins's swagger his way of compensating for the damage inflicted by a miserable upbringing? Undoubtedly, but he radiated arrogance so convincingly that

Packard decided to start out his new apprentice with a lesson in humility, assigning Perkins to HP's machine shop, where the Harvard-educated hotshot MBA spent three months running a lathe. Perkins then moved into sales, becoming sales manager for California, HP's largest market. As an MBA-worthy side project, he reorganized order processing for the entire company, which, in his view, "had become almost impossibly cumbersome."[6]

Perkins lasted just three years in his first go-round at HP. Frustrated by what he considered the slow pace of his advancement, he quit in 1960 to take a job in the San Francisco office of a prestigious management consulting firm at twice the pay. Just twelve months later, a contrite Perkins called Packard and asked to return to HP.

Packard wasn't quite ready to welcome back his wayward protégé and steered him instead to Optics Technology Inc. (OTI), a fledgling laser company in which both Bill and Dave had invested personally. For the first time, OTI put Perkins in what would become a familiar position for him as a venture capitalist: on the ground floor of an emerging technology of potentially great but undefined commercial promise. Perkins would make his first million in the laser business while exacting a measure of hard-earned revenge against a hated rival.

OTI's mastermind was Narinder Kapany, a young Indian-born scientist with boundless charisma and ambition to match. Perkins, who joined OTI as director of marketing, emerged enthralled from his job interview with the Sikh scientist but soon came to despise Kapany with a fervor that still burned half a century later. "Dr. Narinder Kapany and I developed what is fortunately a rare thing in life: a mutual hatred of near biblical proportions," Perkins wrote in *Valley Boy*. "Years afterward I told anyone who would listen that I wanted engraved on my tombstone: 'I still hate him.' Perhaps it's time to cancel that request. I'll start to think about it, one of these days."[7]

Kapany, who, like Perkins, still lives in the Bay Area, admits to owing a copy of Perkins's autobiography but hastens to add that it gathers dust on a shelf, its denunciations of him unread. "My children saw it and they were quite upset," Kapany told me. "My son actually bought one. He wrapped it up nicely and handed it to me. I never opened it. Look, I'm eighty-one years old. At this age, you understand that in this life, you can't live with everybody in love with you. He may have some animosity toward me. Who cares?"[8]

Kapany was born and raised in the Punjab, the scion of affluent, upper-class parents who sparked his interest in optics as a teenager by giving him a box camera. Narinder earned top marks at a fine Indian university, worked briefly for a military contractor in his native land, and then flew to London to study optics at the Imperial College of Science and Technology. In time, he no doubt would have returned home to start an optical business of some sort had not the renowned British physicist Harold Hopkins hired him in 1952 to assist with what proved to be landmark experiments in fiber optics. PhD in hand, Kapany headed to the United States in 1955 in pursuit of grander opportunity than either England or his native land offered.

Scores of scientists on both sides of the Atlantic did groundbreaking work in fiber optics in the 1950s and 1960s, but it was Kapany who won global acclaim as the "father of fiber optics." He inserted this epithet into his curriculum vitae, infuriating Hopkins, who had begun accusing Kapany of exaggerating his contribution to their joint research before the ink on his protégé's PhD thesis was dry. Like Perkins, Hopkins cultivated a hatred of Kapany that lasted a lifetime. In 1994, a few months before

Hopkins died, he took a parting shot in an interview with the science writer Jeff Hecht, insisting that Kapany had "contributed nothing to the brains of the project: he was a pair of hands."[9] Hopkins went too far, but Hecht found that Kapany's claim on paternity was indeed overstated; today, his technical innovations are widely regarded as less crucial than those of a handful of other, less visible pioneers. When it came to speaking and writing about fiber optics, though, he was prolific beyond compare. From 1955 to 1965, Kapany was the lead author on forty-five scientific papers and the co-author of ten more—a staggering 30 percent of all papers published on fiber optics during this time. "His greatest gift may have been for promotion, though he dislikes the word," Hecht concluded in his 2003 book *City of Light: The Story of Fiber Optics*.[10]

As Hecht tells it, Kapany commanded attention wherever he went. His turban and full beard were set off by the sharply tailored western business suits that he favored even in the privacy of his research laboratory. Silver-tongued in any setting, "Dr. Singh," as he always introduced himself, punctuated his conversation with a booming laugh that contrasted charmingly with his high-gloss manners and regal bearing. The unthinking slights and deliberate insults that white-bread America reflexively meted out to "exotic" visitors failed to dent Kapany's formidable self-possession. He was so secure in his Sikh identity that he once volunteered to answer the door at a faculty Halloween party at the University of Rochester, laughingly explaining to his hosts that the trick-or-treaters would assume that he, too, was in costume.[11]

In 1960, Kapany headed to Silicon Valley, raised a few million dollars from the San Francisco venture capital outfit Draper, Gaither & Anderson, and founded Optics Technology Inc.

A physicist employed by the billionaire recluse Howard Hughes had demonstrated the first working laser less than a year before Kapany established OTI, which, as its name implied, was conceived not as a fiber optics company per se, but as a vehicle for commercializing scientific advances across the entire field of optics. As OTI's president and research director, Kapany used most of his seed money to build a first-rate lab staffed with half a dozen accomplished physicists recruited from industry and academe.

At OTI, the formidable challenge of shepherding the "wonder ray" out of the laboratory and into the marketplace fell mainly to Perkins, the lone MBA at a company long on PhDs. A hefty dose of frustration was built into this task, for laser science was not nearly the stuff of the military and commercial fantasies its invention had inspired.[12] Although the technology advanced by leaps and bounds, the business of lasers would fall well short of blockbuster status. Even Spectra Physics, the world's largest laser company (on whose board Perkins sat for years), never reached $1 billion in sales. "The laser industry did not achieve 'greatness' because, as Herb Dwight [Spectra Physics' CEO] once said, 'The laser is the second-best solution to every problem,'" Perkins said.[13]

Had the odds not been stacked so steeply against success, OTI might have grown at a rate sufficient to accommodate two personalities as outsize as Perkins and Kapany. Or perhaps not, for Perkins struggled greatly to control his temper and was loath to defer to a boss who was only a few years older than he, no matter how impressive the man's résumé. Actually, Kapany's elite credentials only exacerbated Perkins's discomfort. At MIT, theoretical physics was the obstacle that had defined the limits of his aptitude, and now here he was surrounded by PhDs, the odd electrical engineer out in the corporate equivalent of an Ivy League physics department.

Perkins directed the anger that often welled up in him during staff meetings not at Kapany, but at the one member of the OTI brain trust whom he could plausibly engage as a peer. "Because Perkins was a sort of frustrated technologist and also because he did his degree in engineering, he would argue with the vice president of engineering—in public!" recalled Kapany with born-again exasperation. In part because of such gross offenses against collegiality, Kapany never granted his marketing director the title of vice president—a largely symbolic slight that increasingly infuriated Perkins during his four years in Optics Technology's employ.

Perkins did not know the first thing about lasers when he joined OTI, but his high-energy curiosity had a way of turning the sales calls he made to major scientific laboratories around the country into impromptu seminars. At MIT, his alma mater, Professor Ali Javan provided a private demonstration of his recent invention, the helium-neon laser, which was the first laser to emit a continuous (rather than pulsed) beam of light. Perkins, who'd never seen a laser in action before, was mesmerized by Javan's prototype. "That shaft of intense red light was unforgettable," he recalled. "I thought that if we could, somehow, make lasers like this available there would be a good demand for them."[14]

Perkins brought the idea to Kapany, who was resolutely unimpressed. As OTI's founder saw it, the business of the company was commercializing the work of its own scientists, not turning other people's inventions into marketable products. In concept, Perkins didn't disagree with this emphasis on proprietary research. In practice, though, OTI's resident geniuses never could come up with the sort of ideas that a marketer could build a dream on. One of the company's most technically impressive—and labor-intensive—inventions was a fiber-optic camera for scanning the insides of nuclear submarine reactors. "Alas," Perkins sneered later, "the navy needed only one of those."[15]

Perkins convinced an OTI engineer to help him work up a poor man's version of the Javan device that he sold to high schools and colleges as an instructional tool. To stimulate demand for this makeshift laser, which sold for a few thousand dollars, Perkins spent many nights at his kitchen table writing a textbook that OTI published in soft cover as *Experiments in Physical Optics Using Continuous Laser Light*. Perkins's classroom device was hardly the "killer app" that OTI needed, but it did sell in large enough numbers over a period of two years to belatedly pique Kapany's interest in the profit potential of budget-priced gas lasers.

OTI devoted a full year to the development of model 170, which cost about $100 to produce. It was a fine little machine; on that, at least, Perkins and Kapany could agree. But the director of marketing insisted that its optimal price was $200 and his boss was equally insistent that it retail for $400. "I made the mistake of taking the issue to the board," Kapany admitted.[16] In the end, OTI split the difference and model 170 became one of the best-selling early lasers at a price of $295. Perkins took no joy in this validation of his commercial instincts, for by the time that OTI introduced its new hit laser in January 1966, he had parted ways with Kapany.

For Perkins, the last straw was the press conference Kapany called to announced his invention of color X-ray or "color-translating radiography." It sounded impressive, but it amounted to nothing more than color tinting. "Ultimately, it was a ridiculous idea," said Perkins, his old anger flaring anew. "You're just changing the colors on a film. It adds no new information at all. Zero." That Kapany's supposed breakthrough coincided with preparations to float OTI's first public stock offering only added to Perkins's outrage. "This is bullshit, Narinder!" he claims to have told his boss.[17]

In *Valley Boy*, Perkins asserted that he "decided to quit by asking the board to choose between Narinder and me."[18] In other words, instead of quitting in the usual way—by resigning—Perkins delivered an ultimatum to his bosses' boss. Why take the trouble, unless he thought there was a chance he might succeed in ousting Kapany? There was no angry final showdown with Kapany, who was OTI's chairman as well as its president. Instead, Perkins sought an audience with Don Lucas, a partner of Draper Gaither, OTI's largest shareholder, and told him in so many words that everything about Kapany's approach to business was dead wrong. Draper disagreed, apparently, leaving Perkins no respectable alternative but to resign. Kapany, who would not learn of the coup attempt until years later, happily accepted Perkins's sudden resignation, no questions asked. As far as he was concerned, it was a non-event. "His leaving had no effect on the business," Kapany recalled.[19]

Perkins again went to Packard and asked his substitute father to readmit him to the Hewlett-Packard family. This time, Dave complied. But even as Perkins put in long days at HP, Kapany and the laser business preoccupied his thoughts. A few months after he rejoined HP, Perkins went to Packard for permission to start a company on the side to develop a laser capable of outdoing OTI's hot-selling model 170. "Sure, I wanted to make some money. But I really wanted to put Optics Technology out of business, because I really detested Narinder Kapany in, I suppose, a very vindictive way," Perkins acknowledged later.[20]

Perkins had two partners in his revenge project: Richard Jaenicke, a talented and relentlessly cheery young electrical engineer who had worked under him as a salesman at OTI, and Henry Rhodes, a long-haired, pot-smoking glassblower who rented loft space on University Avenue in Berkeley, near the University of California campus. Together, Perkins and Jaenicke worked out a schematic design that could, they hoped, make a gas laser as simple and reliable to operate as a light bulb and at a fraction of the cost of the 170. Rhodes's contribution was to turn their idea, which existed only on paper, into a working prototype of a device that Perkins dubbed the "Lasertron."

With his wife's blessing, Perkins put their life savings of $15,000 into the new company, which took its name—University Laboratories Inc. (ULI)—from the location of Rhodes's shop. A few months of intensive tinkering produced a working "light-bulb" laser. Turning the Perkins-Jaenicke design into a bona fide prototype was mostly Jaenicke's doing; as ULI's president he routinely put in eighty-hour weeks. In Jaenicke's view, though, the comparatively limited hours that Perkins could spare for ULI were no less crucial. "Tom would come to the lab at all the critical moments," Jaenicke recalled. "I doubt if we would have gotten there without him."[21]

Perkins also worked hard to secure a series of bank loans and to raise $200,000 in venture capital from various sources (Draper, Gaither & Anderson pointedly not among them). With the additional funding, University Labs was able to move into new design and production space, hire dozens of employees, and begin cranking out Lasertrons by the hundreds. Perkins and Jaenicke each ended up with 40 percent ownership of ULI after jointly buying out Rhodes, who purchased a sailboat and left for parts unknown.

To drive from Hewlett-Packard's offices in Palo Alto to ULI's lab in Berkeley, as Perkins did three or four times a week in 1966, was to be transported from a corporate milieu of white button-down shirts and slide rule holsters into the tie-dyed heart of hippiedom on the eve of the Summer of Love. For a time, ULI's quarters were separated by a thin partition from a drug lab run by Owsley Stanley, a pioneering sound engineer for the Grateful Dead who was probably the first individual to manufacture LSD in bulk.[22] Perkins certainly was conspicuous in his tie and jacket, but he was intrigued by his exposure to Berkeley scene. He joined Businessmen Against the War and subscribed to *The Realist*, Paul Krassner's left-wing satire magazine. "I've always been outspoken—from the left at that time and now from the right," Perkins said.[23]

Priced at $195 to $295 (depending on the model), complete with instructional kits on holography and the like, the Lasertron was a hit with the very sort of education customer that Perkins had been cultivating for years. Optics Technology sued not long after the Lasertron's mid-1967 debut, accusing ULI of stealing not only its customer lists but also its laser wavelength, which, as Perkins later quipped, had been "determined either by God or Albert Einstein"—not Narinder Kapany.[24] Perkins settled this nuisance suit with a small payment and ULI went on to sell lightbulb lasers by the thousands.

As it turned out, there was room enough in the market for both Perkins and Kapany to prosper, at least for a time. Buoyed by a couple of particularly noteworthy inventions—a holographic camera and a laser blood coagulator—OTI succeeded in going public in the "go-go" stock market of 1968, temporarily making Kapany a rich man on paper. Meanwhile, ULI hired an optics PhD and a Harvard-educated marketer and developed

an array of new premium-priced lasers for use in science labs
and on building sites. ULI set the industry standard for construction lasers that added speed and precision to such tasks as laying
sewer pipe and aligning elevator shafts.

Perkins easily could have matched Kapany and sold shares
in his company to outside investors, but he wanted no part of
the added managerial burdens of running a publicly held company. University Labs was growing so fast that it was starting
to get away from him and Jaenicke. "I likened their place to a
Maoist bomb factory," recalled Herb Dwight of Spectra Physics.
"It was right in the heart of Berkeley, and you walked in and it
just seemed to be complete chaos, with PhDs everywhere."[25]

Perkins invited Dwight to visit because he had decided to
sell ULI in lieu of quitting HP a second time to work full-time
at his burgeoning laser company. Jaenicke was not eager to sell
out, but loyally deferred to Perkins, as always. "Tom had a near-
genius capability in all he did, besides being a wonderful guy,"
Jaenicke said.[26] By early 1970, Perkins had come to terms with
Spectra Physics, which was one of Optics Technology's main
competitors. Perkins and Jaenicke each got about $2 million in
cash and shares (equivalent to about $11 million in 2009 dol-
lars).[27] Jaenicke moved into a senior executive position at Spectra
Physics and Perkins joined its board.

The fortunes of Perkins and Kapany diverged sharply after
the sale to Spectra Physics. Perkins had shrewdly cast his lot
with a well-managed enterprise on its way to dominating the
laser business. Largely because of a profit surge supplied by ULI,
Spectra Physics' share price more than tripled in the three years
following the acquisition, adding to Perkins's seven-figure net
worth. Meanwhile, OTI struggled as it lagged behind the pace

of product innovation set by Spectra Physics and other competitors. In 1972, OTI's fourth consecutive money-losing year, its board removed Kapany as CEO and piled insult atop injury by replacing the self-styled father of fiber optics with an executive from the cement industry.[28] By 1974, OTI was out of business.

For Perkins, the laser had indeed proven to be a wonder ray. He had moonlighted his way to entrepreneurial triumph in the classic manner, turning an idea into a small, well-secured fortune. That University Labs succeeded largely at the expense of Kapany and Optics Technology made it a whole lot sweeter, of course.

Perkins's new wealth brought him comfort, both psychic and material, but at a cost, for his success brought out the worst in his parents. Harry, who had retired on meager savings, was envious and resentful—all the more so because he had predicted not only that University Labs would fail but also that HP would fire his son for giving his day job short shrift. "At first, he was very, very much against it, because he thought it would upset HP," Perkins recalled. "Then it started to work and was doing well. I was explaining it and he'd say, 'You sound just like the Kingfish'"—the ne'er-do-well character on the old Amos 'n' Andy radio show who was forever hatching crazy get-rich schemes. Elizabeth, on the other hand, was overeager to share in her son's good fortune. "She told me, 'I want one million dollars,'" Perkins recalled. "I thought she was kidding. She wasn't."[29] He declined to make a seven-figure payment but did put his mother on a monthly salary for the rest of her life. (After Elizabeth died, Perkins discovered that she had squirreled away most of the money he'd given her in obscure banks up and down the Central Valley. The deposits exceeded $1 million.)

Perkins's parents weren't exactly Ozzie and Harriet, but his life was good and getting better even so. Still a few years shy of his fortieth birthday, Perkins was married to a woman he adored and was father to a little boy, Tor, and a daughter named Elizabeth, after his mother. He had a million dollars in the bank, a mansion in Belvedere perched spectacularly above San Francisco Bay, a fancy sports car in the garage, and a new yacht at the dock. So why not just declare victory over Kapany and move on? Why hold tight to an undying hatred of an enemy so thoroughly vanquished? Not even his wife understood. "At the time, Gerd kept saying, 'Forget Kapany!'" Perkins recalled.

This question moves us from the quantifiable certitudes of business into the murk of human psychology. Kapany certainly had his faults, immodesty chief among them. Worse, he was essentially inept as a businessman. By his own admission, though, Perkins's hatred of Kapany was rooted as much in his errant perceptions and judgments as in his employer's failings. "I think it started off as a sort of love affair. I mean, I was overwhelmed by the guy," Perkins said. "He's very charming and entertaining and open, apparently. I went for it just hook, line, and sinker. . . . And then, bit by bit, it dawned on me that he wasn't any of these things I thought he was."[30]

* * *

THE LASER BUSINESS made Perkins rich, but it was the work he did simultaneously at Hewlett-Packard that produced the larger achievements of the pre–Kleiner & Perkins phase of his career. At HP, as at OTI, Perkins's considerable talents seemed inextricable from his propensity for offending his titular superiors. When one of HP's fusty Old Guard executives took away his corporate car in punishment for a supposedly insubordinate act, Perkins dipped into his laser windfall and bought a red Ferrari roadster. "The grinding of teeth overcame the grinding of gears when I parked it in front of headquarters," he recalled. "How stupid I was! How wonderful it felt!"[31]

Perkins managed to survive—and, for a time, thrive—during his second go-round at the company by making himself indispensable to the two HPers who mattered most: Bill and Dave. Packard and Hewlett affirmed their reputations as shrewd judges of character by deploying Perkins as a kind of human icebreaker. When the founders were looking to set a new and difficult course, they used him to smash through the status quo. Perkins's energy and effrontery played a critical role in HP's most important strategic move since the company's founding—its entry into the computer business.

By the mid-1960s, the scientists and engineers to whom HP catered were looking to use computers to enhance the speed and accuracy of their laboratory instruments. The 2116A, which HP introduced in 1965, fit the bill beautifully. It was easy to use, extraordinarily rugged, and a bargain at $22,000. And yet HP's Palo Alto division, which manufactured and marketed the device, sold only five of them in its first year on the market—a keen disappointment to Packard, who had personally championed its development over the misgivings of Hewlett and other senior executives.

Packard convened an all-day meeting at headquarters in late 1967 to address the 2116A's underwhelming debut. Perkins knew little about computers, but attended along with a hundred other employees. A pep fest it was not. "The first half of the meeting was mostly excuses as to why nothing had happened," recalled one attendee. "A number of problems were evident. The principal one was that very few people wanted to go into the computer business except Dave Packard."[32] The madder Packard got, the higher he rolled the sleeves of his white dress shirt. By meeting's end, they were almost to his shoulders. Perkins was uncharacteristically silent, speaking only once, when called on by Dave. Even so, a few days later Packard effectively dumped the 2116A in Perkins's lap by naming him marketing manager of the Palo Alto division.

Perkins's essential contribution was to substitute utter conviction for queasy ambivalence. HP had not only backed into the intensely competitive computer business, but had done so on tiptoe, as Bernard Oliver, its longtime research and development chief, later admitted: "We had a way of acting humble in those days because we felt—rightly or wrongly—that IBM, the computer giant, could become annoyed at us at any point and simply squash our computer business."[33] Top management had gone so far as to forbid employees from referring to the computer as a computer, even in casual conversation with one another, much less with customers. (Acceptable euphemisms included "information processor" as well as "instrument controller.")

Perkins not only insisted on calling a computer a computer as loudly as he could, but also deemphasized (and in some cases discontinued) traditional scientific instruments also handled by the Palo Alto division to put the 2116A front and center. He ventured outside HP to hire salesmen and product managers with computer experience and insisted on doing his own advertising, public relations, trade show promotions, and so on instead of relying on various headquarters departments. "The computer had to have its own sales force—its own everything really," Perkins recalled.[34]

Sales of the 2116A picked up as if on cue, with a twist that delighted Perkins and surprised his bosses. As it turned out, a large majority of buyers used the new machine and the new and improved models that followed hard on its heels not as instrument controllers for automatic measurement, but as stand-alone computers for a variety of other applications. In other words, the company's customers forced it to embrace a reality that most of its senior management had sought to deny: HP was in fact in the computer business, IBM and Digital Equipment Corp. be damned!

Even so, Perkins's every move raised the hackles of at least one home office executive with a bigger title than his own. His immediate superior, the general manager of the Palo Alto division, soon suffered what Perkins termed "a minor collapse, perhaps an anxiety attack (having me as a direct report was not the cause . . . I think)."[35] Packard transferred the poor man to a job out of the line of fire and promoted Perkins to Palo Alto GM. "I couldn't conceivably have done what I needed to do if Dave Packard didn't wish for me to win those battles," Perkins said.[36]

Soon after, HP solidified its commitment to computers by spinning the operation out as a separate division, headed by Perkins and housed in Cupertino. There, a dozen miles from headquarters, Perkins presided over what passed for HP's counterculture. In a company where white shirts and steel-toed shoes were de rigueur, many of Cupertino's four hundred employees wore blue jeans and sandals and flouted HP's regimented work schedule. Software chief Roy Clay led a group of programmers who took to playing golf a few mornings a week, arriving late to work. They might have escaped the home office's notice had not their number included a recent college grad named Jim Hewlett. One afternoon Clay got an angry call from Jim's father, Bill, reminding him that the HP work day started promptly at 7:45 A.M. Jim had played his last nine holes, but his co-workers played on, confident that Perkins had their backs.

Not that Perkins was a soft touch. On the contrary, he was a demanding and temperamental boss who often berated his managers even as he tried to insulate them from interdivisional politics. "Sometimes Tom and I would get to the point of almost screaming at each other and my being fired," Clay recalled. "I don't know how much we liked each other, but we respected each other."[37]

By the late 1960s, Perkins was in charge of the largest and fastest-growing of HP's seventeen divisions. Each new model Cupertino developed—the 2116 A, B, and C were quickly followed by the 2115A and the 2114A—was significantly faster, smaller, cheaper, and more adaptable than its predecessor. Perkins was laying the foundation of Silicon Valley's first major computer-making franchise, nearly a decade before the founding of Apple Computer. And then came the disaster called Omega. "Upon reflection," Perkins conceded later, "Omega was certainly the biggest mistake of my entire career."[38]

The object of the project code-named Omega was undeniably audacious: to develop the first 32-bit computer, a machine that offered the promise of twice the speed and thousands of times more memory than the 2116A and its 16-bit successors. "Omega was Tom's idea, and he was pushing it very hard," recalled William Terry, a veteran instruments executive who often clashed with Perkins. "It was a big, giant leap forward."[39] If Omega had succeeded, HP might well have vaulted over all of its competitors into a position of preeminence in minicomputers worldwide. As it was, though, the project's failure toppled Perkins from his perch in Cupertino.

Product development at HP tended to be an incremental process of baby steps forward. Failure was not uncommon, but rarely did a division sink enough money into a new product to do serious damage—either to its financial results or to the careers of its managers. Omega, though, was a truly radical departure: At a projected cost of $10 million, it was by far the costliest undertaking in HP's history.

Cupertino's best minds—some eighty people all told—gravitated to Omega and did a brilliant job of developing the hardware for a 32-bit machine. And why not? HP had always been a hardware company par excellence. But the software was a mess. "In the beginning no one outside of the division understood software, its importance, its cost, and its long-term implications," Perkins said. "Frankly, it took me a while, too, to absorb these fundamental differences." A few months into the project, Perkins realized that Cupertino lacked the necessary expertise. "The bottom line was simple," he said. "A freestanding division simply couldn't bootstrap itself into the 32-bit computer league."[40]

Perkins begged the home office for additional funds and technical resources, but his timing was awful. His champion, Packard, had just taken a leave from HP and moved to Washington to begin a three-year stint as deputy secretary of defense, leaving Hewlett solely in charge. Hewlett remained deeply ambivalent about the computer business, and Perkins had not a single ally among his peers, the other senior executives. "I think it's fair to say that my vertical support, upward to Dave and Bill and downward to the people in my exploding division, was excellent," he recalled. "But my horizontal support among my peers, the other GMs, was beyond terrible—they hated my guts."[41]

Perkins felt, in the end, that he had no alternative but to kill Omega. "I cancelled Omega, but really the 'system' shot it down," he said. "I should have understood the quicksand that I had led the troops into, so it was a huge failing on my part."[42] Cupertino staffers quit by the dozens and many of those who remained donned black velvet armbands in mourning for the 32-bit machine of their dreams.

Project Omega certainly exposed Perkins's managerial shortcomings, but the larger failure was probably Hewlett's. There is general agreement today that in letting the Omega die HP committed an epic error. It was not until 1978—eight years later—that Boston-based Digital Equipment Corp. (DEC) finally introduced the first 32-bit machine, the hugely successful VAX, and parlayed it into dominance of the minicomputer market. Packard, who never directly criticized Hewlett, nonetheless used the story of the demise of the "promising" Omega project to illustrate the pitfalls of HP's "cautious approach to computers" in his 1995 memoir, *The HP Way*.[43] Bernie Oliver wasn't nearly as tactful, declaring flat-out in several post-retirement interviews that HP was wrong to terminate Omega. "I think it would have done a terrific job, made history," Oliver said.[44]

In Packard's absence, it was Hewlett who gave Perkins a soft place to fall. In early 1971, the CEO invited Perkins to move to headquarters and occupy an office just outside his own as HP's first director of corporate development. Despite the impressive title, Perkins was keenly aware that his authority and status had greatly diminished. "Having been a management consultant, I understood the powerlessness of a staff job," he recalled. "If you picture a dog lying on its back, legs in the air, in abject surrender before the other dogs in the pack, you will get some idea of the posture I felt I needed to adopt."[45]

Perkins tried to make the best of it, organizing budgets for Hewlett's review and tending to the mechanics of small acquisitions while keeping an eye peeled for something Big and Important. It arrived in the form of a brochure from the Boston Consulting Group titled "How Do You Allocate Resources Among

Competing Corporate Entities?" The answer, BCG argued, was to value above all—profits included—the rapid accumulation of market share early in a product's "life cycle." This then-novel approach struck Perkins with the force of revelation, not least because it apotheosized the very arguments he had made while running the computer business. He worked up an impressive analysis of the theory's application to HP and persuaded Hewlett and the executive council to implement what amounted to a seismic shift in the company's planning. "The entire budgeting process became infested with this thinking," Perkins recalled.[46]

With an assist from BCG, Perkins thus managed to increase funding for the computer business and prevent the Omega from becoming an evolutionary cul-de-sac. The 32-bit Omega was reengineered as a 16-bit general-purpose computer called the HP3000, which overcame a couple of horrendous marketing missteps to eventually establish HP as a force in computing. According to HP historian Michael Malone, "The HP3000 became (in terms of total revenues) probably the most successful product in Hewlett-Packard history—and one of the most popular computers of all time. The model 3000, in its many variants, would live on in the HP catalog for 31 years."[47]

Dave Packard returned from Washington to active duty at HP in early 1972, having resigned his Pentagon post out of frustration at the disastrous course of the Vietnam War and his own inability to command the vast military bureaucracy. Packard's mood only darkened after his return upon the realization that in his absence Perkins had gotten the whole company dancing to the market share tune of Boston Consulting Group. "Somewhere we got into the idea that market share was an objective," complained Packard, in a tongue-lashing administered to a group of senior managers. "Anyone can build market share, and if you set your prices low enough, you can get the whole damn market. But I'll tell you, it won't get you anywhere around here."[48]

Actually, the changes in budgeting and planning that HP had implemented in Packard's absence were not only immediately beneficial but also essential to HP's eventual transformation from an electronic instruments maker into a computer giant. But if Perkins was looking to the future, Packard was reasserting the primacy of what he believed to be the eternal verities on which HP rested, failing to recognize how musty some of them had become over time. Packard's real quarrel was with Bill Hewlett, who as CEO had approved Perkins's every innovation, but HP's co-founders had never clashed, at least not overtly, and they never would.

Shortly after he resurfaced in Palo Alto, Packard summoned Perkins to his office and told him that he was through as director of corporate development. Perkins gladly would have returned to Cupertino, but there was no opening there for him, or at any of HP's other Silicon Valley divisions. Rather than accept the corporate equivalent of a transfer to Siberia and spend years working his way back into favor in Palo Alto, Perkins resigned from HP for the second time in five years.

Perkins left HP with decidedly mixed feelings. Like most ambitious executives, he had hoped to climb the corporate ladder all the way to the top and become CEO of Hewlett-Packard one day. On the other hand, Perkins recognized that he did not fit the profile of the classic corporate overachiever and was better suited to the more freewheeling realm of venture capital investing. "I don't consider myself a kind of a corporate executive at all, although I was pretty successful at it," he said. "I think both Hewlett and Packard recognized in me a different kind of executive, a person who could manage but who was restless and

ambitious and aggressive. I think I was a difficult person to manage but worth the trouble."[49]

Although Perkins's sacking as corporate development chief
had more to do with political expedience than his own performance, he was not embittered by it. At Kleiner & Perkins, he
would back numerous start-up companies that competed with
HP, but none of these investments was motivated by a desire for
revenge. On the contrary, he continued to hold HP in high regard
and took pains to remain on good terms with Packard and
Hewlett, who jointly approved a sizable investment by HP's employee retirement fund in one of Kleiner & Perkins early venture
funds. Packard also accepted Perkins's invitation to join the
board of Genentech Inc., the biotech company that was perhaps
K&P's greatest success.

In 1989, Perkins and Packard both arrived early for a Genentech board meeting and retired to a couple of bar stools to kill
time before the other directors showed up. HP was suffering
through a bad patch at the time, and Packard had just come out
of retirement to usher the CEO who had succeeded him into premature retirement. "Before we had finished our drinks, there
was a pause in our conversation about HP and its problems,"
Perkins recalled. "Dave turned his bar stool toward me and with
a wistful smile said: 'Tom, how did I ever let you get away from
HP?' I was taken aback and very flattered. This was the most
significant compliment of my life."[50]

CHAPTER THREE

I, CHAIRMAN

MORE OFTEN THAN not, it was as chairman of the board that Tom Perkins exerted Kleiner & Perkins's dominion over the many companies in which it invested. At the peak of Perkins's influence, he was chairman or lead director of fifteen companies at the same time, making him in all likelihood the most active chairman in modern business history. Without question, he was the first executive to serve simultaneously as chairman of three companies listed on the New York Stock Exchange: Tandem, Genentech, and Accuson. "I was very involved in all of those companies—way, way beyond just directors' meetings," Perkins recalled. "I've never worked harder in my life."[1] Such was the force of Perkins's personality—not to mention his mastery of boardroom politics—that he also was able to dominate many of the numerous other corporate boards to which he belonged over his career without chairing them.

That Perkins was as much professional chairman as he was professional investor was a function not only, or even primarily, of his compulsion to dominate but also of the high-risk, high-reward nature of venture capital itself. Although talented VCs certainly compile a higher batting average than .300 hitters in baseball, they strike out at rates that would bring disqualification in most every other form of investing. Kleiner & Perkins's first $8 million was an emphatic case in point. Seven of the first seventeen investments made were losers and in some cases the firm lost all its money. However, these failures were more than offset by two tape-measure home runs: Tandem Computers and Genentech. On balance, Kleiner & Perkins parlayed its original $8 million into asserts worth $400 million over a ten-year period; this worked out to an average annual return to the firm's outside investors of 47 percent.[2]

K&P's impressive performance resulted from a whole lot of heavy lifting. Until Perkins barged into the business, elbows flying, venture capital investing tended to be an altogether more decorous exercise than implied by its risk levels. The typical venture capitalist spent his days in an office poring over business plans and financial reports in search of companies worthy of financing. But Perkins was accustomed to running businesses instead of charting their progress from a distance. In other words, he was an operator, not a financier, and he continued to look to Dave Packard as a role model as he built Kleiner & Perkins into a new kind of venture capital firm. "I did things the way I think Dave would have done them if he was building businesses outside of HP—very hands-on, very technically involved, very willing to start small and build it, not requiring a full-blown plan or clear course of action," Perkins said.[3]

That said, the VC model pioneered by Kleiner Perkins turned HP's classically establishment approach to corporate governance inside out. In most large public companies then and now, the CEO also held the title of the chairman and even the largest shareholders were doing well to get a single seat on the board. The result was that the CEO had no real boss. In Kleiner Perkins companies, the chairman was almost always someone other than the CEO. The CEO was still in charge, at least nominally, but every aspect of the business was intently scrutinized by a board staffed mainly by partners of Kleiner Perkins and of allied VC firms.

Perkins first entered the rarefied realm of public company boards a few years before he moved into venture capital. While assisting Bill Hewlett as HP's corporate development director, Perkins had negotiated the acquisition of a small company controlled by Fred Adler, a New York lawyer turned venture capitalist. Afterwards, Adler invited Perkins to join the board of Applied Materials Inc., a start-up that supplied semiconductor manufacturers with equipment for fabricating silicon chips. Perkins jumped at the opportunity, even though Adler, Applied Materials' chairman, was notorious among early venture capitalists for the bullying tactics he used to dominate the companies he invested in. "They consider me to be too tough," Adler acknowledged, referring to his VC peers.[4]

As a director, Perkins was fascinated by the "playful, but tough, interaction" of Adler and Michael McNeilly, the company's young CEO and principal founder.[5] Adler once bounced a roll off McNeilly's head, transforming a board of directors dinner into an all-out food fight—a scene that so amused Perkins that he included a version in his potboiler novel, *Sex and the Single Zillionaire*. In the end, though, the laughs ran thin for McNeilly, who left in his prime to start another company. "One can guess that Adler became too much, though, as I learned later, Mike had plenty of his own demons," recalled Perkins, who resigned from the Applied Materials board himself soon after founding K&P in the belief that his time was better spent doing venture capital deals (one of which, as it happened, was making a sizable investment in Applied Materials).[6]

For Perkins, the three years he spent on the Applied Materials board was mainly useful in refining his knowledge of semiconductor technology and in defining the acceptable limits of VC intrusion. "Fred [Adler] was too strong a personality to be effective ultimately," Perkins said. "He stifled the managements with whom he was involved, in my opinion."[7]

Even with strangers the New Yorker could come on too strong. Perkins recalled that a friend of his once found himself seated next to Adler on a flight from San Francisco to New York and was in such a rush to get away from his overbearing companion after the plane landed that he broke his leg in a headlong fall down an escalator.

Even as Perkins bowed out of Applied Materials, he held tight to his directorship of Spectra Physics, the Silicon Valley laser company in which he had become a large shareholder through its acquisition of University Labs. Spectra Physics was barely a decade old when Perkins became a director, but its board already had outgrown the VC model; Herb Dwight was both CEO and chairman. Perkins proved an exceptionally vigilant and assertive board member, taking copious notes on a steno pad during every board meeting and frequently dropping by Dwight's office between sessions to talk. For a time, Perkins even took it upon himself to write advertising copy for the company, just as he had for University Labs. "Tom had very well-defined thoughts about how image and brand should be projected in the public eye," recalled Dwight, who invited Perkins and one other director to join him on the board's executive committee.[8]

By his own admission Perkins "nearly drove [Dwight] nuts with my 'help'" during his dozen years on the Spectra Physics board.[9] Dwight, an engineer by training, was a poised but intense executive who became so exasperated by Perkins's criticisms during one meeting that he leapt atop the boardroom table and shouted out his rebuttal as he walked up and down. Perkins was (briefly) stunned into silence. "I was really out of line in my comments," he later admitted.[10] While neither man now can recall the specifics of this day's disagreement, Dwight said that his frequent high-decibel debates with Perkins invariably were about basic issues of strategy. "Tom has his quirks, but he is not a petty individual," he said. "We would get real pissed off at each other sometimes, but for the most part we were able to put that behind us."[11]

Although Perkins never would resort to table-stomping, he gained new respect for Dwight (and even Adler) as he learned to cope with the pressures and frustrations of chairing a board himself. On balance, he acquitted himself well as chairman of the companies in K&P's portfolio. But his performance—like the firm's investment results—was a wildly mixed bag. Of the fifteen companies Perkins chaired or lead-directed, only two (Symantec, LSI Corp.) still survive as independent entities. Most of the rest were bought out by other companies at a price that easily exceeded what Kleiner Perkins had originally paid for its stock. However, three of them (Alliant, Internet Systems, Focus Semiconductor) failed outright, wiping out K&P's investment. Although the firm's losses were manageable in each case, Focus Semiconductor's demise made a fool of Perkins. "I was so embarrassed," he admitted. "I hadn't done my homework."[12]

Focus had reunited Perkins with Mike McNeilly, who had fled to Sun Valley, Idaho, after quitting Applied Materials in 1978. Eight years later, McNeilly returned to Silicon Valley and to Kleiner Perkins with new ideas for greatly enhancing the technology on which he'd founded Applied. Because he already knew McNeilly—or thought he did—Perkins dispensed with the usual personal background checks and confined his due diligence to the technology, which intrigued him. Perkins quickly agreed to back McNeilly in a new commercial venture, but wisely limited K&P's investment to $1.7 million, instead of the $7.5 million requested.

Focus Semiconductor began as a mutual admiration society masquerading as a company. Perkins considered McNeilly a "near genius PhD in chemistry."[13] As for McNeilly, "Mike liked to share his thoughts and experiences on everything . . . but his favorite topic of conversation was Tom Perkins," recalled Jim Hansell, the company's chief financial officer.[14] Perkins was the chairman of a board whose only other member was McNeilly. Board meetings, which took place once a month in the CEO's office, consisted mainly of intricate tech talk, according to Hansell, who doubled as board secretary. Perkins "was different from 99 percent of the other venture capitalists because of his technical management skills," observed Hansell, a Silicon Valley start-up veteran. "He and McNeilly were able to discuss in detail every chemical, electronic, or mechanical engineering issue related to any problem that arose."[15]

Hansell and other executives at the company were struck by the weirdness of McNeilly's behavior right from the start. Moody and distracted, the CEO routinely left the office early and did grievous damage to the undercarriage of his company Volvo by driving it over the raised medians of roads to make U-turns. He lifted $50 from the petty cash lock box a couple of times a week until he smashed it apart with a hammer. Yet McNeilly managed to behave himself around Perkins, who gave the CEO the benefit of the doubt even after he had fired three executives without cause. Balking at drawing up the papers for the third termination,

Hansell tried unsuccessfully to reach Perkins. Floyd Kvamme, a new Kleiner Perkins Caufield & Byers partner who had just joined the Focus board, told Hansell that "it was a Kleiner Perkins policy to let the CEO run the company as he saw fit."[16]

The dime didn't drop at Kleiner Perkins until a secretary walked in on McNeilly freebasing cocaine in his office. Perkins belatedly did a background check on the CEO that turned up what he later described as "a Sun Valley horror story: drugs, crime, bankruptcies."[17] After McNeilly denied that he was abusing cocaine, Perkins forced him to submit to a medical examination that revealed massive damage to his nasal passages. McNeilly agreed to take a medical leave and enter drug rehab in Santa Fe (paid for by KPC&B), but dropped out before completing the program.

One morning a frazzled-looking McNeilly showed up at KPC&B's offices on short notice. "He was raving but the essence of it was that he was in huge debt to 'the Italian guys in black suits'"—meaning the Mafia, Perkins recalled. "If I didn't fork over $250,000 in five days, they would kill me!"[18] He threw McNeilly out and never saw him again.[19] Perkins was pretty sure that the Mafia threat was nothing more than cokehead paranoia, but hired a bodyguard for a few weeks just in case.

Although Perkins remained a director of Focus Semiconductor, he never attended another board meeting, effectively shifting responsibility for the company to Kvamme. Focus blundered on for a few more years under a new chief executive promoted from the ranks. Kleiner Perkins invested more of its own money and helped the company organize three rounds of additional financing, bringing in other venture capital investors and raising $40 million in total. This accomplished nothing more than compounding the financial disaster that was Focus, which in four years of trying never managed to parlay McNeilly's technological advances into a revenue-producing product.

In Perkins's own estimation, he'd committed a much worse error in continuing to invest in Focus Semiconductor even after it had become apparent that McNeilly had been incapacitated than in misjudging him in the first place. As Perkins practiced it, venture capital was more like jazz than classical music; what counted was how well you improvised. "I've always had the attitude that the momentum and the initiative are more important in some ways than the ultimate accuracy, because if you made a mistake you can fix it on the way," he said. "And if you can't fix it, you just say, 'That's it' and pull the plug. You lose all your money but so what? If you've done it right, it isn't that much."[20] In Focus Semiconductor's case, KPC&B's loss was much greater than it would have been had Perkins adhered to his own professed standards of ruthlessness. Did he let his preexisting admiration for McNeilly cloud his judgment? Of course, but his larger failing seemed to be lack of focus, so to speak: Perkins was too busy with other companies that mattered more to him to ever pay Focus sufficient attention.

* * *

ONE OF THE most idiosyncratic aspects of Perkins's style as a VC jazz master was his rhythmic versatility. The key measure of the initial success of a venture capital investment is the rapidity with which a start-up company puts its original investors in the money either by selling out or going public. Urgency came naturally to Perkins, who raced cars and yachts when he wasn't hustling initial public offerings to market *prestissimo*. For most venture capitalists, an IPO was as much a winding down or termination of their involvement with a company as a taking of profits. Yet one of the hallmarks of venture capital à la Perkins was the extraordinary longevity of his involvement with his favorite companies. In numerous instances, he remained chairman long after K&P's investment had dwindled into insignificance. "We would tell entrepreneurs when we put the original money in that we hoped they were as ambitious for their company as we were, and that they couldn't get rid of us by going public," Perkins said. "Our intention was to continue with the company long after an IPO, because we wanted that company to be the biggest and best it could be."[21]

That Perkins's ambitions transcended venture capital per se was hardly surprising for someone who thought of himself as a businessman rather than a moneyman. For Perkins personally, venture capital prowess was doubly rewarding: He could invest big money at what was far and away the most lucrative stage of corporate development and then stick tight as a corporation amassed size and significance in the world. Chairing such a company engaged Perkins's intellect even as it flattered his ego, given that the complexity of a business tends to grow apace with its scope and scale. "You continually learn from these companies," he said. "It's an umbilical [connection]: we provide, but we get nourishment, too."[22]

Perkins's legacy was disproportionately defined by two companies, Tandem Computers and Genentech. He was a director of Genentech for twenty years, fifteen of them as chairman. He chaired Tandem for all twenty-three years that it existed as an independent company and extended his tenure by another nine years, in a sense, first by becoming a director of the company

that acquired Tandem—Compaq Computer—and then by joining the board of the company that in due course acquired Compaq: Hewlett-Packard.

Many parallels existed between Tandem and Genentech,
as one might expect of siblings born two years apart in a family
as tight-knit as K&P, but the essential one was the close, complicated, and ultimately anguished relationship that Perkins had
as chairman with the founder/CEOs of these companies. Both
James Treybig of Tandem and Robert Swanson of Genentech
had once been employees of Kleiner & Perkins and, despite the
magnitude of their success, were never able to move out from
under Perkins's intensive brand of sponsorship to true independence. There is no question that Perkins admired these two
visionary entrepreneurs and yet, in the end, he took the lead in
removing each of them as CEO of the companies they'd founded.
"For years and years, we were quite good friends," Perkins acknowledged. "It was only at the end that we came apart."[23]

Perkins actually hired Treybig twice, the first time at Hewlett-
Packard just after the transplanted Texan had earned an MBA
at Stanford. Although Treybig got his start as an engineer, he
made his mark on Perkins's fast-growing computer division in
sales and marketing. Despite his back-country affect, he had
come of age in the big city, Houston, which he remembered
fondly as a place "where you start playing poker at the age of
six."[24] Rarely has the poker player's shrewdly calculating intelligence come more disarmingly packaged than in Jimmy Treybig,
whose irrepressible good humor and utter lack of vanity en-
deared him to colleagues and journalists alike. "His eyeglasses
still refuse to perch properly on the bridge of his nose," one reporter noted approvingly, "preferring to park themselves crazily
at the other end."[25]

From the moment Perkins met him, Treybig exuded an audacious self-confidence that would serve him well as an entrepreneur. In his first job interview, Treybig declared that he would gladly accept employment at Hewlett-Packard, but only if he was hired into a position where eventually he would have twenty people reporting to him. Why twenty? "I wanted to learn to manage, and twenty was just a number," Treybig recalled. "So Tom and I argued about that for a while and I said, 'Look, Tom, you're going to fail if you don't hire me,' or something like that. That was too much maybe, but he knew that I meant what I said about the twenty. I don't bluff. I am not afraid."[26]

The idea of creating a "fault-tolerant" or "fail-safe" computer came to Treybig about a year after he had followed Perkins to K&P. At HP, Treybig had dealt with big banks that were starting to build networks of automated teller machines. Unlike branch offices, ATMs never closed. To operate them properly, banks needed computers that were always on line. "The problem was, once you start running a business that way, your computer cannot ever fail or lose data," Treybig said. "And it had to have a very fast response time, because people only waited at terminals so long."[27] The supposedly fail-safe systems being sold by HP and IBM were just lash-ups of conventional computers, unreliable and inefficient. Treybig envisioned a whole new kind of system in which multiple computers would work smoothly in tandem and could be used for a wide range of "mission-critical" applications in banking and industry.

Perkins and Treybig spent many an afternoon together drawing diagrams of exactly how the logic of such a system would work, succeeding only in proving that it might. "Tom is very technical, more technical than me, I'd say, but still not technical enough to design from scratch a whole computer system," Treybig explained.[28] K&P laid out an initial $50,000 to retain as consultants three former HP computer engineers who first proved out the feasibility of the concept and then designed the architecture of a failsafe tandem system, under Treybig's supervision. The innovation they arrived at after months of work—the "nonstop kernel"—was one of the great breakthroughs in computing.

Treybig spun out of Kleiner & Perkins in late 1974 to found Tandem Computer, which began in a warehouse in Cupertino, Perkins's old stomping grounds. The company started with eighteen employees, nine of whom had once worked at HP. K&P daringly supplied all of its $1.5 million in seed capital from its $8 million fund. (Perkins had scoured the Valley in search of other investors, but had found no takers.) Tandem raised $1.5 million more in venture funds in 1975, fixing K&P's ownership at 40 percent.

A few weeks after Treybig went out on his own, K&P replaced him with Bob Swanson, a fledgling venture capitalist who had entered the firm's orbit through Gene Kleiner. Swanson, who had degrees from MIT in organic chemistry and management, had become bored working in San Francisco for Citibank's venture capital arm. He struck up a friendship with the avuncular Kleiner in trying to salvage Citi's investment in a troubled tech company that K&P also had backed. Impressed with Swanson's energy and tenacity, Kleiner got Perkins to agree to add him to the K&P payroll. "I wanted to get in and run something, and they said, 'Why don't you join us for a year and maybe you can find the right thing to do,'" Swanson recalled.[29]

What Swanson settled on after months of intensive research was the nascent field of genetic engineering, or the cutting and splicing of DNA strands to create artificial genes. The prevailing view was that it would be many years before recombinant DNA technology could be used to create commercially viable products. But the more research papers Swanson studied and the more scientists he pestered over the phone and buttonholed at conferences, the more the conventional (albeit expert) wisdom confounded and even offended him. It was obvious that society had an urgent need for new drugs to do things like treat diabetes or to cure cancer. Why wasn't there a corresponding sense of urgency among the scientists capable of realizing biotechnology's enormous life-saving potential? Why not start a company and give it a go?

That Perkins was never as chummy with Swanson as he was with Treybig had nothing to with personality differences. In terms of basic temperament, Swanson was pretty much a Florida-reared version of Treybig—cheerful, sociable, fun-loving, and yet diligent and hugely ambitious. However, Perkins was not well versed in biology and thus was incapable of helping refine Swanson's entrepreneurial ideas to the degree he had Treybig's. He sensed that Swanson might be onto something with genetic engineering, but the prospect of funding an open-ended research project that might never result in an actual business opportunity increasingly grated on him.

At the end of 1975, K&P made what was probably the costliest error in its history by firing Swanson, more or less. He was allowed to keep coming in to the office every day and sit at the same desk doing what he'd been doing for months, except that he no longer drew a paycheck and had to get by on $410 a month of unemployment. Had K&P kept Swanson on salary, it probably would have been able to finance Genentech on much more advantageous terms, adding hundreds of millions of dollars to its eventual profit. "Tom Perkins told me that one of his biggest mistakes was in cutting Bob loose without a salary," recalled Fred Middleton, Genentech's first chief financial officer. "I don't think at the time he had a tremendous amount of confidence in Bob. Tom is a man of action and a bit of an impetuous guy."[30]

Swanson's entrepreneurial notions rapidly coalesced into a business plan after he joined forces with Herbert Boyer, a young professor of microbiology at the University of California San Francisco who had co-led the first successful gene-splicing experiments two years earlier. Businessman and scientist each put up $500 and incorporated Genentech in April 1976 with the immediate aim of producing insulin in the lab.

Although Perkins was highly impressed with Boyer, he remained skeptical of Swanson's business concept, even so. "This idea was verging upon pure research [and] everyone knows that's a ticket for losing millions," he said.[31] But when Swanson and Boyer came up with a plan to outsource most of the critical early laboratory work to two universities, Perkins kicked in $100,000 to pay for it. In retrospect, this sum "just seems so small—almost a joke—but that was enough to remove much of the risk from the entire venture," Perkins said.[32] The initial experiments worked like a dream, and Genentech methodically secured a golden future by filing for fundamental patents in every direction.

Swanson was equally shrewd in his dealings with K&P. Before he presented his business plan to Perkins, Genentech's CEO labored mightily to line up financing commitments from a couple of other VC firms. In the end, Swanson opted to rely entirely on K&P's money, but only had to give up 25 percent of Genentech's equity in exchange. "He knew all my tricks," Perkins conceded.[33] When Genentech raised an additional $850,000 in venture money in 1977, Swanson again put the squeeze on his old employer. "Tom thought Bob would need to come back to him for more money, and he could buy more of it then," according to CFO Middleton. K&P did invest another $100,000, but the lion's share came from two rival firms, Inco Venture Capital Management and Mayfield Fund. "Kleiner Perkins put in a little bit, but the valuations and terms were decided by these new investors," Middleton added.[34]

Taking Genentech public was a hugely contentious undertaking, pitting chairman against CEO. When Perkins began pushing the idea of a stock offering in 1979, Genentech hardly fit the standard profile of an IPO candidate. Its revenues were negligible, its profits were marginal, and it was still many months away from bringing a first product to market. Genentech had assembled a solid foundation of invaluable research, and it was Swanson's life ambition to methodically build a world-changing company atop it. However, Perkins's immediate priority was turning a buck. By this time, K&P had exhausted its $8 million in initial capital and was preparing to raise a second, much larger fund. Booking a big gain on Genentech would exalt the firm's investment results and supercharge its fund-raising like nothing else.

Perkins would have been just as happy to sell Genentech to a big, deep-pocketed pharmaceutical company as to take it public. Over Swanson's demurrals, the chair initiated a discussion with Johnson & Johnson at which it was intimated that Genentech could be had for as little as $80 million. By the time Perkins led a Genentech delegation to Indianapolis to meet with Eli Lilly Co., the asking price had risen to $100 million. After Lilly and J&J both passed, Perkins fixated on the IPO alternative, which really put Swanson's back up.

Push came to shove at a meeting of the board, which consisted solely of Perkins, Swanson, and Boyer. When the CEO suggested waiting at least a year to float a public stock offering,

Perkins had a fit, according to Middleton, who attended as board secretary. "He took a pencil and threw it down on the table and said, 'That's the most ridiculous thing I ever heard! Why don't I just sell all my stock and resign from the board. I think we ought to put this to a vote right now,'" Middleton recalled.[35] First, though, Perkins asked Boyer how he intended to vote. "Well," the scientist carefully replied, "I will vote with the majority of my friends."[36] There were big laughs all around, and the meeting proceeded on a much friendlier footing.

Perkins finally turned Swanson around with the argument that the first biotech company to go public would so excite investors that it would garner a disproportionate share of the available funding. The longer Genentech waited to cash in on the public's wonderment over the promise of genetic engineering, the greater the risk that an also-ran like Cetus, Biogen, or Genex would beat it to market.

To this day, Genentech's 1980 IPO stands as the ultimate hot new tech issue. Opening at $35 a share, the stock rocketed to $89 in the first hour and a half of trading as buy orders poured in from all over the world. A weary but elated Perkins placed an early morning congratulatory call to Swanson, waking him from his slumbers. "You're the richest guy I know, Bob," Perkins said.[37] Perkins didn't do too badly himself. Kleiner & Perkins's $200,000 investment in Genentech was now worth $160 million, an 800-fold increase. Both Perkins and Kleiner hung onto most of the shares they owned personally and were rewarded with another 550-fold rise in the share price by 2007. To Perkins, Genentech was "the wonderful faucet that never turned off."[38]

* * *

TANDEM'S BOARD OF directors was a "guidance" board par excellence, in Perkins-speak. That is, it was a small board packed with venture capitalists, it was thoroughly dominated by Perkins as chairman, and it closely involved itself in every aspect of the business. Tandem "fully validated the K&P approach of hands-on management of ventures, which became our trademark," Perkins asserted. "I, as chairman, participated in every major step in its history."[39]

Treybig worked hand in glove with his chairman but also sought guidance from other directors, particularly Tommy Davis, who was one of the most distinguished West Coast venture capitalists of the generation preceding Perkins and Kleiner. Soft-spoken and amiable, Davis seemed the gentlest of souls, but he had fought in World War II as an OSS operative in the jungles of Southeast Asia and cut his business teeth running a big land company in Southern California. When Tandem ran into trouble, Davis liked to take Treybig to lunch and stiffen the CEO's spine with cryptic but inspiring tales of his adventures. "That was valuable, but different than Tom Perkins, because Tommy was such a gentleman," Treybig recalled. "Tom would be in your face with, 'This is no good.' He couldn't call you fast enough when he saw something wrong."[40]

In 1982, Tandem had an unexpectedly bad quarter, knocking its stock price down a peg or two. The day before the results were announced, Treybig jotted down eight steps he planned to take to improve the company's performance (immediately cancelling all vacations was one of them) and hopped on a plane to present his list to Perkins, who was in New York City at the time. "If I had not faced up that we had a problem," Treybig said, "Tom would have flown to find me." For all the power Perkins wielded, though, Treybig never felt that his chairman encroached on his prerogatives as CEO. "He didn't try to run the company. We would have had a *big* conflict about that. I can look back at things where we did what I wanted and I wish I'd done what Tom wanted, and probably vice versa. But the point is there was no conflict between us that didn't get resolved."[41]

Treybig, who took great pride in the strength of Tandem's board, collaborated with Perkins in recruiting several prominent directors, notably longtime Citicorp CEO Walter Wriston, who became a Tandem director in 1986. Wriston, in turn, convinced George Schultz to sign on after he stepped down as Secretary of State in 1989. According to Wriston, Schultz was so offended by the informality of the Tandem board that he rebuked Perkins after his first meeting and nearly quit on the spot. "We calmed George down," recalled Wriston, referring to himself and Perkins. "We said, 'these entrepreneurs, they don't have staff and briefing books. They want to do business.'"[42]

Genentech's enlarged, post-IPO board was equally high-powered, but was designed mainly to the specifications of Swanson, not Perkins, who was the lone VC among the directors. The diminution of K&P's typically dominant role followed from Genentech's strategy of using directorships to cement alliances with other companies useful to it. "What you want is help in building the business," explained Swanson, who made room on the board for the CEOs of Corning Glass Works, Flour Corporation, Time-Life, and Alpha-Laval and who also happily welcomed Dave Packard, a Perkins recruit.[43] "At Dave's very first meeting, it dawned on me that I'd put the proverbial eight-hundred-pound gorilla on the board," Perkins said. "If Dave had disagreed in any way on anything and had spoken up in the boardroom, his opinion probably would have prevailed over mine. He never did that. I can't remember any difficulty we ever had in a board meeting."[44]

To cement Genentech's alliance with Corning Glass, Perkins agreed to become a director of this old-line manufacturer, which was headquartered in upstate New York and still ruled by the family that had founded it in 1851. For a few years, Perkins served as the "West Coast high-tech guy" on a board that epitomized the clubbiness of the traditional Eastern corporate establishment. So many cigars were smoked during meetings that "the air turned blue and you could hardly see through it by the end," recalled Perkins, who admired a few of his fellow directors (particularly Robert McNamara, the former Secretary of Defense) but could not resign fast enough after Corning cashed out its interest in Genentech.[45]

Genentech was K&P's crown jewel, so it was only natural that Perkins should devote more time to it than to Tandem or any other of his companies. He spent at least a day at its headquarters in South San Francisco almost every week and frequently joined Swanson for long, brainstorming lunches. "Swanson, for a young guy, had incredible vision. I'd never seen anything like it before," Perkins said.[46]

A few years into Genentech's development, Swanson and Perkins came to a meeting of the minds on a critical strategic issue with little fuss. The question was whether the company should use its patents as a barrier to competition or license its proprietary technology to other manufacturers. Genentech took the licensing route, reasoning that its technology was so fundamental that it would find itself ensnared in endless patent litigation if it tried to maintain exclusivity. (As it turned out, Genentech's legal bills were exorbitant anyway.) Licensing had the added advantages of generating immediate revenue and reducing the company's capital spending. Failing to acquire Genentech in its entirety for as little as $100 million thus proved a costly error for Eli Lilly, which ended up paying hundreds of millions of dollars in royalties to the company under its insulin license alone.

Perkins always kept a respectful distance from Genentech's research department, which was Swanson's bailiwick, concentrating instead on marketing and finance. Even with its royalty revenues, Genentech needed a lot more cash in its formative years to fund clinical trials and to build manufacturing plants than conventional financing sources could supply. The necessity of bridging this cash gap made the biotech company as much a hotbed of financial creativity as of science, raising about $3 billion in Perkins's fifteen years as chairman. Although Perkins contributed significantly to such innovations as clinical R&D partnerships and junior common stock, the lion's share of the credit belonged to the company's CFO, Fred Middleton.

By the mid-1980s, Perkins's top priority as chairman was keeping Swanson "at the grindstone," as he put it. "Bob kept saying, 'I'm exhausted. I don't have a minute's time for my family. . . . I've got to get help,'" Perkins recalled.[47]

Help arrived in 1985 in the person of G. Kirk Raab, a veteran pharmaceutical industry executive, who filled the new positions of president and chief operating officer and also took a seat on the board. Although Raab was twelve years older than Swanson, who was just thirty-seven, he joined Genentech with every intention of moving up to CEO—and the sooner the better. "Here I was, number two—but with a lot more experience than the number one," Raab said.[48] The new recruit had not been forced on Swanson by any means, but Raab's room-filling presence seemed to unnerve him. Swanson balked at surrendering the authority promised Raab, who was disinclined to let it pass or to seethe in silence. "I can't remember how many times I had to go down and pull these guys apart, get their hands off each other's throats, recalibrate everybody and reacquaint them with what the mission was," Perkins recalled. "Kirk did a better job of it than Bob."[49]

After a few years of refereeing, Perkins reluctantly concluded that Genentech was suffering from one of the classic maladies of emerging companies: clinging founder syndrome. "Quite a number of times we have had to shift from the founding entrepreneur to somebody else to carry the venture further into the future," Perkins said. "We consider that our role, and it's a very long term role. I would say that companies sometimes outgrow their founders, but they never outgrow us."[50] For Perkins, Swanson was a difficult case in point because he was so easy to admire: "[Bob] was certainly the best entrepreneur I ever worked with."[51]

In 1989, Genentech's stock took a dive. The underlying problem—an unexpected dearth of hot new products to sell—defied hopes of a quick fix. Perkins and Raab persuaded a majority of their colleagues on the board that selling a controlling 60 percent interest to the Swiss drug company Roche Holding was preferable to the risk of being forcibly acquired by another company less willing than was Roche to let Genentech maintain its own, research-driven identity.[52] Swanson was aghast at the prospect of a sale and hated it even more when the Swiss giant, guided by a wink and a nod from Perkins, insisted that Raab move up to CEO as part of the deal. "I probably presented it to Bob as a deal point demanded by Roche, which it was," Perkins acknowledged. "But it may have been put in Roche's head along the way."[53]

Again, Swanson relented, but not before extracting heavy tribute. Perkins stepped into the peacemaker's role, shuttling among Roche, Swanson, Raab, and Genentech's other directors with proposals and counterproposals. "[Swanson] had ten unalterable demands that I guess I boiled down to about four," recalled Perkins, who greased the skids of compromise by surrendering his chairman's post to Swanson.[54] Roche refused absolutely to accede to Swanson's demand of a seat on its board, but it did agree to buy out his stock options at a premium, pay him $500,000 a year as chair (Perkins had received only a nominal payment), and provide him with an office and a secretary.

Perkins unhappily coexisted with Swanson on Genentech's board for five more years. By the time he finally resigned as a director in 1995, he and Swanson were barely on speaking terms. "Although he agreed with every step along the way, each step came with a loss of his prestige," Perkins said. "Unfortunately, my name and fingerprints were all over each step. You just add up enough of them, and I think there was a resentment that was fairly serious."[55]

Perkins also was beleaguered by events at Tandem Computer, which had spiraled into a major crisis of its own as it struggled throughout the mid-1990s to adapt to the advent of open-system computer architecture. As Tandem evolved from selling costly proprietary computer systems to becoming more of a commodity vendor, its revenue growth ground to a halt and Treybig had to eliminate hundreds of jobs to keep the company in the black. The computer business was consolidating with a vengeance, and Perkins and a majority of his fellow directors arrived at the conclusion that Tandem was just not big enough to survive much longer as a freestanding company.

In 1996, the board replaced Treybig with Roel Pieper, a much younger executive who ran a Tandem subsidiary. In the end, the CEO went quietly, submitting to a face-saving shuffle much like the one Perkins had arranged at Genentech; Perkins gave up the chairman's position to Treybig and became chair of a new executive committee of the board. After just one meeting as chairman, though Treybig resigned from the board, left Silicon Valley, and moved back to Texas. "When you've been a CEO for so long and you built a company from no people to a lot of people, it's hard to go to board meetings and dismember everything," Treybig said. "I really didn't want to be chairman, and I thought it would be better to have Tom stay as chairman."[56]

Compaq Computer acquired Tandem for $3 billion in 1997, about a year after Treybig departed. For Perkins, who personally received $70 million for his Tandem shares, this was an all-in-the family sort of deal. Kleiner & Perkins was a major early investor in Compaq and still owned a big slug of stock in the company, whose board was cast in the same VC-dominated mold as Tandem's had been. Perkins was the only Tandem director who was invited to join the Compaq board, which was chaired by his friend Ben Rosen, a Wall Street stock analyst turned venture capitalist. And it was Compaq that would soon lead Perkins back to where it all began for him: Hewlett-Packard.

Although both Tandem and Genentech were financial bonanzas for Perkins, his ruptured relationships with Swanson and Treybig were beyond repair. Treybig has yet to reestablish contact with Perkins, but he acknowledges that his ex-mentor did the right thing in forcing the sale of Tandem to a larger company and is delighted that the business he founded eventually was folded into HP. "It's probably true that things can never be the same between Tom and me, but that doesn't change anything that I feel," said Treybig, who eventually reinvented himself as a venture capitalist after leaving Tandem. "I admire Tom very much. However, he is a very aggressive, smart, quick-acting person. We often had valuable but volatile interactions."[57]

Perkins did enjoy a bit of a rapprochement with Swanson after Genentech's co-founder was diagnosed with brain cancer in 1998. But Swanson died the following year at age fifty-two without ever publicly acknowledging Perkins's contributions to Genentech in any detail. In fact, he barely even mentioned him in an extensive series of interviews he did a few years before his death as part of an oral history project at the University of California, Berkeley. Luckily, Fred Middleton, who had been Swanson's roommate at MIT before becoming Genentech's first CFO, addressed this issue in the reminiscences he provided to the same Berkeley archive.

"Bob and I both had a tremendous amount of respect for Tom Perkins as a highly visible promoter, marketer, strategist, and financier," Middleton said. "Bob felt that if you needed to climb mountains, and you needed to go out and establish a beachhead somewhere new, that Tom was the guy to lead the charge. He was capable and adept at promoting and being a front man for the company. . . . Tom had a think big, spend big, make it big mentality, which was the mentality that Bob was interested in himself, personally. And which he was inspiring everybody else to. There's one story I heard. Bob was taking the founding scientists to Tom Perkins's house for dinner in Belvedere. It's a pretty spectacular place. And he said to all the scientists, 'See guys, this is what we're working towards. Right here.'"[58]

CHAPTER FOUR

HP'S OTHER WOMAN

BY THE TIME Tom Perkins joined Hewlett-Packard's board of directors in the spring of 2002, he was seventy years old and retired from Kleiner Perkins Caufield & Byers. He owed his seat on the board not to Dave Packard or Bill Hewlett, both of whom were dead and gone, but to Cara Carleton Fiorina, the most improbable of the co-founders' several successors. In her three years as chair and CEO of Hewlett-Packard, Fiorina's audacious blend of talent, arrogance, and glamour not only had enthroned her atop lists of the world's most powerful female executives, but had also established her as a superstar CEO identifiable by a single name, "Carly" having become the business-world equivalent of "Madonna" or "Tiger."

The Fiorina-Perkins union was a marriage of convenience, cemented by the shared belief that Compaq Computer should be folded into Hewlett-Packard. The $20 billion acquisition of Compaq would prove to be the signature triumph of Fiorina's tenure as HP's chief, but it was a mega-deal born of weakness, not strength. The price of computing power was falling much faster than the cost of manufacturing it, undermining the basic economics of the computer business. The struggles of HP and

Compaq were greatly exacerbated by their inability to match Dell's prowess at selling computers at a discount over the Web.

The strategic choice confronting Fiorina and her board in 2001 was stark: either shrink HP or get a whole lot bigger. The consensus on Wall Street was that HP should downsize, preferably by off-loading its flagging computer division to concentrate on the high-margin bonanza that was its printer business. But Fiorina wouldn't hear of it. She aspired to make HP "the world's leading technology company," not chop it in half to conform to what she derided as defeatist views of its prospects. She was a buyer, not a seller. The idea of acquiring Compaq appealed to Fiorina because of the big-time economies of scale it would bring to HP, which essentially would be doubling down on its investment in the computer trade. In addition, the two companies' product lines were generally complementary, with HP dominating in the consumer segments of the market and Compaq on the commercial side. And Compaq was available—very available.

Compaq's acquisition of Tandem Computer had not worked out nearly the way Perkins had hoped it would. Even before Compaq had finished absorbing Tandem, it had rashly had made the much larger acquisition of Digital Equipment Corp. (DEC). According to Perkins, he and Compaq's other directors fired CEO Eckhard Pfeiffer in 1999 (just about the time that HP was hiring Fiorina), mainly because he had made a mess of fitting Tandem and DEC into Compaq. Under a new up-from-the-ranks CEO named Michael Capellas, Compaq had straightened itself out operationally but was unable to grow at a rate acceptable to Wall Street or, for that matter, its board of directors. The computer industry was continuing to consolidate inexorably, and the same bigger-is-better logic that had convinced Perkins that Tandem needed to partner with Compaq now convinced him that

Compaq should merge with HP. "It was clear to us on the Compaq board and to Carly that billions could be saved by combining these companies," Perkins said. "It wasn't so clear to the HP board."[1]

HP's directors had reason to be skeptical. Few big tech mergers had ever worked out (Compaq's recent misadventures being a particularly pertinent example), and this would be the largest combination ever attempted. But after lengthy and occasionally heated discussions, HP's directors closed ranks behind Fiorina, with one defiant exception. The prospect of further diluting the "HP Way" by absorbing a Texas-based gunslinger of a company appalled many longtime HP shareholders and employees. They rallied around Walter Hewlett, the last of HP's family directors, who led a proxy fight that plunged his late father's company into a state approximating civil war for the better part of a year and put Fiorina's back squarely against the wall.

Shortly after HP and Compaq had reached a preliminary merger agreement, Perkins called Fiorina to offer to help her promote the union in any way he could and to invite her to dine with him at the Village Pub in Woodside, a celebrated hub of Silicon Valley deal making. Over dinner, Fiorina asked the venture capitalist if he would be interested in joining the HP board if the merger came to pass. Perkins jumped at the chance. "We kicked it around and I told Carly that I would like to be very active on the board and that I thought that my role would be on the technology and marketing side," Perkins said.[2]

Perkins came out swinging from Compaq's corner, talking up the benefits of the merger deal to any reporter who wanted a quote. Just before Christmas 2001, the San Jose *Mercury News* profiled Perkins at length as "one of the most outspoken backers of the merger." As the paper noted, the VC's championing of the deal had brought him into awkward conflict with the descendants of the mentor he still revered, Dave Packard. Perkins "believes the heirs have misunderstood the HP tradition," the story declared. "In part, Perkins is fighting for Compaq. But he also is fighting for his right to interpret the legacy that Packard and Hewlett left for Silicon Valley."[3]

The article prompted a searing letter to the editor from Dave Kirby, a retired HP executive who was a preeminent keeper of the Packard flame. Kirby had been public relations director for twenty-seven years and had helped Packard write his autobiographical book, *The HP Way*. Kirby accused Perkins of exaggerating his contribution to HP. "Tom often had a difficult time at HP because people tired of his immense ego and flashes of arrogance," Kirby wrote. "Many managers commented that this attitude was the antithesis of the HP Way."[4]

Stung, Perkins immediately responded with his own letter to the editor. "Dave Kirby is a skilled wordsmith who could have helped tremendously all those years ago," he concluded. "He chose rather to align with the old guard who resented the emergence of the computer business."[5]

For what it's worth, Perkins was certain that he'd gotten the better of this venomous exchange. "I put one right down the smokestack and that was the end of that," he boasted later. "I've never been shy about a fight."[6]

In the end, Fiorina prevailed by the thinnest of margins over Walter Hewlett, garnering slightly more than 50 percent of the votes cast at a raucous special meeting of HP shareholders held at the Flint Center in Cupertino. The 2,400-seat auditorium was packed with small stockholders allied with Hewlett and openly hostile to Fiorina, who was unyielding in the face of scores of angry questions and comments from the floor. "No matter what her opponents threw at her, Carly Fiorina wouldn't break. They could insult her, boo her, or even appeal to her tender side. It wouldn't work," observed a journalist in attendance. "She would emerge from this meeting an iron-willed survivor."[7]

All in all, Carly's resolute championing of the Compaq acquisition proved to be her finest hour. "You have to hand it to Carly, who saw it from a strategic point of view and pushed it through," said Perkins, who was one of four Compaq directors who joined HP's board. "In my opinion, only Carly could have made it happen."[8]

***

PERKINS WAS SO bedazzled by Carly and her great oxygen-sucking celebrity that at first he barely noticed the other woman in HP's boardroom, fellow director Patricia "Pattie" Dunn. Privately, Perkins dismissed the earnest, even-tempered Dunn as a "mouse" undeserving of a seat on the board of HP or any other big-time company. As for Dunn, the legend of Perkins as Silicon Valley colossus seemed to loom a lot larger in the abstract than the man did in person. "Tom seemed slightly depressive to me, actually," Dunn recalled. "He wasn't rude or anything, but he was kind of slumped in his chair and certainly didn't try to dominate the meetings."[9]

Events would force Perkins to admit that he had grossly underestimated Dunn, who soon would inspire HP's board to take the boldest, most convulsive action in the company's history: the firing of Carly Fiorina. Dunn was the unanimous choice of her colleagues to replace Fiorina as chair and head the search for a new CEO. As chair of HP, Dunn would reduce Perkins to such spluttering irrelevance that she came to supplant even

Narinder Kapany as nemesis and revenge object. "I thought she was mild-mannered, but she is *not* mild-mannered," Perkins said. "She is highly controlled, with an extraordinarily strong will."[10]

Perkins's failure to accurately take Dunn's measure was not entirely his fault, for she had made a career of being underestimated by presumptuous men. Born in 1953, Dunn earned a place in the vanguard of the first generation of women to shatter the so-called glass ceiling and climb to the top of the largest corporations in the United States. In 1999, *Fortune* magazine ranked Dunn eleventh on its first annual list of "the most powerful women in business," just three slots behind Martha Stewart.

Like everyone else on the HP board, Perkins barely understood what Dunn did for a living, much less comprehend how she had risen from the position of temporary secretary to CEO of Barclays Global Investors even as the San Francisco–based firm emerged from obscurity to become the world's largest money manager, with more than $1 trillion in assets. As a lifelong employee of BGI, Dunn was a pure product of a risk-averse, high-precision approach to investing that in many ways that was the opposite of Perkins's ballsy brand of venture capitalism. In its original incarnation as Wells Fargo Investment Advisors (WFIA), BGI had pioneered "quantitative" investing, which substituted rigorous, computer-driven analysis for the guesswork that had long passed for scientific method on Wall Street. The object was to outsmart and outperform the market averages, but in tiny, hard-thought increments that would have constituted utter failure for Kleiner & Perkins.

Dunn was not herself a quantitative analyst, or "quant," lacking a PhD in finance, economics, mathematics, physics, or the like. But she did marry one—her husband, Bill Jahnke, was a top executive of WFIA—and was a quick learner. A smarter, prettier, and grittier version of the proverbial girl next door, she also mastered the art of self-advancement through self-effacement. This required some doing, because Dunn radiated energy and a feisty magnetism from the start; she was noticed. But this secretary-cum-executive would never admit to any ambition grander than doing a good job and made herself indispensable to a succession of BGI bosses, culminating with Frederick Grauer, the mentor whom she ultimately replaced as CEO. When asked about Dunn years later, Grauer gave a terse reply and then lapsed into a sulfurous silence. "There's a lot there," he finally snapped, "but I keep it in a box."[11]

Dunn insisted that she had been scrupulously loyal to Grauer and did not conspire in his downfall. "All I can say is that I don't go behind people's backs and stab them," she said. "I've never done it to anybody I know of. I've fired people, but I stabbed them in the chest, not the back."

Dunn laughed and stole a sly glance across her dining room table at her public relations minder, who urged that I strike her comment from the record. "Not a good quote," Dunn conceded, and then laughed even harder.[12]

* * *

ALTHOUGH DUNN GREW up in a show business family, she was a long time finding the spotlight herself. For years, she took her cues from Grauer, an erudite former finance professor who saw no need for a serious-minded and purely institutional business like BGI to promote itself to the world at large. But after Dunn supplanted Grauer, she immediately set out to raise BGI's profile as the firm made a daring bet on the nascent retail market in Exchange Traded Funds. In 1999, a year after Dunn became

CEO, the *Financial Times* featured her in its "Business Lunch" column, duly noting her "big blow-dried hair, power shoulders, perfect fingernails," and "white-toothed smile."[13]

Dunn and Fiorina were similar in many ways: bright, driven and stylish women of substance. Born less than two years apart, each of them had happened into business as an accidental calling after starting out in entry-level secretarial jobs. Dunn's climb was more arduous, if only because she started well below Fiorina, whose father was a nationally renowned constitutional scholar, and really had to struggle to gain a foothold on the next rung up the socioeconomic ladder.

Dunn's father, Henry Dunn, was an old-fashioned singing comedian who traveled the country more or less continually during vaudeville's long twilight in the 1930s and 1940s. Dunn was an adopted name that Henry claimed to have chosen because it fit on a marquee better than the Jewish surname he was born with: Levine. Born into abject poverty in Boston in 1898, Henry was the only one of thirteen siblings to survive to adulthood. A self-taught pianist blessed with perfect pitch and a powerful tenor voice, he landed his first gig at age thirteen as a cantor in a Boston synagogue. Dunn was best known as the "broad-shouldered, stoutish" half of Cross and Dunn, which from 1932 to 1950 appeared at virtually every major theater and nightclub in the country and also toured Europe at least once.[14] Their specialty was satiric songs on topical issues of the day, with titles like "One Hamburger For Madame," "We're Behind in Our Whittlin'," and "It Could Only Happen in the U.S.A." According to the *New York Times*, "Cross and Dunn were never top headliners, but they were never very far from there either."[15]

Late in his performing career, Dunn became a labor union activist, rotating through various leadership positions in the

American Guild of Variety Artists. Founded in 1939, the AGVA was the latest in a series of unions that had attempted to organize variety entertainers, among them circus and vaudeville performers, comedy and animal acts, night club singers, and "exotic" dancers. Although many of its 30,000 members lived hand to mouth, their number also included such stars as Bob Hope, Bing Crosby, and Dinah Shore. The well-traveled Dunn was so popular among his peers that he was elected chairman at the AGVA's first national convention in New York in 1948.

"Contrary to the glamorous association of theater and the actor, the performer's life isn't filled with champagne and roses," Dunn declared in a radio address he gave in 1950. "Operators of theaters and nightclubs, always ready for a bargain, do not as a rule pay what is necessary to live, but try to keep the expense down. The actor is the first and last person who is always asked to consider the plight of an employer and to take as little as possible." Dunn was especially critical of circus operators, noting that the AGVA had just blacklisted Ringling Bros. and Barnum & Bailey for refusing to negotiate over improvements in working conditions for performers. "Fantastic situations of human abuses by a fellow human being are still being practiced [by circuses]," he said. "Conditions similar to peonage are not rare."[16]

Shortly after Dunn retired from the stage, he married Ruth Marie Tierney, who was twenty-five years his junior. Pattie once publicly described her mother as "a redhead in every way— mercurial, feisty, extremely funny, wacky."[17] Growing up poor and Catholic in the Coney Island section of Brooklyn, Ruth was a superb student who left home as a teenager to study Latin at a special school in Albany. She went on to college nearby, but could not finish for lack of funds. She met Henry Dunn when he tried to organize a theater in Philadelphia where she was appearing as a scantily clad Miss Liberty.

In 1952, the Dunns moved from New York to Los Angeles, where Henry worked as a talent agent, opening an office in Hollywood for the celebrated English impresario Sir Lew Grade. The following year Ruth gave birth to Pattie, her second daughter, in a hospital directly across the street from Walt Disney Studios. Pattie was afflicted with such a bad case of strabismus, or wandering eye, that she was unable to attend kindergarten or first grade. "Pattie was very shy and self-conscious when we played with other kids because they would tease her," recalled sister Debbie, who was just fifteen months older.[18] From age two, Pattie wore Coke-bottle-thick glasses with plaid frames that she frequently hid from her parents by burying them in the back yard. It was not until she was sixteen that her strabismus was finally cured by surgery.

The family moved to Las Vegas in 1958, buying a modest house in one of Sin City's first subdivisions, at the edge of the desert. Henry made a decent living as head meeter-and-greeter and talent booker first at the Dunes and then at the Tropicana. He knew everybody worth knowing in show business. There was no telling whom he might bring home for dinner on Sunday night, when most Vegas showrooms stayed dark. Don Rickles, Sammie Davis Jr., and Dean Martin all graced the Dunns' table, as did a troupe of harmonica-playing midgets. Lena Horne once embarrassed Ruth by insisting on entering the house through the back door. "Honey," she told Ruth, "they won't let me in the front door at the hotel, so I'm not coming in the front door here."[19]

The racism of the Las Vegas casinos galled Henry, who'd chaired the AGVA convention at which eliminating discrimination against black performers was adopted as an official goal of the union. Although Dunn's labor crusading days were over, he was an active, longtime member of the National Conference of Christians and Jews. He organized and hosted a multidenominational Christmas pageant at the convention center in Las Vegas that became an annual event.

Much as Pattie admired her father, who doted affectionately on his kids, her drive to achieve was implanted by Ruth, who entrusted her daughters' education to the knuckle-rapping nuns at Our Lady of Las Vegas and pressed upon her girls the importance of a college diploma virtually from the cradle. Pattie especially excelled in the classroom, just as Ruth had, but during her summers away from school she and her sister accompanied their father to "The Trop" every day and made it their playground. Nobody minded, not even "the guys with the crooked noses," as Henry referred to the casino's mob bosses. The Dunns and their daughters were front-row fixtures at all the best shows, including Barbra Streisand's famous Vegas debut at the Riviera opening for Liberace. "It was not exactly 'Leave it to Beaver,' but we were a very close family," Pattie said. "I think we felt very secure and safe and all that good stuff."[20]

The idyll ended abruptly in 1965, when Henry died of a heart attack at age sixty-six, leaving a modest estate, three children (Paul, the youngest, was not yet two), and a widow who coped pretty well at first. A year later Ruth decided that Sin City wasn't such a fine place to raise kids after all. She sold the house, attached a U-Haul trailer to her big white Cadillac, and drove out to the "Welcome Las Vegas" sign on the city's western outskirts. "OK, girls, where to?" she asked.[21] The choice, democratically arrived at, was San Francisco, where the family had once vacationed.

Ruth rented a little town house north of the city, in San Rafael, where Pattie pulled straight A's at Terra Linda High School and managed to graduate as a National Merit Scholar even as her home life turned nightmarish. The responsibility of caring for Paul increasingly fell on the teenaged Dunn sisters as their mother succumbed to alcoholism and depression. Periodically, the highway patrol would find her pulled over on a shoulder somewhere, paralyzed by a panic attack. According to her daughters, Ruth completely collapsed emotionally after she married a practiced con man who played the adoring hubbie only long enough to clean out her bank account.

By this time, Pattie had moved to Eugene to attend the University of Oregon on a scholarship and Debbie had enrolled at California State University, Chico. A month passed before the sisters realized that Ruth had been evicted and was driving aimlessly around Marin Country with Paul in her Caddie, sleeping at the side of the road. Debbie brought them to Chico and took a job washing dishes to support her destitute mother and little brother for a year. Then it was Pattie's turn. After completing two years at Oregon, she returned to the Bay Area, landed a job as service agent at an office complex in San Francisco, and rented a tiny apartment in Daly City.

After a year or so under Pattie's care, Ruth had recovered to the point where she at least could hold down a part-time job as a retail clerk. At her mother's insistence, Pattie returned to school, winning a scholarship to the University of California, Berkeley, where she majored in journalism and dreamed of being the next Tom Wolfe. Despite a commute that consumed four hours a day round-trip, she completed her last two years of college in five quarters, graduating in December 1975. "I tried to zoom through because I needed to get back to work," she said. "We needed to pay the rent and buy food."[22]

* * *

DUNN ASPIRED TO a career as a reporter, but her mother had other plans and sprang them on her when she returned home from her last day of classes. "Good news," Ruth said, "I've got you a part-time job. You're starting at Wells Fargo Bank on January 2."

"I don't want to work for a bank," Pattie replied.

"It's only temporary."

"I don't even want to temporarily work for a bank. Banks are horrible places."

Ruth said, "You can do it for a few days and find another temporary job."[23]

On Dunn's first day as a secretary in sales and marketing at Wells Fargo, her boss asked her to type up the copy he'd written for a new brochure. Figuring she had nothing to lose except a job she didn't want, Dunn took the liberty of rewriting it entirely as she typed, and handed it back to him half-expecting to be fired on the spot. Instead, she was pressed into service as the writer/editor of every brochure and letter her department sent out. For two years, Dunn determinedly maintained her temp status as a marketing assistant while chasing freelance writing assignments after hours. In 1978, she finally gave up on journalism and accepted the bank's fifth—and final—offer of permanent employment.

Happily, Dunn had wandered into an intriguing little hotbed of financial sedition. She worked for an obscure offshoot of the bank called Wells Fargo Investment Advisors, which in the 1960s had become the first money manager to embrace the quantitative revolution in academic finance. In 1971, WFIA introduced what would become quantitative investing's first commercial break-through: the index fund. It was derived from the heretical notion that the typical investor was better off buying funds that repli-cated market indices than trying to beat the averages by picking stocks or bonds with superior prospects. Wells Fargo's index fund was a megaton bomb of innovation with a slow-burning fuse. There were lots of technical and logistical problems to solve in creating and managing index funds. Mainly, though, years of cajolery were required to convince the pinstriped custodians of institutional wealth to break the habits of generations and en-trust their funds to a bunch of PhDs who spouted weird notions in a vocabulary that seemed to consist mainly of Greek letters.

Enter Dunn, who absorbed the fundamentals of quant while rotating through a series of junior-level positions at a firm that employed fewer than a hundred people at the time she joined. Attractive, quick-witted, and sincerely interested, Dunn found plenty of willing instructors among her senior colleagues—many of whom once had been professors, after all—for intensive one-on-one instruction in the Oxford University mold. In 1980, Dunn wrote an original research study on a fairly complicated invest-ment topic. It was solid work, but nothing in it was as revelatory as the stage presence that she exhibited in presenting the paper at a WFIA client conference in San Francisco attended by William Sharpe, a future Nobel Prize–winner in economics and a consultant to the firm. "I remember Sharpe saying, 'Wow!'" recalled Mary "Cary" Zellerbach, a WFIA quant who'd studied under Sharpe at Stanford. "With all of us, she just knocked our socks off that day."[24]

Dunn rose through the ranks at Wells Fargo not on the strength of her original ideas, but rather her ability to translate her colleagues' often abstruse notions into clear, eloquent English for clients and others who hadn't had advanced training in finance. WFIA also needed someone who could order chaos, a familial role that the precociously self-possessed Dunn had filled since adolescence. WFIA's investment ideas emerged from a maelstrom of freewheeling intellectual debate but had to be codified and implemented with great precision. "Pattie is so subtle in the way she does things that she organized the place around these people and they didn't even know it," said John Casey, a consultant to pension funds and other institutional investors, who befriended Dunn in her second month on the job. Dunn's talents aside, it helped her enormously that WFIA was, as Casey put it, "one of the first, if not the very first, organizations in money management that was absolutely gender neutral."[25]

From 1979 to 1981, Dunn worked as Grauer's assistant. This Stanford PhD was only six years older than Dunn but far more experienced, having taught finance at Columbia and MIT and worked for a big brokerage house before joining WFIA to run its pension fund consulting unit. "I was very much second banana, but we were a team," Dunn said. "Fred was by far the most important person in my career."[26]

Dunn was even closer to Jahnke, a computer systems expert nine years her senior whom she started dating after he divorced his wife in 1980. As office romances go, this one wasn't particularly problematic—at least not until Jahnke and Grauer ended up on opposite sides of a bitter power struggle that polarized senior management. Dunn and Jahnke were married in 1981, just a month after Grauer was fired. (Grauer did not respond to the wedding invitation Dunn sent him.) Jahnke had four children, three of whom (ages sixteen, six, and four) came to live with the newlyweds. In speeches, Dunn liked to say that she married four people.

At first, Ruth was disconsolate over her daughter's choice of husbands, not only because of Jahnke's age and status as a recent divorcé, but also because she objected to his libertarian political philosophy. "My quip about Ruth was that she was to the left of Lenin," said Jahnke, who in time would win over his mother-in-law over through his good humor, patience, and financial generosity.[27] Ruth never completely escaped her demons before her death from cancer in 1992, but stabilized considerably after she moved into a house purchased for her by her daughter and son-in-law. "Pattie was always incredibly understanding of our mother's plight," said her sister, now Debbie Lammers. "There were times when I'd be frustrated or disappointed, but my sister never had a single disparaging word to say about her."[28]

Dunn stopped working with her husband in 1983, when Jahnke was fired for objecting to a radical restructuring plan imposed by Wells Fargo's new CEO. Jahnke took eleven employees with him and founded an investment software company. About the same time, William Fouse, WFIA's chief investment officer, and Tom Loeb, Dunn's boss, resigned and set up a competing quant shop at Mellon Bank using software systems supplied by Jahnke's new company. A half dozen of Dunn's closest colleagues also quit to join Mellon Capital. Dunn yearned to join them, but she was never offered a job.

Fouse said later that he had been advised by Mellon's lawyers that if the talent exodus left WFIA unable to service its customers, Wells Fargo might succeed in getting an injunction against Mellon Capital. "Someone had to stay behind," Fouse told me. "It actually was a compliment to Pattie that we thought she could hold WFIA together by herself."[29] Dunn found Fouse's belated explanation hard to believe, given that Mellon Capital started out trying to take all the business it could away from Wells Fargo. In any event, Dunn certainly was not flattered to be the one left behind. "It hurt my feelings terribly," she admitted.[30]

By this time, Dunn was responsible for administering all of WFIA's investment portfolios, some $25 billion in assets. She was an assistant vice president, making only $18,000 a year, but the entire management hierarchy above her had been eliminated, and she now reported directly to Robert Joss, the Wells Fargo executive who had fired her husband (and who later would become dean of Stanford's business school).

Dunn had arrived at the first of three turning points in her career at WFIA. She suspected that she would be demoted or fired by whomever Wells Fargo brought in to run WFIA. Spying the glint of opportunity amid the chaos, she went to Joss and demanded an extra $25,000 a month for as long as it took him to hire a new CEO. "I never expected to stay," she said. "In effect, I was negotiating a severance package in return for which I was going to deliver intact a set of relationships and portfolios to my successor. Everybody wins. Goodbye."[31] Joss grumbled, but acceded to her demand.

Three months and $75,000 in extra salary later, Dunn got a call from Grauer, who invited her over to his office at Merrill Lynch. "I want to be the first to tell you," he said. "I'm coming back." Dunn, who'd urged Joss to bring Grauer back as CEO, was delighted. "I want you to stay," Grauer continued. "But I

want you to give the money back."[32] Grauer explained that he
didn't want her reputation besmirched by a malingering mer-
cenary taint. Dunn refused on the spot and never heard another
word about it from Grauer or anyone else, though there were
red faces all around when a private quip of Jahnke's accidentally ended up in a national magazine. "Pattie's picture is now
next to the picture of Black Bart in the Wells Fargo history
room," *Institutional Investor* quoted him saying. "She's stolen
more money from Wells Fargo than Bart"—a legendary stage-
coach thief.[33]

Over the next decade, WFIA grew by leaps and bounds, as
indexing belatedly came of age and tens of billions of dollars
in new money rolled into the firm. "Pattie Dunn was one of
four or five people who made important contributions to the
firm's success, but Fred [Grauer] was the man," said Donald L.
Luskin, a longtime WFIA executive. "Even for a rugged indi-
vidualist like me, it was really quite easy to fall in step behind
and follow him."[34]

In one of two deals that transformed WFIA into a global
money manager, Grauer persuaded Wells Fargo's initially reluctant executives to sell a full 50 percent interest to Nikko Securities in 1989. The joint venture legitimated WFIA in Japan, but
was generally disappointing. Six years later, Grauer orchestrated
an even bolder deal with Dunn's help: the sale of the entire firm
to the giant British bank Barclays PLC for $445 million; WFIA
was reborn as Barclays Global Investors. Martin Taylor, Barclays'
CEO, recalled that Grauer and Dunn acted as a team throughout
the negotiations. "Fred fronted the thing up front. He had a lot
to say and he said it," Taylor said. "Pattie sat very quietly on
the side, occasionally interjecting things, more or less in paren-
thesis, which were always to the point and very observant."[35]

Grauer recognized Dunn's own contribution by repeatedly promoting her. In 1985, he named her one of three executive vice presidents. And when Grauer was awarded the additional title of chairman in 1987, he elevated Dunn to president and chief operating officer. Dunn's only serious internal rival for power and position during this grandly expansionary era was Jeffrey Skelton, a gregarious former UC Berkeley finance professor who joined WFIA as its chief quant in 1984 and was promoted in tandem with Dunn. For some years, he and Dunn shared the title of co–chief investment officer and each reported separately to Grauer even as they spent a lot of time traveling together to visit clients and prospect for new business.

Skelton initially mistook Dunn for a pushover, because he heard her crying on the phone as he waited outside her office before meeting her for the first time. A famously nasty pension fund consultant was berating Dunn, threatening to urge his clients to pull their money out of WFIA. About a year later, Dunn and Skelton traveled to New Jersey to meet with her nemesis's most important clients. Their object: to sell a roomful of skeptical middle-aged men on a novel market-timing fund that moved money among stocks, bonds, and cash. The consultant opened by trashing the fund and Skelton followed with a dry, math-intensive presentation that was cut short by Dunn, who spoke impromptu for an hour. "Through an easy logic and charm, and some feminine wiles, to be perfectly honest, she had these guys in the palm of her hand," Skelton recalled. "We walked in there under threat and walked out almost to applause."[36] In the end, the pension fund not only put money into the new fund, but also fired the consultant who had given Dunn such a hard time.

Skelton resigned in 1994, shortly after Grauer elevated Dunn to the post of co-CEO. (Grauer remained the firm's sole chairman until 1997, when he decided to share that position with Dunn, too.) A dozen years after Dunn had aced him out, Skelton's bitterness was still evident beneath his surface good humor. "Pattie is a very ambitious and charming person who knows how to use an organization to get what she wants," he said. "I have a lot of affection for her, but she is someone you underestimate at your peril. She disarms you—literally—and she'll also disleg you."[37]

It appears that Grauer's downfall was as much a matter of overestimating himself as of underestimating Dunn. Seemingly unable to reconcile himself to his firm's subordinate status, Grauer antagonized his bosses, first at Wells Fargo and then at Barclays, with insistent, importunate demands for one thing or another. As it turned out, the sale to Barclays was a reverse takeover in the limited sense that it left the San Francisco contingent in charge of the British bank's large but undistinguished BZW (nicknamed "Beezwim") asset management division. Grauer insisted on this arrangement, and yet in the end this concession only sharpened his sense of grievance. In merging WFIA and Beezwim to form BGI, Grauer and his team effectively turned dross into gold. He expected to be paid accordingly.

Grauer's employment contract expired in the fall of 1998, as did Dunn's, for that matter. Grauer asked Dunn, who was much more politic in her dealings with BGI's London masters, to "witness" his compensation negotiation with Martin Taylor, Barclay's CEO. "I knew what Fred was looking for and I knew what Barclays was willing to do, and I tried to mediate between them," said Dunn, who failed, to say the least.[38] In mid-1998, Grauer took Taylor aside after a meeting at Barclay headquarters and demanded a colossal pay raise. Taylor made a counteroffer that Grauer dismissed as an insult. "We were a very, very, *very* long way apart," Taylor told me. "Fred said, 'I'm out of here then,' and I said, 'I deeply regret it, but there you are.'"[39]

Dunn, who was vacationing in Italy with her husband when Grauer resigned, had arrived at the second great turning point of her career. "Had Fred come to me and said, 'I want you to quit with me,' I don't know what I would have done," Dunn said. As it was, though, Grauer gave her no advance warning and did not even call her after he had delivered his unsuccessful ultimatum. Instead, Dunn heard the news from Taylor and, at his request, was in London within hours. The very next day, Barclays announced Dunn's promotion to CEO and chair of BGI.

By most accounts, Grauer's disappointment that Dunn had failed to support him by volunteering on her own to resign had morphed into cold fury as he came to believe that she had secretly opened a back channel to Taylor through which she had plotted his overthrow. Both Dunn and Taylor denied that they had conspired to oust Grauer. However, Taylor clouded the matter a bit by acknowledging that he was emboldened in his dealings with Grauer by the knowledge that Dunn would stay at BGI. *How* did he know? "Actually, I didn't," he replied. "I just had a sense of it. Certainly I never doubted that Pattie could do the job."[40]

For a second time, Dunn had to hold a traumatized firm together, only this time she was responsible for 2,000 employees and $600 billion in assets. It helped enormously that Grauer held his tongue, sparing Dunn the taint of illegitimacy. Although Grauer was sorely missed, many of BGI's executives soon rallied to Dunn's equally energetic but much more collaborative management style. Over the next few years, Dunn would travel to London a dozen times a year, maintaining a solid relationship with Barclays even after Taylor was replaced by Matthew Barrett in late 1999. In her solicitous, methodical way, she overcame pervasive resistance within Barclays' senior management group to secure a $45 million investment that would vault BGI into a hugely lucrative position of complete dominance in exchange-traded funds. She also succeeded where Grauer had failed in finally persuading Barclays to set up a generous stock option plan for BGI executives that in time would make multimillionaires of many of them.

As CEO, Dunn would have her failures as well as her successes, but none of them pained her as much as her estrangement from Grauer, who rarely returned her phone calls or responded to her emails and letters. "What I came to understand much after the fact was that Fred felt I had engineered him out of the business. He felt that I had gone to Barclays and said, 'We don't need Fred. I can do this by myself,'" acknowledged Dunn, who had worked side by side with Grauer for fifteen years. "Believe it or not, I have very few sources of heartbreak in my life. That's one of them."[41]

* * *

IN 1998, HEWLETT-PACKARD became the first company to ask Dunn to join its board of directors, and this affirmation of her ascent into elite corporate ranks could not have been more providentially timed. She attended her first HP board meeting just ten days after Grauer's unexpected resignation had left her solely in charge of Barclays Global Investors. "If anyone thought that I wasn't up to the job of being the CEO," she recalled, "the fact that HP had asked me to become a director was confirming."[42]

Dunn's name was on a short list of director candidates that the executive recruiting firm Russell Reynolds Associates had submitted to Lewis Platt, HP's chairman and CEO. The board's designated investment expert was retiring, and Platt wanted to replace him with someone of equal expertise. If this person happened to be a CEO and a woman, so much the better, Platt having made "diversity" one of the hallmarks of his tenure, which began in 1992. Dunn met all these criteria and impressed in her interview with Andrea Redmond of Russell Reynolds. "She was gracious, thoughtful, intense, and busy," Redmond said. "This was not someone who was the slightest bit flaky."[43]

The selection of Dunn was a step forward in Platt's fitful campaign to professionalize the vestigial founder's board that he'd inherited from his predecessor and that still included four representatives of the families of Bill Hewlett and Dave Packard. Platt had strengthened the board considerably with the addition of the CEOs of Boeing and Pacific Telesis, but he had yet to begin disassembling the family bloc, which, whatever the individual merits of its members, was an impediment to change for a company burdened by excessive reverence for a distant golden age.

Not long after Dunn joined the board, Platt put forth a bold restructuring plan. The idea was to revitalize HP by spinning off its oldest part—the original scientific instruments founded by Bill and Dave—into a brand new company called Agilent Technologies, which would start with $8 billion in revenues and 40,000 employees. If all went according to Platt's plan, the family directors would either retire or go with Agilent, shattering the family bloc once and for all. In March 1999, Dunn voted with the majority of directors in approving the divestiture, which would also prove to be Platt's swan song.

Although Platt was only fifty-eight years old, it had become evident to key directors that on his watch HP had failed utterly to anticipate the emergence of the Internet as the new fulcrum of high tech. This was particularly galling to Dick Hackborn, who also sat on the board of Microsoft and had watched admiringly as its CEO, Bill Gates, completely reoriented that company around the Internet over the preceding few years. Platt sealed his fate by commissioning a critique from a Silicon Valley consultant, who concluded that he was ill equipped to manage change (the Agilent spin-off notwithstanding). Platt dutifully reported this finding to the board, which not only strong-armed the CEO into early retirement but also denied him the traditional courtesies of remaining as chair and of choosing his own successor. The board's only concession to Platt was to put him on the four-person committee formed to search for a new CEO.

The committee's essential member was Hackborn, a revered, quasi-mystical figure within HP. Working from the obscurity of an HP satellite office in Boise, Idaho, Hackborn had created the first mass-market laser printer in the early 1980s and parlayed it into a franchise of such fabulous profitability and enduring dominance that it reduced HP's instruments business to second-class status. Packard was so eager to promote Hackborn to CEO that in 1992 he offered to relocate HP headquarters to Boise to accommodate him. Hackborn turned the promotion down, even so (much to the delight of Platt, Packard's second choice), for he was a kind of hermit genius who remained at HP as it grew around him, but who was almost pathologically averse to the organizational complications and social entanglements that follow from business success. Hackborn did consent to join HP's board, and there he hauntingly remained, a silver-haired should-have-been-successor to Bill and Dave.

The search committee cast a wide net, and in the end made a daringly unconventional choice in Fiorina. Her gender wasn't the half of it: She was unacquainted with the computer business, she had never before held the position of CEO, and she had never even run a successful division at Lucent, the telecommunications giant at which she had spent most of her career as a marketing executive. Brimming with self-assurance, energy, and charm, Carly was spellbindingly persuasive in any setting. She had dazzled Hackborn, cinching his approval by inviting him to partner with her as HP's future chairman. "Come on, Dick," she said, "you can't tell me there's a better person to do it."[44]

Like most of HP's directors, Dunn had played no part in Fiorina's selection, other than to rubber-stamp the search committee's choice. In fact, she hadn't even set eyes on Carly until after she'd been chosen and made her first presentation to the board as CEO. Dunn was content to defer to Hackborn, who held nothing back in recommending Carly to his colleagues. "We may be getting one of the top two or three CEOs of our generation," he declared. "She could be the next Jack Welch."[45] For many directors, Dunn included, Hackborn's newfound willingness to postpone his long-threatened retirement from the board and become chairman also worked to Fiorina's great advantage. As Dunn put it, "The nice thing about picking Carly for CEO was that it saved Dick Hackborn for HP. That can't be overestimated."[46]

At Carly's debut board meeting, she spoke at length without notes, artfully using colored pens and an overhead slide projector to sketch out a bold vision of the digital future and of HP's place within it. "I remember thinking, 'This is either an incredible tour de force by someone who already has her head completely around the most important decisions that are going to have to be made affecting the way the company operates for the next decade, or she doesn't know what the hell she's talking about and is just faking it,'" Dunn said. "To me, a lot of it did make sense. I looked around the room and the general reaction was, 'Wow, we're really lucky to have her!'"[47]

* * *

FOR DUNN, THE drama of HP's scorched-earth proxy war paled in comparison to a reversal in her personal fortunes that made 2001 to 2002 the most difficult stretch of her adult life by far. Dunn was diagnosed with breast cancer in September 2001, just a week after HP had announced its plan to acquire Compaq. Although breast cancer had killed her mother not ten years earlier, Dunn took the diagnosis in stride. Not that she dawdled: She had surgery in November and started daily radiation therapy two months later. But she just didn't give the disease much thought as she went about her daily business, keeping to the same grueling work schedule she always had. "It just sort of went over my head," she said. "I didn't understand the ramifications of it."

Dunn also was greatly distracted by the press of events at BGI. Although she was far more diplomatic in interacting with Barclays than Grauer had been, she soon began to chafe under the UK bank's ownership and concluded that the firm would be much better off as an independent company owned by its employees. She had little trouble convincing the San Francisco private equity house of Hellman & Friedman to partner with her in proposing a $1.4 billion management buyout of BGI in early 2002. The mechanics of the deal, which was code-named Project Amethyst, proved hellaciously complex, involving dozens of disparate national tax regimes and scores of regulators. The insuperable problem, though, was that Barclays' management did not want to let BGI go and in fact only grew more averse to the idea as the negotiations deepened its understanding of the subsidiary's underlying value. In advocating a buyout as long and hard as Dunn did, she inevitably alienated her London bosses, just as Grauer had. "I say that Pattie did a pretty good job pushing on a string," said Matthew Barger, the Hellman & Friedman partner who worked most closely with her on the buyout. "Honestly, though, it ended up a mess and took forever and was irritating to all involved, me included."[48]

In May 2002, Dunn's health turned from bad to worse as she was diagnosed with a second form of cancer—melanoma. This time, Dunn was devastated emotionally. Her doctors planned a program of intensive chemotherapy to augment her radiation treatments for the breast cancer. "I had no idea how I was going to do that and still be CEO," she said.[49]

Dunn ended a three-week agony of indecision by resigning in June. Some BGI insiders assert that her standing with London had eroded to the point that she could not have effectively carried on as CEO even in good health. Like Grauer, in other words, she overreached in the end. She was not asked to recommend a successor. Blake Grossman, the American half of the trans-Atlantic team of co-CEOs that replaced her, had been tepidly supportive of the buyout at best. Dunn, who knew Grossman well and thought highly of him, moved to a smaller office at BGI headquarters and into a well-paid but largely ceremonial position as vice chairman. However, Dunn never seriously considered giving up her seat on the HP board. "I didn't want to crawl into a hole," she explained. "I felt that HP was a fairly light list compared to being CEO."[50]

Barclays not only terminated the buyout negotiations but later refused to acknowledge that they had ever taken place. This was only to be expected, because selling BGI in 2002 would have been a stupendous mistake. Over the next five years, its annual earnings would soar eightfold, to $1.1 billion, as capital investments made under Grauer and Dunn paid off beyond even the most optimistic of the projections underpinning the buyout plan. By 2007, BGI was worth some $20 billion, Barger estimated. "This was the one that got away—a colossal home run," Barger lamented.[51] Had the deal happened, Dunn personally would have added as much as $500 million to the $50 million net worth she had already amassed, putting her on the fringes of the neighborhood inhabited by her new colleague on the HP board, Tom Perkins.

Dunn's advocacy worked to the great benefit of her BGI colleagues even though the buyout never came to pass. Taking to heart the concept underlying the failed deal, Barclays instituted a much more generous stock option plan for BGI's senior executives. By 2009, when Barclays finally did sell BGI, a few hundred insiders owned about 9 percent of the firm. Of the $13.5 billion that BlackRock paid for BGI, some $1.2 billion went to the firm's employees. Dunn did not share in the bonanza, having cashed out her options at a lower price when she resigned as vice chairman in 2005.

Dunn had left tens of millions of dollars on the table, but her preoccupation was time, not money. In early 2004, less than two years after she had been diagnosed with breast cancer, Dunn's lungs had suddenly filled with fluid, leaving her gasping for breath. She was rushed to the University of California, San Francisco, where doctors made a grim diagnosis: Yet another kind of cancer had invaded her body. She now had ovarian cancer and it was roaringly active, having already had advanced to Stage IV, the final phase. Although Dunn was being continually monitored for a recurrence of breast cancer, tests had shown that she did not have a gene that would put her at risk for ovarian cancer, which is difficult to detect and asymptomatic until late in the growth process, according to Dr. Bethan Powell, a UCSF gynecological cancer specialist who cared for Dunn. Dr. Powell, informed Dunn that the median life expectancy for a patient in her condition was just three years.[52]

Dunn quickly settled on the most aggressive treatment option—chemotherapy followed by a four-hour operation on her abdomen and pelvis and then six more rounds of chemotherapy—hoping all the while that the melanoma and breast cancer remained in remission. While still undergoing treatment, Dunn joined the board of the Charlotte Maxwell Clinic, an Oakland organization that assisted low-income and indigent women with cancer. "One of the things that I began to understand after my first experience with cancer was how well off I was," Dunn said. "Here I am dealing with the big problem, but with access to the best medical care, with financial resources. If I'm not feeling good, I can go home. I have a nice house. I have someone to bring me tea. It will be all right. But there are women with cancer who have to sleep on a bench."[53]

CHAPTER FIVE

JAY KEYWORTH'S CELESTIAL PROXY

THE REMOVAL OF Carly Fiorina as HP's chairman and CEO in 2005 was a most improbable act, and not just because it came so soon after her triumph in the Compaq campaign. Perhaps the greatest systemic failing of the American system of corporate governance is that boards of directors rarely take decisive action to avert crisis until the damage done is so utterly obvious as to be irreparable. The odds against the timely firing of a CEO are long indeed—particularly one as forceful and egotistical as Fiorina. That HP became an exception to the rule was Fiorina's own fault; she not only lost the confidence of her board but needlessly antagonized many of its members with her high-handed behavior. Even so, push might never have come to shove had not two HP directors stepped to the fore amid the contention and chaos of the moment, first George A. "Jay" Keyworth II and then Pattie Dunn.

Keyworth, a nuclear physicist who had held high position in the first Reagan White House, was HP's longest-serving director, having joined the board in 1986. A voluble, incisively opinionated man, Keyworth was deeply knowledgeable about HP and took great pride in being the last remaining board member who had been appointed by Dave Packard. He believed that the close, quasi-familial bond that he had forged with Packard during the industrialist's difficult final years, coupled with his unrivaled tenure as a director, conferred upon him both a special status and a solemn duty to safeguard Packard's corporate legacy. That Keyworth's career had traced a steady downward slope after precocious early success only deepened his attachment to HP. By the time Fiorina became CEO, if not earlier, his seat on the board had become the keystone of his identity and also an important source of income. "HP was my whole world," he said after he'd been forced to resign.[1]

Keyworth was a self-styled Westerner with a classic Eastern Establishment pedigree. Born in Boston into a prosperous family that owned a furniture-manufacturing company, he attended an elite New England prep school and graduated from Yale University in 1963 with a bachelor's degree in physics. He went on to do graduate work at Duke University, earning a PhD in nuclear physics in 1968. Keyworth immediately headed west to New Mexico to take a staff job at what is now called Los Alamos National Laboratory, the high-security U.S. government research complex near Santa Fe where the first atomic bomb had been developed during World War II.

That Keyworth rose through the ranks to become director of the physics division at Los Alamos was a tribute to his intellect and work ethic, for he certainly did not do it on tact and discretion. "Keyworth was quick to grasp the implications of scientific discoveries and perhaps just as quick to dismiss those who disagreed," observed the authors of a book about the inner workings of the weapons laboratory, adding that he was also "renowned at Los Alamos for his love of fine food, cars, and accommodations." This account suggested that Keyworth did manage upwards effectively, becoming a protégé of Harold Agnew, the top man at Los Alamos throughout the 1970s. Agnew, a dyed-in-the-wool skinflint, "warmed to [Keyworth's] energy and forceful persona," even as he chided the young physicist for his "champagne tastes."[2]

Although Keyworth did not succeed Agnew as Los Alamos director, he followed in his footsteps, in a sense, even so. Just after the United States and China established normal diplomatic relations in 1978, Agnew visited Beijing at the invitation of the Chinese government. After meeting with many of China's top nuclear physicists, he agreed to provide the Central Intelligence Agency with a tantalizing glimpse into one of the world's most secretive nuclear weapons development programs. Agnew retired shortly after his return home. In casting about for someone to send back to China in his stead, Los Alamos's own intelligence chief tapped Keyworth, who was initially reluctant to go to China, according to *A Convenient Spy*, an account of the U.S. government's unsuccessful espionage prosecution of Wen Ho Lee, a Taiwan-born programmer at Los Alamos: "Keyworth had been to the Soviet Union and disliked it immensely, being especially disdainful of the lack of stalls, seats, or sanitation in restrooms."[3]

The CIA sent a team of field operatives to Keyworth's house in Pojoaque, a small town on an Indian reservation near Los Alamos, to instruct him in spycraft and to brief him on hundreds of questions about the Chinese weapons program that the agency was hoping he could help answer. "I was stunned to learn how little we knew about it," Keyworth told the authors of *A Convenient Spy*.[4] Washington also assigned Keyworth a diplomatic objective: to convince China to stop testing nuclear weapons in the atmosphere, as the U.S. and the USSR already had done.

Keyworth made several trips to China in 1980 and 1981, staying weeks at a time. In Beijing, he bunked in a presidential guest house with bugs in the walls and guards at the doors. Each night, Keyworth turned his shower on full blast as he recorded his observations on micro-cassettes that he hid inside his pillow while he slept and carried with him at all times during the day. His visits amounted to an elaborate high-stakes game of cat and mouse, in which he tried to get his Chinese counterparts to provide substantive answers to his queries without giving up classified information in return. "No question, one had to be on one's toes," Keyworth recalled. "You had to be tricky."[5]

Although Keyworth's stint as a scientist-spy was a considerable success on balance, producing reams of useful information, he also was accused of inadvertently providing the Chinese with an intelligence coup of their own. On one of his trips, Keyworth came under especially aggressive questioning about U.S. techniques of laser fusion, a topic heavily shrouded in secrecy at the time. Keyworth finally fended off his most persistent questioner with what he intended to be a simple, playful analogy about the two gases used to fuel the process. "You just make a ball of it," he said. "If you drop the ball on the floor, it will go off. It's that easy."[6]

Keyworth thought he'd acquitted himself well under pressure, but dutifully reported the incident to intelligence officials upon his return home even so. "When I came back, I used this example many times to show how completely benign conversations could turn into uncomfortable situations in China," Keyworth recalled. However, some of his colleagues at Los Alamos feared that Keyworth's disclosure actually was not so benign, that his analogy had been too revealing and amounted to an indiscretion. Years later, in 1999, a House select committee investigating China's nuclear thefts and illicit technology transfers studied the episode and concluded in its final report that it "involved the inadvertent, bordering on negligent disclosure of classified technical information." In an interview with the *New York Times*, Keyworth criticized the committee's finding. "I most certainly did hold scientific discussions in China and many of those discussions did run right up against the rules of propriety, no question," he said. "But I don't believe those bounds were crossed."[7]

The FBI had investigated the incident not long after it occurred, but apparently found nothing untoward, for in 1981 Keyworth was appointed to the prestigious post of science adviser in the Reagan White House. He was a surprise nominee, to put it mildly. Just forty-one years old when he left Santa Fe for Washington, Keyworth was not preeminent in his own field of nuclear physics and virtually unknown to the larger scientific community. That he was a scientist with a conservative political bent who had devoted his entire career to making nuclear weapons only intensified the backlash to his nomination. "The reigning mandarins of science . . . mounted an increasingly virulent campaign of abuse and vilification against Keyworth," recalled Martin Anderson, a senior Reagan adviser who was responsible for vetting the nominee. "The anti-Keyworth letters poured in."[8]

Reagan's aides stuck with Keyworth even so, seemingly because he fit their downgraded specifications for the job to a T. What the new administration wanted was not the traditional kind of eminent, independent-minded science adviser inclined to speak truth to power, but rather one who would support its policies and otherwise do what he was told to do as chief of the White House Office of Science and Technology Policy (OSTP). According to Gregg Herken, author of a history of presidential science advising, the conditions attached were so off-putting that a dozen more prominent candidates had turned down the post before it was offered to Keyworth, who once told members of the OSTP staff that they should consider themselves "the President's slaves."[9] That Keyworth hailed from a weapons lab was "a bonus," Anderson observed, because it meant that he "was not hostile to using science to help defend the country."[10]

In his own estimation, Keyworth ultimately got the nod as science adviser only because Edward Teller wanted him to. Teller had made important early contributions to U.S. nuclear weapons programs but had been ostracized by other leading physicists because of his hawkish views (he was an inspiration for Dr. Strangelove) and his reputation for distorting the scientific record to advance his personal interests at the expense of colleagues. In reaction, Teller shifted the focus of his promotional efforts to military and government circles, becoming a darling of the far right for his strident anti-Communism and championing of American military and technological supremacy. Reagan's election in 1980 completed Teller's transformation from a largely discredited old warhorse of the nuclear arms race into "America's number one scientific celebrity," according to biographer William Broad.[11]

Keyworth admired Teller from a distance before befriending him in the mid-1970s. As head of the physics department, the much younger physicist was instrumental in Teller's rehabilitation at Los Alamos, where, after two decades of estrangement, he had returned to consult and lecture. In recommending Keyworth as science adviser, Teller more than repaid the favor, thus enhancing his already considerable influence over the Reagan White House. Keyworth freely acknowledged his debt to Teller, telling friends that he regarded him as a father figure. "Bluntly," Keyworth admitted later, "the reason I was in that office is because Edward first proposed me, and the president very much admires Edward."[12]

In other words, Keyworth came to Washington under obligation to two masters—Teller and Reagan—whose ambitions overlapped most consequentially in support of the deployment of defensive nuclear weapons. As science adviser, Keyworth dealt with dozens upon dozens of important initiatives spanning the entire scientific spectrum, but his tenure was dominated and defined by a single apocalyptic issue: the Strategic Defensive Initiative, better known by the derisive nickname "Star Wars." The idea was for the United States to jettison the doctrine of Mutual Assured Destruction, which had long defined its Cold War standoff with the USSR, and gain a strategic advantage using high-tech defensive weaponry to create an impenetrable missile shield.

Much as Keyworth idolized Reagan, he did not always toe the administration line. Before Star Wars loomed as the acid test of his political loyalty, he had damaged his standing within the administration by opposing it on a number of issues, including its plans to build a huge space station (which he mocked as a costly "motel in the sky" and even potentially "a lead balloon") and its dismissal of acid rain as a serious environmental threat.[13] By some accounts, he also annoyed his masters in the West Wing by talking too freely with reporters covering the administration. Liberated at last from the secrecy shackles of Los Alamos, Keyworth found that he quite enjoyed interacting with reporters. "I had a lot of contacts in the press, hundreds—and some very close ones," Keyworth said later.[14]

Like most scientific and defense experts, Keyworth was deeply skeptical of the technical feasibility of SDI, including the cutting-edge nuclear X-ray technology that Teller envisioned as its centerpiece. He was often critical of the concept of anti-missile defense in speeches to elite scientific audiences, including one that included Teller. But in meetings at the White House he said little, encouraging the misperception that he was a Star Wars enthusiast. Keyworth played for time by setting up a panel of a dozen preeminent scientists who spent a full year evaluating various anti-missile technologies. The group concluded that none of them was nearly ready for prime time, including Teller's precious X-ray laser, which it dismissed as "blue sky."[15]

When Reagan abruptly decided to commit to SDI in defiance of its many critics, though, Keyworth signed onto the project and never looked back. He helped edit the President's famous speech announcing Star Wars in March 1983 and then spent the rest of his term as science adviser acting as the administration's chief spokesman for SDI. "Rather than trying to close the gap between the administration and the nation's scientists over SDI. . . . Keyworth's public statements seemed almost calculated to make that rift grow wider," noted Herken in his history of presidential science advising.[16] Keyworth responded to the barrage of criticism leveled at him by turning on those he deemed his fair-weather friends in the press. Drawn from a "narrow fringe element on the far left of our society," the media were "skewed toward an apparent joy in attacking anything that resembles the 'Establishment,'" he charged.[17]

Keyworth was so vociferous and intemperate in the self-described role of "cheerleader" for SDI (he objected to the Star Wars appellation) that the Republican defense eminence Brent Scowcroft finally took him aside and advised him to tone it down for his own good. "You are throwing your career away for something that isn't yours," Scowcroft said. Keyworth thanked him for the advice and then ignored it, soldiering on as SDI's chief mouthpiece even as he became "one of the most hated scientists in the country," by his own description. "In some ways," he told me, "I never recovered. I have not walked a life of simplicity all the time."[18]

Luckily for Keyworth, he crossed paths with Dave Packard during his time in the White House. He had known Packard only by reputation when he called in 1982 to invite HP's co-founder to join a blue-ribbon advisory panel to the science adviser that also included Teller and Agnew. "I became addicted to Dave's judgment," Keyworth said. "He was a man of very few words, but impeccable judgment."[19]

When Keyworth decided in late 1985 to resign as science adviser, the first person in whom he confided was Packard. "I've done my best to help you," replied Packard, who'd retired from HP management but remained chairman at age seventy-three. "Now I need you to come and help me."

About the same time that Keyworth joined the HP board in 1986, he also hung out his shingle in Washington as a corporate consultant. At Packard's urging, President Reagan in 1983 had formed the President's Commission on Industrial Competitiveness, which reported to Keyworth and was chaired by John Young, Packard's successor as CEO of Hewlett-Packard. The commission never did much in the way of neutralizing the threat posed by Japan Inc., but at least it provided Keyworth with useful personal contacts, staffed as it was by top executives of Pfizer, Texas Instruments, Westinghouse, and other big companies.

Keyworth gave Washington's famous revolving door a couple of twirls, but failed to convert his connections into a sustainable business. He first set himself up as a consultant on security and intelligence in partnership with Herbert Meyer, a former special assistant to Reagan's CIA chief, William Casey. Keyworth-Meyer International quickly imploded, with Keyworth exiting after a few months to form his own firm, The Keyworth Co., which advertised itself as a corporate helpmate in "developing strategies for growth based on emerging and changing technologies." Keyworth's little advisory firm thrived for a time, counting the aluminum giant Alcoa and the Mexican billionaire industrialist Alfonso Romo Garza among its most active clients. But the half dozen or so professionals Keyworth hired to assist him melted away along with his paying clients over a period of a few years, reducing his chairmanship of The Keyworth Co. to little more than a line on his résumé.

Keyworth's Hewlett-Packard tie was not the only enduring affiliation he fashioned after stepping down as science adviser. He was a longtime fellow (and, for two years, research director) of the Hudson Institute, a pillar of Washington's conservative establishment, and in 1993 he joined with Newt Gingrich and others to found the Progress and Freedom Foundation. To this day, Keyworth remains chairman of the latter think tank, which applies a libertarian philosophy to digital-technology policy issues. Keyworth also is now in his fifteenth year as a board member of General Atomics, a nuclear physics and defense contractor best known for manufacturing the unmanned Predator aircraft.

Unquestionably, though, Keyworth's seat on HP's board was the centerpiece of his professional life in the twenty years that followed his White House service. For nine of those years, Packard continued to dominate the board as its chairman, despite his failing health. After Packard's wife died in 1987, Keyworth began spending a week or so every month with Packard at his home in Los Altos Hills. There was little small talk between them—Packard had always been averse to it and was all but deaf now, in any event—but much instructive discussion of HP. Keyworth often literally took notes and soon found himself acting as Packard's public relations mouthpiece. "Every time someone from the press tried to contact him, he'd always pass them off to me," Keyworth said.[20]

One of Packard's most pertinent lessons was how to remove a CEO. John Young had succeeded Bill Hewlett as CEO in 1978 and had outlasted his effectiveness by 1991. Something had to be done, and Packard put a special committee of the board in charge of figuring out what it should be. The group proved so ineffectual that Packard finally stepped in and ushered Young into early retirement himself. The main failing of the committee was ignorance, concluded Keyworth, who was a member. "We did not know enough about the business to be able to say, 'Here's the company's performance' and write a paragraph on it. 'Here's John's performance' and write a paragraph on it," he said. "Worse yet, we couldn't even have written the requirements to give to a search firm to find a new CEO."

"Partly, you have to blame Dave and Bill," Keyworth continued. "They never really thought through what the right board would look like. Some of the people they put on it were good, but it was never done through much of a selection process. It's very hard to select the right people if you don't know what it is you are trying to build in the first place. What you want is a board where every single person is capable of understanding the company and together brings a diversity of skills to that task."[21]

Devastated by Packard's death in 1996—which he recalled as "one of the toughest things I've ever experienced in my life"—Keyworth emerged from a prolonged bout of introspection convinced that he'd done a lousy job as an HP director. "I felt very guilty because I didn't think I'd lived up to Dave's expectations," said Keyworth, who was resolved to be a more diligent and assertive member of a board that in his view had been for a long time passive to a fault.[22]

* * *

KEYWORTH NEVER THOUGHT much of Young's successor, Lew Platt, and was one of a handful of directors who took the lead in forcing him into early retirement in 1999. Although Keyworth was not a member of the search committee that decided to replace Platt with Fiorina, he had no rival in the extravagance of his initial admiration of Fiorina as a "change agent" extraordinaire. In fact, he apparently was so discombobulated by Carly that he publicly praised her as "the son Dave Packard never had"—a compliment all the more bizarre in light of the fact that Packard did in fact have a son, David Woodley Packard, whom Keyworth knew well as a longtime fellow HP board member. "While it was a cruel thing to say about his friend David, Jay meant that I both understood and had passion for the business Dave had built," Fiorina commented.[23]

In Keyworth's view, the Compaq merger in 2002 confirmed Carly's greatness as a strategist and leader while providing the HP board with a desperately needed infusion of new talent in the person of Tom Perkins. Despite their shared veneration of Packard, Keyworth and Perkins had never met. Keyworth had long admired Perkins from afar as a great Silicon Valley venture capitalist, but was surprised even so at the breadth of his new colleague's scientific knowledge and the perspicacity of his understanding of HP's business challenges. For his part, Perkins immediately recognized Keyworth as a kindred spirit and a "powerful director" who could make a useful boardroom ally. "We became very close very quickly," Perkins said.[24]

Fiorina was wary of Perkins, whose reputation as a domineering director preceded him, but made a tactical error even so in granting his request to organize a technology committee of the board consisting of himself as chairman and the only two colleagues he deemed technologically worthy: Dick Hackborn and Jay Keyworth. Although the nominal purpose of the tech committee was to help guide HP's $5 billion in annual research-and-development spending, Perkins defined its purview in practice as Everything That Really Mattered. The panel effectively functioned as an executive committee, which Perkins had used at Genentech and other Kleiner & Perkins companies to exert added leverage over strong-willed CEOs. Much as he admired Fiorina, Perkins was accustomed to deference from corporate executives. If he couldn't compel it as chairman of the board, then the chairmanship of a tech committee would have to do.

HP's tech committee was not a total disaster for Fiorina by any means. Perkins, Keyworth, and Hackborn made valuable contributions in three important areas: improving HP's haphazard management of its patent portfolio, diminishing the company's reliance on Intel as a source of microprocessors, and raising its game on the Internet. "In general, when they stuck to technology strategy they were insightful," Fiorina conceded. "When they strayed into other areas, however, they were disruptive. And they didn't know what they didn't know." On the contrary, she added, "they thought because the understood technology, they understood everything."[25]

Fiorina's budding resentment of the tech committee's intrusiveness into what she considered the prerogatives of management probably cost Perkins his seat on the board in January 2004. Because he was about to turn seventy-two, the board's mandatory retirement age, he could not be nominated for another term unless Fiorina as chair took measures to exempt him from disqualification. She chose not to do so, much to Perkins's chagrin. As he put it, "I left because Carly didn't plead with me to stay. I said, 'I think I'll retire,' and Carly sort of said, 'Hmmmm. OK!'"[26]

The only board members for whom Fiorina manifested high regard were those that were or had been CEOs of "Fortune 50 companies," as she put it. There were two: Philip Condit, chairman and CEO of Boeing Corp., and Sam Ginn, chairman of Vodafone and former CEO of AirTouch. "I would rely on them heavily, and their voices carried great weight in the board room," Fiorina acknowledged.[27] But not for long. Both Condit and Ginn quit the board in January 2004, at the same time Perkins departed. "Would the outcome have been different if the two experienced CEOs, Phil Condit and Sam Ginn, had remained on the board?" Carly mused after she'd been fired. "Or if we'd been able to recruit more board members sooner?"[28]

This was disingenuous at best. By most accounts, Fiorina never made more than a token effort to replace her dynamic duo with CEOs of equal stature. Fiorina added only one new CEO in her entire six-year tenure: Robert Knowling, CEO of Covad Communications, a mid-size telecom company of no great distinction. Knowling, who resigned from Covad shortly after he joined HP's board, discredited himself as an independent director from the start by publicly swearing fealty to Fiorina, HP shareholders be damned. "I didn't join HP; I joined Carly," he told a reporter. "If she left tomorrow, I'd resign tomorrow."[29] Knowling would be true to his word, but his devotion wasn't nearly enough to save Carly from the consequences of allowing the fourteen-person board she had inherited to shrink to just nine members, thus reducing the number of votes required to remove her to just five.

By the fall of 2004, Keyworth's admiration for Fiorina had given way to the belief that she was wrecking HP and must be removed as chair and CEO, one way or another. Like many of his fellow directors, he had become progressively disillusioned by Carly's pursuit of celebrity. Few CEOs have ever cultivated a high profile as relentlessly as did Fiorina, who traveled constantly, making dozens of speeches and personal appearances every month, many of which had no direct connection to the business of Hewlett-Packard. Fiorina's star turn at the Davos conference in 2003 inspired her to organize her own "Renaissance Weekend" in California, at which she hosted fifty carefully selected luminaries. After discussing her plans for the event at an HP board meeting, she extended what several directors considered an insultingly halfhearted last-minute invitation to join in.

Although Carly had attempted to ingratiate herself with the few directors she considered her peers, she had exhibited a worrisome tendency toward self-aggrandizement right from the start. The flattering deference she had shown Hackborn in her job interviews vanished shortly after she moved into the corner office. Hackborn soon tired of the chairman's post, complaining to some board colleagues that Carly rarely sought his counsel and often did not even return his phone calls. Hackborn never really settled into the role of chairman, holding the title for about a year before relinquishing it to Fiorina.

It hadn't taken long for HP's directors to decide that the best way to raise problematic issues with their imperious CEO was to designate a representative to meet with her privately and speak with a single voice for the whole board. Usually, the assignment fell to Ginn as chairman of the Nominating & Governance committee and later to his replacement, Knowling. At one time or another, though, almost every director was drafted into the role of emissary. Dunn's turn came after Fiorina gave short shrift to an employee survey that pointed to a festering morale problem in the ranks. Over dinner in an HP conference room—the first and last private meal she ever shared with Fiorina—Dunn tried to get the CEO to take the survey more respectfully than she had at the board meeting. She got nowhere. "Anyone who ever had to tell Carly something that she didn't want to hear would have a really hard time getting her to accept the message," Dunn said. "The term of art on the board became, 'I had my head handed to me.' Everyone would commiserate with the latest victim. 'Oh, yeah,' they'd say, 'I know exactly what you're talking about.'"[30]

Fiorina could get away with turning Silicon Valley's largest company into The Carly Show as long as the company performed well, as indeed it did into 2004, her fifth year on the job. HP did a good job of melding Compaq's operations into its own, a Herculean undertaking that consumed eighteen months. Formerly skeptical Wall Street analysts applauded as the cost savings that HP realized through its contentious mega-merger exceeded the most optimistic projections. But a funny thing happened on the way to Carly's enthronement as the next Jack Welch: All those nicely realized economies of scale failed to translate into profit growth. The problem, in a nutshell, was that HP was still losing market share to Dell, IBM, and other competitors and thus was failing to add to its revenues at anything close to an acceptable rate.

HP's stock traded down sharply from its post-merger highs to levels so low as to incite an unwanted buyout offer from a private equity group or perhaps even a rival corporation. After HP reported conspicuously disappointing results for the second quarter of 2004, Fiorina publicly pinned the blame on three subordinates, all of whom she fired, and then committed the company to meeting wildly optimistic future performance levels that she was accused of pulling out of a hat.

By now, it was apparent to most HP directors that Fiorina had neither interest in nor aptitude for the hard, unglamorous work of managing a complex company day to day. Operations had been the forte of Michael Capellas, the former CEO of Compaq, but he had quit in frustration after just six months as Carly's "Mr. Inside," spurning Perkins, who had pleaded with him to stay. Instead of replacing Capellas, Carly assumed many of his responsibilities as president and chief operating officer. It worked all right for a while, if only because the Compaq deal had added a lot of talented executives to HP's senior ranks. After a year or two, though, many of the company's best managers tired of playing supporting roles in the Carly drama and began quitting in droves, further exposing Fiorina's managerial shortcomings.

Keyworth, who signed an email to Hackborn "a worried Jay," started spending more and more time at HP headquarters in Palo Alto after he'd replaced Perkins as chairman of the tech committee, popping into Fiorina's office unannounced with unsolicited and unwelcome advice. "Mostly he wanted me to buy things. AMD, Apple, TiVo, Veritas—his list was long and varied," the CEO recalled. "He was impatient with the practical details. He argued strenuously that these acquisitions made strategic sense and that we could figure out the rest. Jay seemed more and more impatient with me as I rejected his many suggestions."[31]

Unwisely if unwittingly, Fiorina made an enemy of the one director who believed that he carried Dave Packard's celestial proxy in his pocket. "I did not just plain like David Packard," Keyworth told me. "To this day, if I'm faced with something really tough, I ask myself, 'What would Dave do?' because he was the best example I ever had in my life." What would Dave have done about Carly? Keyworth had no doubts: get rid of her. "I do not believe that Carly would have been removed if not for me," he said. "I believe that eventually it would have been done in some external way that would have been very destructive for the company. So, at that stage of the game, I felt that I had done what Dave would have wanted me to do."[32]

With as much discretion as Keyworth could muster, the former scientist-spy began his covert campaign to remove Fiorina by approaching each of the directors he knew to be unhappy with her and trying to persuade them to commit their vote to fire her if it came to that. He was not encouraged by the response, concluding that he could count on the votes of only two directors other than himself: Hackborn and Lucille Salhany, a television executive and former Compaq director who was chummy with Perkins. Two directors were so adamant in support of Fiorina that Keyworth didn't bother approaching them: Knowling and Larry Babbio, a top executive at Verizon and another of the ex–Compaq directors. Dunn clearly was displeased with Carly, but Keyworth doubted whether she would favor decisive action in the end. He also classed as uncertain Bob Ryan, the CFO of Medtronic and a recent addition to the board; Sanford Litvak, who was so preoccupied with his duties as general counsel of Walt Disney Co. that he seldom attended board meetings; and Bob Wayman, HP's longtime chief financial officer.

Keyworth decided that the best way to tilt the odds in his favor was to get his friend and ally Tom Perkins back on the board. The first obstacle to his scheme was Perkins himself.

Completely absorbed in the complex technical challenges of designing *The Maltese Falcon*, he had taken no interest in events at HP in the year since he'd retired as a director. In October 2005, Keyworth traveled 5,500 miles to get Perkins's attention, spending a few days with him at his manor house in England. Perkins was persuaded that Carly should be removed, and he agreed to rejoin the board, if Keyworth could broker his reinstatement.

Keyworth returned home and worked the phones, making a case for the venture capitalist's return to each of his fellow directors, not all of whom were thrilled by the prospect of Perkins redux. Confident that a majority supported the idea even so, Keyworth called an executive session at the November board meeting and put the matter to a vote. When Fiorina joined the meeting later, Keyworth said, "Carly, some of the board members feel that we should bring Tom Perkins back onto the board. We're having trouble recruiting another technical expert to fill in for Dick Hackborn when he chooses to retire."[33] Against her better judgment, Fiorina agreed to welcome Perkins back. "I should have said no to all of it," she recalled. "No one else on the board expressed any reservations, however."[34] Although Perkins would not officially resume his board post until HP's annual meeting in March 2005, he immediately joined in Keyworth's behind-the-scenes maneuvering against Fiorina.

* * *

AS DISCONTENTED AS many directors were with Fiorina by the time of Perkins's return to the board, they were equally unhappy with one another. Some members were barely on speaking terms. "The Carly situation drew out of this group an underlying dislike, lack of trust, and suspicion," Dunn said.[35] It certainly didn't help that the seniormost director, Keyworth, considered many of his colleagues unworthy of their board seats, according to Fiorina. "Jay was always opinionated about everything, including his fellow board members," the CEO recalled. "He had been derisive of Pattie Dunn's capabilities ever since I'd known him."[36] Dunn had no idea that Keyworth disdained her or had been badmouthing her to Fiorina until she read it in *Tough Choices*. With Larry Babbio, at least, Keyworth's hostility was all in the open. Keyworth and Babbio, a canny, plainspoken New Yorker, were constantly at odds. As Dunn put it, "With Jay and Larry it was like a two-males-with-antlers thing—visceral and really rough."

Most of the directors got along no better with Perkins, who was far too contentious a figure to forge a boardroom consensus over as radical an act as firing a CEO. It was Dunn who effectively sealed Fiorina's fate by bringing a modicum of civility and order to a rancorous board, temporarily making common cause with both Keyworth and Perkins.

Dunn and Fiorina had never been close or even very friendly, despite—or perhaps because—the similarity of their backstories as secretaries who had climbed all the way to the top in the man's world of big business. "There were board social events at which I found Carly to be great company, but no, there was never a sisterhood thing going on between us," Dunn said. On the contrary, did Carly's acclamation as America's supreme distaff executive inflame Dunn's competitive impulses? "Oh, God, what bullshit!" scoffed Dunn, who dropped off *Fortune*'s list entirely after resigning as BGI's chief executive. Clearly, though, she was miffed that Fiorina treated her as dismissively as an old-school male CEO might have. "I don't think Carly had any idea what I did for a living," she said. "I don't think she ever asked me what

I thought about anything. I don't know why she thought I was on the board—probably because I was a convenient woman."[37]

What divided Fiorina and Dunn was not merely the inevitable clash of well-toned egos, but also divergent philosophies of how corporations should be managed and evaluated. As Dunn put it, adapting a cliché usually applied to male-female mutual incomprehension, "I did feel like she was from Venus and I was from Mars." Actually, it was more like Carly was from Earth and Pattie was from Pluto, for Fiorina's outlook was pretty standard, while Dunn's decades of on-the-job training at BGI had instilled in her a passion for scientific measurement that was increasingly prevalent among big institutional investors but highly unconventional within corporate boardrooms.

Hewlett-Packard posed a corporate analytical challenge of the highest order, consisting of dozens upon dozens of different businesses that spanned much of the information technology panoply, not to mention 110 countries around the world. To the quant, the traditional performance yardsticks on which HP relied (market share, profit margin, earnings per share, and the like) offered little more than more than a jumping-off point to true understanding, Dunn explained. "I thought that we as a board should require HP management to introduce more sophisticated measures that it could use to evaluate all the businesses in terms of whether they are creating or destroying shareholder value—and that the board itself also could use over time to evaluate management."[38] Dunn's comments in this vein at board meetings tended to leave Fiorina and most of her fellow directors scratching their heads. As Carly put it in her book, "[Dunn's] opinions were frequently hard to discern."[39] At one point, Fiorina mistakenly concluded that Dunn favored splitting HP into separate computer and printing divisions—a notion that the CEO held

in contempt. What Dunn actually advocated was precisely mea-
suring the performance of each of HP's component parts. Could
this have served as prelude to HP selling off some of those parts?
Perhaps, but this was not a case that Dunn ever made.

Dunn remained supportive of Fiorina even so until HP began
to falter financially, as documented even by standard measures.
As a career investment executive, Dunn was especially distressed
by the erosion of HP's credibility on Wall Street. "Toward the
autumn of 2004 I started feeling that Carly was in a real pickle
with the Street," she said. "Although analysts can be so narrow-
minded and annoying, if you lose their confidence—as Carly
had—it's very, very hard to get it back."[40]

Dunn's views might have puzzled her colleagues at times,
but she was a conciliator by nature and worked at maintaining
cordial relations with every other board member, including Keyworth. When he and Babbio butted heads, it was Dunn, not Fiorina, who typically stepped in as peacemaker. "I did not seek a
leadership role," she insisted later. "I was like Rodney King. I
just wanted everyone to get along."[41]

Could someone as accomplished as Dunn truly be devoid of
personal ambition in such a situation? Fiorina certainly didn't
think so, noting that "Pattie seemed extraordinarily pleased to
be playing a more leading role" on the board in the weeks preceding her ouster as chairman and CEO.[42] If Dunn did in fact
aspire to the chairmanship of HP, her usurpation of it will go down
in the annals of corporate intrigue as a scheme of almost Zen-
like beauty. Soft-pedaling her own opinions, she listened patiently
to what each of her colleagues had to say about Fiorina—and
one another. Even the strong-willed Keyworth seemed to fall
under her velvety spell. At one point, Dunn ended an email to
her fellow directors by apologizing for its length. "You most cer-

tainly are not running on," Keyworth replied. "In fact, you may be mending all the communications gaps that matter."[43]

Toward the end of 2004, Dunn took the lead in organizing a series of conference calls exclusively for the independent directors, which is to say behind Fiorina's back. She volunteered to record what was said and worked up her notes into a succession of memos, finally consolidating the various complaints against Fiorina into a comprehensive 500-word critique titled "Confidential to Independent Directors Only: Board Communication to the CEO." Said Dunn, "It finally got to the point where no one could legitimately object to any of the words on the page because they were what everybody had agreed to."[44]

Dunn's memo made three main points: 1. "The Board is concerned about its relationship with the CEO, including the CEO's unwillingness to seriously consider the Board's input on key issues, insufficient communication from the CEO to the Board outside of formal board meetings and lack of involvement by the Board in determining meeting agendas"; 2. HP's "competitive position in the computing and services businesses is unsatisfactory and it is unlikely these businesses will achieve market leadership under the Company's current strategy and organizational structure"; and 3. "The market is unlikely to accept that the company strategy will achieve competitive results, and its unwillingness to correct course is adverse to shareholder value creation."[45]

Keyworth set up an appointment with Carly, and he, Hackborn, and Dunn met with her at HP headquarters on January 5, 2005, two days before the board was to hold its annual planning session at the Park Hyatt in downtown San Francisco. They took turns reading each of the memo's sections as Fiorina did a slow burn. "Jay seemed particularly overwrought, so much so that I asked him straight out why he was so angry," Fiorina recalled.[46]

On this point anyway, Keyworth and Fiorina were in agreement. "Of course I was overwrought," he acknowledged later. "Anybody who wasn't overwrought at one of the greatest corporations in the world being on its knees with jackals hovering around shouldn't be on a board."[47]

The confrontation ended well, even so. Fiorina clearly was offended—she later said that the trio's "suggestions came out of left field and were half-baked"—but maintained a steely composure throughout.[48] No ultimatum was delivered, after all. The directors asked only that Fiorina set aside her agenda for the planning review to deal with the board's grievances. This she agreed to do. Afterwards, the ever politic Dunn sent a reassuring email to Knowling. "I think you and the other directors would have been comfortable with the tone on both sides," she wrote. "Jay got a little emotional at one point, but Carly called him on it and things went smoothly from there." Replied Knowling: "I have been nervous all day. This is great news."[49]

Fiorina was true to her word. She opened the San Francisco meeting by inviting the directors to get up one by one and speak their minds. Dunn remained resolutely in mediator mode throughout, but could not smooth away all the differences that surfaced. There was general agreement that Carly held too much power, but no consensus on the issues of how it should be redistributed and to whom. Fiorina made no commitments, but listened, for a change, and also kept her temper in check. Most directors came away feeling mildly encouraged that Carly would do what needed to be done to start fixing the company. Dunn was so sure that crisis had been averted, at least for the time being, that she flew off to Bali for a vacation with her husband. Fiorina marked the meeting's end by hosting a dinner at a swanky restaurant named Rubicon—an apt choice, in fact, for she was about to cross the point of no return in her tumultuous relations with the board.

A week after the Rubicon dinner, the *Wall Street Journal* published a front-page story headlined, "Hewlett-Packard Board Considers a Reorganization." Although the story cast Carly in an unflattering light, the criticisms it contained were pretty mild compared with what Keyworth and others had been saying privately. What was shocking was how much its author, HP beat reporter Pui-Wing Tam, had learned about the board's innermost workings from a source or sources she had quoted only anonymously. "It is hard to convey how violated I felt," declared Fiorina, assuming that it was a director who was sniping at her from behind Tam's blind of anonymity. "Until a board makes a decision, its deliberations are confidential. Whoever had done this had broken a bond of trust with me and every board member. . . . Trust is a business imperative."[50]

And so is controlling the dissemination of inside information. Corporations put great emphasis on communicating to the outside world with one consistent if often unforthcoming voice. Public companies especially are under heavy obligation to conform to the laws and regulations governing the disclosure of "material" information, which tends to move stock prices. Their overriding aim, though, is promotional: to create a narrative that allows a company and its CEO to put their best foot forward. However, journalists have their own objectives and requirements, and making a company and its leaders look good as they want to look tends not to be their priority.

Hewlett-Packard was a very special case, less because of its fame as a company than because of Fiorina's transcendent celebrity. Privately, a number of directors had long doubted that Carly's pursuit of the spotlight furthered HP's business interests.

Without question, she was confident and adept in her personal dealings with reporters, and yet, under her, HP's press relations had taken a turn for the pugnacious. The tone was set by Allison Johnson, a marketing executive who amassed wide influence within the company as the self-appointed manager of the "Carly brand." She punished the authors of stories she considered unfair or merely insufficiently flattering by restricting their access to company executives. "You're on Isolation Island," was her signature catchphrase.[51]

The natural reaction of a banished reporter was to redouble her efforts to develop unauthorized inside sources—of which there were plenty. Under Fiorina, HP was much leakier than most other Silicon Valley companies, recalled a veteran technology journalist: "The cool kids clique at HP was very small and well-dressed. Old-time HPers weren't happy and a lot of them were willing to talk." A number of HP beat reporters came to suspect that HP management not only was going to great lengths to ferret out the identities of their anonymous sources, but also was monitoring the telephone and email communications of the HP media relations employees with whom they dealt. At the same time, though, members of Carly's in crowd freely bad-mouthed former company executives (and each other on occasion) to reporters. "It was insanely political," one reporter said. "Especially after the [Compaq] proxy fight started, it was no holds barred." Needing all the help she could get in the struggle for the hearts and minds of HP shareholders, Fiorina took the muzzles off the directors early in the battle, encouraging them to stand with her in making the case for merger in speeches and press interviews. They answered her call on a scale that exceeded the communications department's ability to manage the process. Keyworth was particularly active, making use of his old Washington contacts when possible and also speaking to scores of other reporters, among them the *Journal*'s Tam.

Coverage of HP's civil war was voluminous and larded with anonymous quotes from both the Fiorina and the Hewlett camps. Sensitive documents detailing HP's post-merger employee compensation plans were leaked, infuriating Carly. "The media seized on these drafts as evidence of yet another CEO's greed," she complained.[52] For his part, Walter Hewlett was incensed when a remarkably detailed account of a private heart-to-heart chat he'd had with Hackborn and Keyworth in his father's old office appeared in *Business Week*. The capper was a front-page piece in the San Jose *Mercury News* that featured a word-for-word transcript of a private and quite candid voice-mail message that Fiorina had left on the office phone of CFO Bob Wayman.[53]

The volume of leaks from within HP waned after Fiorina succeeded in annexing Compaq, but waxed anew in 2004 in tandem with the growing discontent over her performance. "I walked into an environment of leaks," said Robert Sherbin, a former Dow Jones reporter who started work in HP's media relations department in the fall of 2004. "There were many discussions of how we might try to stop it. I never took it very seriously, because I thought it was impossible. My basic view was that leaks occur in organizations where there is disaffection, and as long as there is disaffection there will be leaks."[54]

However, the leak to Tam in early 2005 was a particularly egregious violation of boardroom confidentiality that outraged not only Fiorina but also many HP board members. "It was really rotten," Keyworth said. "Somebody really wanted to the hurt the company and the board." On a conference call with all the directors except the vacationing Dunn, Fiorina was, by her own description, "cold as ice," dressing down her board members as if they were misbehaving schoolkids and she their principal. When Fiorina demanded to know which of them had spoken to Tam, there were denials all around, some of them heated. Fiorina strongly suspected Keyworth, who, in her view, was particularly long-winded in explaining why it could not possibly have been him. "Everyone on that call knew that both Tom and Jay were the sources," Fiorina said later. "They were allies. They were the ones pushing for the reorganization described in the article."[55]

Perkins had indeed spoken to Tam but couldn't bring himself to fess up on the conference call. "I was so intimidated by Carly I couldn't tell her," he said. The next day he called Knowling and explained that the *Journal* reporter had called him to tell him that she was going to write about Perkins's impending return to the board. "I said, 'Why don't you wait until it actually happens and then we'll talk about it.' She said, 'No, no,' and then she basically read me her story. She knew everything."[56]

The identity of Tam's inside source has still not been definitively established. Fiorina authorized a quick investigation, but it was superficial and inconclusive. The *Journal* article was outside the scope of the internal investigation that later implicated Keyworth as a leaker, and Tam has kept her confidential source or sources confidential. For his part, Keyworth continues to this day to vehemently deny that he was Tam's informant.

The most outré theory is that Carly herself was Tam's source and only feigned outrage to regain the upper hand over the board. As one director later suggested, "It gave her self-righteousness to use over the board and, man, did she ever wield that club!" A more plausible variant of this theory held that Fiorina genuinely was blindsided by the leak, but exaggerated her response to try to shift the board's focus from her performance to the treachery of its own members. It didn't work, in any event.

Carly's regally indignant reaction to the leak poisoned her relations with the board to a fatal level of toxicity. In talking with
the other directors after returning from Bali, Dunn listened as
sympathetically as ever, but this time she also expressed an opinion: Carly now must agree to a restructuring plan that shifted
some of her operating duties to other executives, or she must
be fired.

The other directors rallied around Dunn as they prepared
for HP's next board meeting on February 7, 2005. In hopes of
minimizing press scrutiny, Fiorina decided to move the meeting
from Palo Alto to an airport hotel in Chicago and kept the new
location secret as long as possible from everyone, the directors
included. The sole exception was Dunn, the only board member
who was out of the country when the leak to the *Journal* occurred and thus absolved of Carly's suspicion. Unwilling even
to trust her own secretary, Fiorina asked Dunn to see to the
arrangements for the Chicago gathering.

Unbeknownst to Fiorina, those arrangements included en-
listing experts to counsel the board on the right way to go about
firing her if it came to that. At first, Dunn was averse to relying
on Larry Sonsini, HP's longtime outside counsel, for legal advice.
There was no doubting the gravitas of "The Great Sonsini," who
was chair of Wilson Sonsini Goodrich & Rosati and generally
considered Silicon Valley's most powerful lawyer. With HP,
though, he had served mostly as an adviser to management, often
dealing directly with Fiorina, as well as Lew Platt and John
Young before her. Could the directors trust his counsel—and his
discretion? After Sonsini persuaded Dunn that he was ready,
willing, and able to guide the board through a CEO firing, she
set up a conference call during which the lawyer successfully
made the same case to all the other directors.

Perkins, who was en route to Istanbul when the board call took place on February 6, was well acquainted with Sonsini. Not only was Kleiner Perkins Caufield & Byers a longtime client of Sonsini's firm, but the lawyer had invested personally—and profitably—in several KPC&B venture funds. "I have known [Sonsini] for 30 years and have never doubted his ethics or ability," Perkins declared in an email to Dunn. "You have my proxy."[57]

Dunn also brought in John Coffee, a professor at Columbia University Law School, as a special counsel for governance, working alongside Sonsini. Coffee wrote a memo titled "Summary of the Board's Fiduciary Duties in the Context of CEO Evaluation and Succession Planning" that was distributed to directors. The night before the board meeting, Coffee and Sonsini sat down to a working dinner in Chicago with Dunn, Keyworth, Hackborn, Ryan, and Perkins.

Despite all these preparations, Fiorina's fate still hung in the balance when the board began deliberating the next day, according to Dunn. "Jay may have wanted to fire her and Tom may have wanted to fire her, but there was not a majority of the board that said a priori, 'This is the end of the line with Carly,'" Dunn said.[58]

Dunn was elected presiding director, meaning that she was to run the board meeting in place of its chair, Fiorina, who read a long, formal statement that she believed to be eloquently conciliatory. It was met with stony silence. Said Dunn, "The basic message the board took from it was, 'You guys don't know what you're doing.' She thought we had no right to judge her because we didn't have the stuff. To which my thought was, 'You've been chairman for five years. If we don't have the stuff, you should have gotten people on this board that do.'"[59] After Fiorina left the room, Dunn presided over three hours of animated discussion but failed, in the end, to persuade Knowling and Babbio to vote with the majority and make Fiorina's firing unanimous.

The board named Wayman to replace Fiorina on a temporary basis as CEO, but not as chair. A rapid-fire discussion of the merits of appointing a non-executive chair ended with Hackborn asking Dunn if she would accept the job. "It was clear to me at that point that it was a complete setup," she said, "because the idea of having a non-executive chair had never even been broached—at least not with me in the room."[60]

The vote for Dunn was unanimous, though by no means uniformly enthusiastic. Keyworth was ambivalent, believing that the position should be his as the board member with the longest experience and deepest knowledge of HP. Perkins, too, would have loved to inherit a title long held by Packard, fulfilling in roundabout fashion his long-ago desire to follow in his mentor's footsteps. But both Keyworth and Perkins realized that, for better or worse, Pattie Dunn was the only director that every other board member would accept in the role of chair.

"Pattie had taken the position, which is not a bad position, that if we were going to fire Carly, we had to do it right, we've got to talk to experts, we've got to talk to lawyers, or otherwise it could blow up in our face," Perkins said. "You can't argue with that. She was right. Pattie had been Miss Compliance, who insisted on doing everything carefully, so she seemed like a safe, default choice for chairman."[61]

Dunn encountered no opposition whatsoever until she flew home from Chicago the day after the board meeting. "They've asked me to be chairman," she told her husband, Bill Jahnke. Although Dunn's breast cancer and melanoma now were in remission, she was still under treatment for ovarian cancer. Medical science had pronounced a death sentence of indeterminate date.

Even as the revolt against Fiorina was building to a climax, Dunn periodically had to absent herself for a day or two at a time to undergo a consolidation round of chemotherapy. In his gentle way, Janhke suggested that assuming the chairmanship of a dysfunctional board that had just fired America's most famous CEO might not be an ideal way to spend the time she had left. "OK, Bill, you have a point," she replied. "But I already told them I'd do it."[62]

HP's Queen was dead, long live the Queen! American business had a new alpha female, one who wore a wig to cover her baldness, took twelve pills a day from a heart-shaped box that she carried at all times, and was lucky to be alive. A year into an intensive twenty-month chemotherapy regimen, Dunn had scored the second great, improbable promotion of her business career. As always, she portrayed herself as accidentally ascendant, although a few insightful reporters did detect a flash of steel beneath the conciliator's façade. As one put it, "Rarely has a stiletto been inserted so bluntly between the shoulder blades of a business chief. For those who come to make the film of Carly Fiorina's remarkable career, the fact that the deliverer of the final blow was another woman will add to the casting excitement."[63]

This catfight undertone in the coverage of Fiorina's dismissal so upset Dunn that she disavowed it in a handwritten "Dear Carly" letter. "I'm not assuming you will welcome a letter from me, but have a compulsion to communicate nonetheless," Dunn wrote. "Along with so many others who feel similarly, you will remain a hero for personifying remarkable energy, commitment, courage, style—the list gets very long. One regret I have is that the press has misconstrued my role in the HP situation. My distress can't be justified in comparison with all you've had to deal with, but it is a source of dismay nonetheless. I wish you the best, Carly."[64] Fiorina chose not to reply.

CHAPTER SIX

MAYHEM BEFORE THE STORM

ON HER FIRST morning as chairman of Hewlett-Packard, Pattie Dunn awoke in a state of high anxiety. A divided board had come together in the end to oust Fiorina, but the experience had been bruising rather than cathartic and had exacerbated the ill feeling among the directors. "As a group, we did not like each other," Keyworth said. "At every board meeting we had, there would be ozone in the air."[1] He and Perkins had gone along with her ascension to chairman, but Dunn suspected that they would try to undermine her authority by moving the tech committee into the power void left by Fiorina. Carly was gone, but the leak that sealed her fate had the directors behaving like houseguests awaiting the drawing-room denouement of an Agatha Christie whodunit. *Was it you, you rotter? Do you suspect me, you cad?* Last but not least, it fell to Dunn as chair to organize the hunt for a new CEO. Dunn had seen to it that Carly's dismissal had been procedurally flawless (as well as leak free), but most CEO candidates would consider HP's executive suite a crime site even so and prefer to let someone else clean up the blood.

That the contours of the position Dunn occupied were ill defined only added to her angst. Shareholder activists long had argued that combining the roles of CEO and chairman concentrated excessive power in one person. The peril inherent in corporate autocracy had been underscored in 2001 and 2002 by the collapse of Enron, WorldCom, Tyco, and other giant U.S. companies led by "imperial CEOs" who had been hailed as geniuses in the go-go markets of the 1990s only to be exposed as scoundrels when stock values receded. As it turned out, the directors of these companies had turned a blind eye to massive fraud perpetrated against shareholders by greedy, power-crazed CEOs. There followed an outpouring of new laws, regulations, and court rulings designed to hold companies and their boards to a higher standard of accountability.

In all its sixty-six years, HP had never had a non-executive chairman. What exactly were Dunn's duties? What was the extent of her authority? Dunn looked outside the company for guidance on these questions, but it really wasn't much help. The truly independent corporate chairman was still a novelty in American business (only about 9 percent of the companies in Standard & Poor's 500 had one) and the position had not been codified or standardized in any meaningful way. Exactly how power was shared varied considerably among the companies that had adopted the reform. In short, Dunn would have to define her job in the doing of it.

The most pressing of the demands that assaulted Dunn on the morning after was the need to stage manage Fiorina's firing. Even as the Securities and Exchange Commission scrupulously regulates the accuracy of companies' financial disclosures, it allows them to routinely issue fictional explanations of dismissals and demotions. Rarely does a U.S. company admit to canning a senior executive. Instead, he or she departs voluntarily to "spend more time with my family" or "pursue personal interests," as the preferred euphemisms of the day would have it. To her credit, though, Carly refused to play along with this face-saving convention. HP's official press release quoted Fiorina saying that she had "stepped down" because of disagreements with the board over "how to execute HP's strategy."[2] This wasn't the whole truth certainly, but it was a lot straighter than the usual crooked tale.

For the first time in her career, Dunn was caught in a media firestorm. In a few days after Fiorina's firing, HP received some 900 phone calls and emails from reporters. The story landed on the front page of almost every major newspaper in the United States and received prominent play all around the world. One HP public relations operative summarized the dominant themes of coverage in an internal memo as follows: "Carly's Story—why she 'failed,' what is the 'behind the scenes' story of her dismissal, what is her severance package and what will she do next (politics, policy or another CEO role?). Some reflection on the success/failure of women CEOs, star CEOs and tech CEOs. Overall coverage included many anonymous sources, especially 'people close to' or 'people familiar with' Board discussions."[3]

After appearing with interim CEO Wayman at a press conference, Dunn conformed to HP's corporate policy of silence even as many reporters turned their focus to "HP's other woman," having exhausted the subject of Carly. The profiles of Dunn were generally favorable, even glowing, as this representative sample of headlines suggests: "As H-P's Chairman, Patricia Dunn Carries Clout" (*Wall Street Journal*); "Cool hand guided HP board to showdown" (*Seattle Times*); and "Dunn makes the show go on at Hewlett-Packard" (*New York Times*). The *Times* quoted ex-CEO Lew Platt, who now looked prescient for having brought Dunn onto the HP board in 1998. "Carly is interested in being out front and in the limelight, and Pattie is not that person," Platt said. Dunn "is quite happy to get the job done without the spotlight on her."[4]

Early in her tenure as chairman, Dunn made a point of visiting every board member in his or her hometown and asking them about their concerns. On an HP corporate jet, she flew to New York City, Boston, Chicago, Minneapolis, and Boise to see Babbio, Salhany, Knowling, Ryan, and Hackborn, respectively. (Both Perkins and Keyworth were local trips, Keyworth having recently remarried and moved from Santa Fe into his wife's house in the East Bay town of Piedmont, just a few miles from Dunn's home in Orinda.) Dunn returned from her listening tour believing that her colleagues wanted her to concentrate as much on stopping the flow of confidential information from HP's boardroom as on finding a replacement for Fiorina. As it turned out, HP's new chairman could hardly have done otherwise, for the search for a new CEO was bedeviled from beginning to end by leaks, as Dunn feared it would be.

"We cannot run a successful search in a fishbowl," she declared in an email to Bob Knowling just three days after she'd been named chair. "On our next board call I plan to hit this one hard: directors cannot speak to ANYONE, period, paragraph, about what happens in the board room. If leaks continue, I will tell them they cannot count on me to continue to serve as interim chairman."[5]

Dunn proposed that Perkins and Keyworth join her on a committee that would "filter" CEO candidates for the full board, which would make the final decision. This made sense logistically because the three of them lived in the San Francisco area and could jointly interview prospects without having to get on a plane. Mainly, though, Dunn had taken to heart the Chinese proverb about keeping friends close and enemies closer. Not that Dunn considered Perkins and Keyworth her enemies exactly, not yet anyway, but she reasoned that it was better to indulge what she saw as their self-importance by involving them from the start rather than risk having them conduct their own shadow CEO search. Perkins and Keyworth were delighted to oblige, believing that they could easily dominate their new chairman and exercise disproportionate influence over the board's CEO selection. Each of them acknowledged later that they misinterpreted Dunn's invitation as a gesture of deference from a chairman whom they fully expected to be defined by passivity and weakness.

Keyworth disputed Fiorina's recollection in *Tough Choices* that he had disdained Dunn right from the start of their association. Initially, in fact, he had taken Dunn under his wing after she had turned to him for orientation advice when she first joined the board, which had preceded Fiorina's hiring by a year. "I found Jay to be approachable, welcoming, friendly," Dunn recalled. "He also seemed to be very well-connected within HP."[6] For his part, Keyworth was unimpressed by Dunn's résumé, which was devoid of the sort of technological expertise that he believed every HP director should have. On the other hand, the newcomer did impress him as hard-working and conscientious in approaching the job of director. "There's no question that she wanted to be good at it," Keyworth said.[7]

Keyworth's opinion of Dunn didn't nosedive until she replaced him as chair of the board's audit committee in 2002, at Fiorina's request. Keyworth was delighted to be relieved of the duty, which he considered pure drudgery. Recent regulatory reforms had imposed higher standards of financial expertise on audit chairs, and Dunn was the only board member who met them. She was no keener on the audit assignment than Keyworth had been, likening the committee's essential functions to "taking a Saturday night bath whether you need one or not," but brought to them her usual diligence and exactitude.

In 2003, Dunn's first full year as audit chair, the committee met twenty-six times—once every two weeks on average—compared to eight times the previous year. According to Dunn, each of these meetings was called not by her but by HP management, mostly to deal with the many new reporting requirements imposed by the Sarbanes-Oxley Act of 2002. The committee also had to deal with the fallout from an HP executive's entanglement in a governmental corruption scandal in Canada. However, Keyworth, who remained a member of the committee, blamed the enormous increase in its workload largely on Dunn's inability to distinguish between "things that were important and things that were unbelievably unimportant."[8] Privately, Keyworth repeatedly urged Fiorina to replace Dunn as audit chair, complaining that she "didn't understand the company and used process as a crutch."[9]

Perkins wasn't a member of the audit committee, but he too was put off by what he saw as Dunn's foisting of its pointless minutiae on the full board, resenting as he did any distraction from the sort of big-picture strategic issues that preoccupied him. "Her audit committee reports to the board were just awful," Perkins said. "They were so long and so detailed and I felt that she was enmeshed in the details."[10]

Like Keyworth, Perkins was disinclined to openly criticize, much less confront, Dunn, who, for her part, was the soul of tact and discretion. The fundamental differences in philosophy and temperament that separated Dunn from Perkins and Keyworth were creating tensions, but at this stage they remained safely sub rosa. Throughout the high-pressure hunt for a successor to Fiorina, these three dissimilar but equally strong-willed personalities maintained a surface civility that served HP and its shareholders well. "Tom and I, along with Jay, worked very effectively together in the search," Dunn said. "I think everyone agreed that in Mark Hurd the board made a surprising but great choice. And it took us all of seven weeks."[11]

Dick Hackborn, who'd led the search that resulted in Fiorina's hiring in 1999, gave most of the credit for landing Hurd to Dunn. "To me, the job you did on the 2005 search committee resulting in the hiring of Mark Hurd was the single biggest contribution of any director during the past 14 years I have been on the HP board," wrote Hackborn in an email he sent Dunn after she was forced to resign from the board in 2006.[12]

* * *

AS THE SEARCH got under way, though, Dunn was convinced that the tech committee fix was in for Richard Belluzzo, a former Hackborn protégé who had quit HP in 1997 after the CEO position he thought he'd been promised went to Platt instead. After a short stint as president of Microsoft, Belluzzo had become CEO of a mid-size tech company in the Valley. In the wake of Fiorina's firing, Hackborn approached Belluzzo and sounded him out about returning to HP. Belluzzo didn't need much encouragement to pursue a position he thought should have been his years before. Both Keyworth and Perkins insisted later that they had started out with open minds, but Dunn smelled a rat. "Tom and Jay wanted me to put a good front on a search, but it seemed to me they'd already decided that Belluzzo was the guy," she said.[13] Dunn had nothing against "Rocket Rick," as he'd been nicknamed at HP in tribute to the rapidity of his rise, but she was determined to run a bona fide search during which every board member could have a say.

Dunn strengthened her hand by persuading the board to hire an executive recruiter she knew and trusted: Andrea Redmond of Russell Reynolds Associates, the headhunter who'd placed her on the HP board. Dunn and Redmond had stayed in touch over the years, bonding over their shared experiences as cancer survivors and as female upstarts in a male-dominated corporate milieu. Other, bigger-name recruiters reacted with outraged disbelief to HP's choice of Redmond and kept working their contacts at the company to try to overturn the board's decision. On February 14, a few days before HP officially hired Russell Reynolds, the relentless Pui-Wing Tam co-authored a story in the *Wall Street Journal* that reported inside details of the board's interactions with two other headhunting firms, citing two sources "close to the situation."[14]

Dunn telephoned Redmond and warned her that HP would pull the CEO search assignment if she or anyone at Russell Reynolds had leaked information to Tam. Redmond assured Dunn that she hadn't talked to the *Journal* reporter, but the leak convinced her to take special precautions even so. At her firm, recruiters were required to share information about their searches by posting regular updates on the company intranet. Redmond knew that reporters were pestering her colleagues specializing in technology for news on HP and she wasn't willing to risk her own reputation on their discretion. From this point on, she instead risked the displeasure of her co-workers by inputting nothing into Reynold's data base about HP until the search was finished.

That same afternoon, Dunn sent an email to all of the board members, notifying them of a conference call she'd scheduled for the upcoming weekend to discuss the latest leak and what to do about it. "I have asked Larry Sonsini to work with me on a strengthened plan for confidentiality, which will probably not be disclosed to anyone else," she wrote.[15] If the culprit was a director—and Dunn wasn't absolutely certain that it was—this message was intended to intimidate them into silence. "I guess that was my attempt at being frightening," she acknowledged later with a laugh.[16]

"This is disgusting!" the normally mild-mannered Hackborn thundered in a private reply to Dunn. "Either we have a Board member who wants to hurt the rest of us and HP. Or there is a 'bug' somewhere in our communications network—either someone's home or at some email node. I cannot think of any alternatives. I wonder if we should have our homes/businesses checked out."[17]

Perkins, too, weighed in, with the first of a series of emails that cast aspersions on insiders other than him and Keyworth—in this instance Ann Baskins, HP's straight-arrow general counsel.[18] Although Dunn was glad that Perkins was paying attention, she gave no credence to his half-baked suspicions of Baskins. That said, she saw to it that no HP executive other than Wayman, who also was a director, took part in the CEO hunt. Baskins, who usually took the official notes at board meetings, now was required to leave the room whenever Dunn, Perkins, and Keyworth updated the other directors on the search.

Two days later, the *Journal* published yet another Tam story revealing that HP had decided to hire Russell Reynolds, citing "a person familiar with the Board's thinking." Dunn now was convinced that Tam's source, at least for the last two scoops, was Silicon Valley's best-connected headhunter: John Thompson of Heidrick & Struggles. Thompson had had every reason to think he would get the HP assignment, because Sonsini had recommended him to the board. Dunn now asked Sonsini to re-buke Thompson for interfering with the search. "I will get on him loud and clear," Sonsini responded. "If this continues, his network to Wilson Sonsini will shrink big time."[19]

A few weeks after Dunn's installation as chair, *Fortune* magazine ran a narrative account of Fiorina's firing—"How the HP Board KO'd Carly"—that leaned heavily on inside sources, none of whom was named. Clearly, it wasn't just Tam who had penetrated HP's inner sanctum. For Dunn, the story was doubly uncomfortable because it highlighted her own role as "the marquee name in this drama," which, author Carol Loomis suggested, was a corporate version of Clint Eastwood's female boxing movie *Million Dollar Baby*. "In a woman to-woman confrontation that never could have happened in the male-dominated executive world of ten years ago. . . . [Dunn] knocked out Carly Fiorina."[20]

After studying the *Fortune* story, Dunn concluded that Loomis's main source had been Carly herself. In an email to Sonsini, she explained her reasoning: "The red flag is this: one fact that Loomis could not ferret out is who else ("one other director") was in the room when Carly was told of the board's decision. If other directors had been the source, this would have been a juicy tidbit given Bob Knowling's known allegiance to Carly. But Carly would have protected him."[21]

HP's press relations department took the view that Carly would continue to seed the news media with stories that questioned the legitimacy of her dismissal by Dunn and the board. Dunn certainly couldn't control her predecessor, and she happily followed the advice given her HP's media handlers, which was to turn down all interview requests until Fiorina's campaign had run its course. Dunn did find a silver lining in the *Fortune* story:

There was no indication that any of the directors had talked to Loomis. But even this realization posed a quandary. "I would like the Board to know that they are not suspects, if they are not, but this would be tricky except one-on-one," Dunn mused in an email to Sonsini. "Maybe my thoughts are in overdrive."[22]

Dunn had wanted to hire Redmond not only because she believed her to be trustworthy, but also because she could be counted on to take a more creative approach than could be expected of her more famous and longer-tenured male counterparts, whose forte was landing the biggest-name CEO they could. "Andrea is more of a hands-on, start with a database of 5,000 people and start filtering type of a person," Dunn said. "Also, I'd worked enough with headhunters to know that when one of them becomes a brand they pretty much dictate the outcome of a search. I thought that this board needed to feel like it was driving the search or it was going to be another source of conflict."[23]

On February 12, just five days after the board had fired Fiorina, Redmond brought an annotated list of about thirty CEO prospects to a meeting at the Four Seasons Hotel in downtown San Francisco with Dunn, Perkins, and Keyworth. Two hours of discussion reduced the roster to eight candidates, ranked in order of preference. Rick Belluzzo was high on the list, as were top executives of IBM, Sun Microsystems, Oracle, Dell, Motorola, and a couple of European companies.

Dunn, Perkins, and Keyworth decided that they would interview candidates jointly or not at all. Most of the interviews took place at Kleiner Perkins's offices in downtown San Francisco, but the Three Musketeers did travel as far Newark, New Jersey, where they met with one leading contender in the Red Carpet Room at the airport. To throw off snoopers, Dunn had the board's secretary set up the meeting under the name of BGI and she also assigned code names to the candidates derived from their initials.

Belluzzo, whose code name was "Robin," recalled his two-hour interview with the filtering committee as "very thorough and grueling."[24] Belluzzo acquitted himself well, though Perkins had given Rocket Rick a bit of a hard time. "Somehow your career reminds me of a penguin on an iceberg floating north from Antarctica," he said. "Everything you get involved with gets smaller and smaller." Belluzzo was flustered, but quickly recovered. Afterward, Keyworth took Perkins aside. "Jesus, Tom!" he said. "How could you say that?"[25] Having passed muster with the committee, Belluzzo then conferred individually with Wayman and each of HP's other directors over the next week or so.

The day after Belluzzo's meeting with Wayman, *Business Week* ran an online story saying that he had emerged as a leading candidate for the CEO job, according to "two sources close to the board."[26] *Business Week* had blown Belluzzo's cover. As far as he knew, his board at Quantum Corp. hadn't a clue that he was pursuing the HP job. Now, he'd have to level with his directors. But what if he didn't get the nod and had to stay at Quantum? Would the board ever trust him again? Belluzzo was, in a word, furious. "HP had assigned me a code name and made me sign a confidentiality agreement," he said. "Here I was following their rules, and out comes a story less than twenty-four hours after I met with Wayman."[27]

Perkins again swung into finger-pointing mode in a hurried email to Dunn: "The leak to *Business Week* is awful—it may scare Robin away—and the references to the others are too accurate to be 'fishing' guesses. This stuff must be coming from the search firms. . . . Extremely dangerous, this sport with the press."[28]

Dunn thought that the Belluzzo indiscretion confirmed her suspicion that John Thompson of Heidrich & Struggles was trying to sabotage the search, to make Russell Reynolds look bad. "The good news is that Robin appears to be hanging tough," Dunn noted, adding that she had asked Knowling, who was a member of Heidrich & Struggles's board, to complain to Thompson's boss and to warn him that "we will take further steps if he doesn't stop."[29]

Although Dunn was dismayed anew over the latest leak, she realized that this was one betrayal that she might be able to parlay to her tactical advantage. Belluzzo had impressed Dunn, but she was not ready to pronounce him the best-qualified candidate. What if there was someone even better who had not made the list of finalists, someone like Mark Hurd, the CEO of NCR Corp., based in Dayton, Ohio?

Several of Redmond's colleagues at Russell Reynolds knew Hurd and spoke highly of him. With Dunn's blessing, Redmond had flown to Dayton a week before the *Business Week* leak to meet Hurd and chat up the HP opportunity for an hour or so. He was interested, and she was impressed. On a conference call the next day, Redmond advised the search committee to interview Hurd. "You have got to see this guy," she declared.[30]

Dunn was willing, but Perkins and Keyworth were disinclined to take the headhunters' advice. On paper certainly, Hurd was definitely not Perkins's kind of CEO, in that he was neither a technologist nor a big deal in Silicon Valley. Like Keyworth, he saw no point in boning up on a dark horse like Hurd with a stud like Belluzzo all set to go. "There's no way anyone from Dayton, Ohio, is ever going to run HP," Perkins said, or meant to say, anyway. What he actually said was Dayton, *Iowa*. Over the next few days, Redmond kept hammering away, but to no avail. "That was the only time on a candidate that I took a strong position," Redmond said.[31]

But once *Business Week* publicly anointed Belluzzo the favorite, Keyworth and Perkins could not very well refuse to even sit down with Hurd without reinforcing the growing suspicion among the other directors that they had made up their minds and were just going through the motions. In her politely insistent way, Dunn urged her colleagues to reconsider, noting that Hurd was about to embark on a West Coast trip. Perkins and Keyworth grudgingly agreed to grant an audience of an hour or so to Hurd, upon whom Dunn promptly bestowed the code name "Mayhem."

Hurd was forty-eight years old and had spent his entire career at NCR. Founded in 1884 as National Cash Register, the company had reinvented itself several times over the decades. In its latest incarnation, NCR was a technology-driven company less than one-twelfth HP's size, but similar in its venerability and complexity. Although NCR was best known as the country's largest manufacturer of automated teller machines, it also operated a variety of different businesses in data management, software, and computer services.

Hurd had gotten his start at NCR as a salesman pushing mainframe computers in competition with IBM and had risen steadily through the ranks on the strength of his intensity, pragmatism, and mastery of the operational mechanics of tech businesses. "Without execution," this operating executive par excellence once declared, "vision is just another word for hallucination."[32] Hurd measurably improved the performance of every NCR division he ran before moving up to president in 2001 and to the top job in 2003. As CEO, Hurd imposed a drastic cost-cutting regimen that eliminated 1,500 jobs and imposed 30 percent pay cuts on many salaried employees. In his two years as CEO, NCR's stock tripled in value.

Hurd enhanced his moral authority as corporate reformer by spurning the imperial trappings of high corporate office in his typically disciplined way. He marked his promotion to CEO by moving out of his spacious, private office into a little cubicle. He carried his own tray in the company cafeteria and parked his car outside in the Ohio winter like everyone else, having converted the executive parking garage into a training center. Hurd shunned the media spotlight in which Fiorina luxuriated and was almost comically self-effacing in the few press interviews he did grant. "I work and I work and I have a family and I work," he once told a reporter in an attempt to deflect her attention from himself to his company. "And I work out some and then I go back to work."[33]

In their eagerness to cast Hurd in the role of the "un-Carly" after he replaced her at HP, reporters misrepresented him in fundamental ways. For a start, he was something of a diva himself, with a quick temper, a thin skin, and a salty tongue. Often described as a "blue-collar CEO" and an "unpretentious Midwesterner," Hurd was in fact a patrician New Yorker whose father hailed from a long line of Yale-educated financiers and whose mother, the daughter of a Park Avenue physician, had been a debutante. Mark attended an elite, boys-only prep school in New York City, but departed from the privileged path laid out for him by attending Baylor University on a tennis scholarship. Although number one on the Baylor team, Hurd was not quite good enough to making a living on the pro circuit, but kept playing tennis (and basketball) as he climbed the corporate ladder. One NCR colleague recalled him as "a vicious athlete and competitor. He would get pretty hot-headed and jaw with people."[34]

What surprised Dunn about Hurd was that he made no effort to ingratiate himself during the job interview she had connived to secure him. It wasn't just that Hurd was nervous, though that he certainly was. In Dunn's opinion, he also came across as diffident. Redmond assured her that Hurd did in fact want the job, but that he was both conflicted by his sense of loyalty to NCR and doubtful that HP would hire him in any event.

As Hurd warmed to the task of fielding the committee's questions, his demeanor was reduced to irrelevancy by the substance of what he had to say over the next hour and a half. He not only exhibited a deep, intuitive understanding of the issues HP faced but also articulated them in the same way company insiders talked about them. By the end of the interview, Hurd had supplanted Belluzzo as the front-runner. Hurd "analyzed HP's problems and prospects with an astonishing precision," Perkins recalled. "Plus, he outlined a plan to fix things quickly and efficiently. When he left my office, the three of us just looked at one another and, virtually simultaneously, said, 'He's our man!'"[35]

It wasn't that simple, actually. There were more candidates to interview, and Hurd still had to pass muster with HP's other directors. Dunn had not forgotten how the board had rushed to judgment in hiring Fiorina, rubber-stamping the selection of a candidate most of them had never even laid eyes on until after she was hired. The Three Musketeers presented a slate of three candidates to the full board: Hurd, Belluzzo and a Motorola executive code-named "Muzak." Hurd was the clear favorite, but his selection was cast into doubt at the eleventh hour when one director complained at a board meeting in Chicago that the committee should have made more of an effort to land a tech CEO who was higher profile and more experienced than any of the finalists. Within thirty-six hours, Redmond found someone who fit the bill and flew him from Boston to Chicago, where he was interviewed by the full board the day after HP's annual meeting. He did well, but Hurd came out on top in a straw poll in which Dunn asked her colleagues to rank the four candidates by order of preference. At the chair's urging, the board made its formal vote unanimously for Hurd.

It wasn't quite a done deal. The terms of Hurd's employment still had to be negotiated. Through Redmond, he told the board that he would accept the CEO position only if Dunn remained as chairman and absolved him of responsibility for managing HP's fractious board. Dunn gladly obliged. Accommodating Hurd financially took rather more doing. Through Larry Babbio, who chaired the compensation committee, the board made an ill-advised but short-lived attempt to acquire Hurd's services on the cheap.

By all accounts, these climactic negotiations were excruciatingly suspenseful for Hurd. Could he reach agreement on a contract before word of his anointment at HP's next CEO leaked to the media? It was of utmost importance to him that NCR's board and its employees hear it first from him, not CNET or the *Wall Street Journal*. In mid-March, Keyworth alarmed Hurd by inadvertently breaking HP's official silence on its CEO search. In a question and answer session following a speech he made at a tech conference, Keyworth let slip that HP would announce the hiring of a CEO very soon.[36] Although Keyworth had not named him, Hurd was upset by the indiscretion and placed an angry call to Redmond, who alerted Dunn. "It was clear that if this sort of thing happened again, we might lose Mark," Dunn said.[37]

A few days later, Peter Burrows of *Business Week* called Hurd at home and said that he had it on good authority that he was HP's choice to replace Fiorina. Now Hurd was really upset. "That was a big bobble," Dunn said. "I think we almost lost Mark there, too."[38] The story *Business Week* published online was carefully hedged, saying only that Hurd was "high on [HP's] short list," not that he was definitely the one.[39] For Hurd, though, the distinction was academic; he was indeed HP's choice and now he had a lot of hurried explaining to do in Dayton. Although the news hit NCR like a thunderbolt, its board decided not to make an issue out of it, letting the CEO out of his contract without a fight.

HP officially announced Hurd's hiring on March 29, 2005, just seven weeks after Fiorina was fired, making this a remarkably expeditious search by big-company standards. Although press coverage was generally quite positive, Tam's story in the *Wall Street Journal* contained confidential details anonymously attributed.[40] "While [Tam's piece] and the rest of the stories are just what we had hoped for, it's most worrying to see that her 'source' is continuing to give her access to what appears to be Board-level thinking," chief press wrangler Bob Sherbin noted in a celebration-damping note to Dunn. "Forgive me if I'm too far out of line, but as your communications person here, I feel it's my duty to send up a warning flare that we're heading down a dangerous path."[41]

On March 31, Hurd's first day on the job, *Business Week* published a commentary co-authored by Ben Elgin and Peter Burrows—"Memo to Mark Hurd"—that included a quote attributed to an unnamed employee in HP's Boise office. The quote was utterly innocuous: "We want to believe. We love this place."[42] But Hurd had already had his fill of leaks and was determined to establish control over the company's increasingly undisciplined interactions with the press. At a meeting of HP's highest-ranking executives in May, he announced a zero-tolerance media policy: Any employee found to have spoken to a reporter without prior authorization would be fired on the spot.[43] Leaks to the press from inside the company are "reprehensible and unacceptable," Hurd said in a speech a few months later. "When I find where this comes from, I promise you I will deal with it appropriately. It is absolutely unacceptable that information does not stay in the company."[44]

CHAPTER SEVEN

SEED OF A SCANDAL

HEWLETT-PACKARD'S DISASTROUS leak investigation began not with a bang but with a forty-five-minute drive from Orinda to Palto Alto. On February 15, just eight days after Dunn had been named chairman, she took Jay Keyworth's advice and drove from her home to HP headquarters to ask HP Security for help in figuring out who was feeding confidential information to Pui-Wing Tam.[1] Dunn met first with interim CEO Bob Wayman, who had long overseen HP Security in his capacity as chief financial officer. Wayman agreed with Dunn that something needed to be done to stop the leaks. "We have people who do this for a living here," Dunn recalled him saying. "I'll have Kevin Huska talk to you right away."[2]

Dunn met with Huska in a guest office near the boardroom. His name hadn't rung a bell, but the chairman recognized the face. Huska was the big, imposing guy who hovered protectively outside the door at board meetings. She'd assumed he was a bodyguard—he certainly looked the part—but his business card identified him by a grand title: manager of the Global Employee Protection Program under the auspices of HP Global Security. Before joining HP in 2000, Huska had worked for the U. S. Department of State as a special agent on the terrorism detail.[3]

According to Dunn, Huska explained that confidential information leaked out of Hewlett-Packard routinely and that HP Security had protocols for dealing with the problem. Huska referred Dunn to Ron DeLia. Dunn assumed that DeLia was an HP employee, but he was a self-employed investigator working out of Boston under contract to HP. "Talk to Ron," Huska urged.

Internal HP documents suggest that Huska was less than forthcoming with Dunn, failing to tell her that the day before her visit HP Security had begun investigating the latest *Journal* leak on its own. At Huska's direction, an HP investigator named Michael Menz was busily searching the company's telephone database to see if anyone had called Tam's office phone from company premises. Menz turned up forty-five such calls, including sixteen placed by Bob Sherbin, HP's chief press handler.

"Do you want to find the home phones for the Target," Menz asked Huska by email shortly after Dunn had departed.[4]

"Yes," Huska replied, "please obtain as much information on this individual as possible."[5]

Menz soon obtained Tam's home and cell phone numbers and also began collecting biographical information on the reporter. She and her husband "have relations in San Diego and [a relative] came from China mainland," he informed Huska.[6]

Shortly after Dunn drove back home from Palo Alto, she emailed Hackborn a report on her meeting with Huska. "There are more things that can be done to track down who may have been in touch with the WSJ reporter, but only if they called from HP or from the Park Hyatt phones," she confided. "In addition they are doing a complete assessment of information security and will report it out to Bob [Wayman] and me." She thanked Hackborn for his support. "Very scary," she concluded.

"I hope our 'come to Jesus' discussion about confidentiality on Saturday had the needed impact."[7]

As it turned out, Dunn would become so preoccupied by the hunt for a new CEO that she would not follow up on the DeLia referral until after Mark Hurd was hired. In the late stages of the search, Andrea Redmond had told Dunn that the time had come to run the customary "deep background checks" on Hurd and the other two finalists. Russell Reynolds routinely checked the professional and personal references that job candidates provided, but left the background checks to client companies because they were much more sensitive, encompassing police and court records, credit reports, divorces, and the like. At Redmond's suggestion, Dunn called Marcela Perez de Alonso, who headed HP's Human Resources Department. "There's a guy we use to do these checks, but you should call him yourself so I don't know the names," Perez de Alonso said. "His name is Ron DeLia."

This time, Dunn immediately followed up on the referral, calling DeLia at his office in Boston. In her thorough way, Dunn asked DeLia to provide some background information about himself, which he did by email. He'd begun his career in the U.S. Army as a military policeman and criminal investigator in 1969. For a time, he worked undercover in Southeast Asia as part of a secret effort to curb the flow of heroin from the region. After leaving the military, DeLia worked for a series of private security companies before setting up his own firm, Security Outsourcing Solutions, in 1998.[8] One of SOS's biggest clients had been Digital Equipment Corp. Luckily for DeLia, DEC's security department survived even after the Boston computer maker was acquired by Compaq and Compaq was absorbed into HP. HP accounted for half of SOS's revenues.

With Hurd safely installed in the corner office, Dunn now had time to focus in a systematic way on the issue of the board's information security, or lack thereof. Huska had promised her a report, but she had never heard back from the monosyllabic ex-bodyguard and chose not to press him. The distraction of the finding a replacement for Fiorina had not been not the only reason she hadn't contacted DeLia after meeting with Huska. Dunn doubted Huska's competency and she worried as well about how HP Global Security fit into the company's larger structure. Could it be trusted to investigate thoroughly and objectively or might it be compromised by corporate politics in ways she knew nothing about? Who ultimately called the shots at HP Global Security?, she wondered.

Dunn's instinctive reaction to her first underwhelming brush with HP's security apparatus was to try to bring in a brand-name investigative firm like Kroll Associates to look into the leaks. Shortly after her meeting with Huska, she'd floated this idea in a memo to the other board members. "I have discussed the prospect of retaining Kroll Associates with Larry Sonsini to see what they can do, within the bounds of ethics and the law, to track unauthorized press communications," she wrote. "I will not know any specifics so that, if this occurs, I will be in the same situation as the rest of the Board."[9] Outside counsel Sonsini didn't give Dunn an opinion one way or the other, but she later recalled that Wayman was strongly opposed, arguing that it was pointless to pay Kroll Associates big money to do something that HP Security could easily handle on it own.

Dunn, who up to this point had been remarkably sure-footed in navigating HP's corridors of power, made a huge error in deferring to Wayman on the question of hiring a third-party investigator. "Oh, God, that was a very poor decision on my part,"

Dunn acknowledged later.[10] Had the leak investigation been entrusted to Kroll Associates, it's entirely possible, even likely, that
scandal never would have ensued. As it was, her worst fears
about HP Security and its bosses would soon be realized.

To this day, Hewlett-Packard claims that the company's first
post-Fiorina leak investigation began on April 19, 2005, when
DeLia emailed a one-page proposal to Dunn for her approval.
This claim was widely accepted as fact, even though it was
patently contradicted by documents that HP itself turned over
to Congress and to the California State Attorney General. In
truth, HP Security began two separate, inconclusive leak investigations well before April 19, 2005, and Dunn was not fully apprised of either of them.

The first of these was the Huska-Menz investigation into
unauthorized disclosures to Pui-Wing Tam that began just before
Dunn established first contact with HP Security. Huska did in
fact write a report to the chairman after the investigation petered
out. But Dunn never received Huska's memo, and it appears that
he never sent it. It read in part:

> HP IT Security investigative group was requested to de-
> termine if HP owned systems were utilized to contact
> SUBJECT's email addresses (work or personal) and/or
> various phone numbers (office, home, mobile) during the
> period of November 15, 2004, to February 14, 2005.
>
> Investigative efforts identified numerous HP employ-
> ees in telephonic contact with SUBJECT during the
> period in question, all from the HP Communications
> department. No employees were identified as having
> routine access to restricted information from the BoD.
> The employees' manager, Bob Sherbin, was interviewed.

Mr. Sherbin indicated that all listed employees had a legitimate professional relationship with SUBJECT as it
related to company business.

Investigative efforts did not find electronic communications (emails) between HP systems and SUBJECT's
listed email addresses. Further investigative efforts and
analysis failed to identify further communications between HP employees or communications systems and
the SUBJECT.[11]

The second investigation was of the leak to *Business Week*
about Rick Belluzzo's emergence as a leading CEO candidate.
After the story appeared, Belluzzo emailed Wayman to complain
that the leak had put him in a compromising position with his
board. Wayman, in turn, informed Dunn that Belluzzo was upset,
but she said that she was not told that DeLia had been assigned
to investigate. The documents that HP later disgorged contain
no explicit references to this probe. They do establish, though,
that on the very day that Belluzzo complained to Wayman, DeLia
did something he would frequently do in subsequent leak investigations: He faxed a long list of telephone numbers to Action
Research Group in Melbourne, Florida. By methods unspecified
on its invoice, Action Research was able to put a name and an
address to all thirty-four of these numbers, at least seven of which
were on HP exchanges.[12]

The next DeLia investigation, initiated by Dunn on behalf
of the board, also focused on a leak to *Business Week*, the one
that generated the story that had so infuriated Hurd. Dunn considered Keyworth and Fiorina the likeliest suspects, with Perkins
a distant third. "We have no control over [Carly's] activities
with the press," Dunn told DeLia, "but we still need to know if

there are leaks coming from 'internal' sources"—namely, the former CEO's unrepentant admirer on the board, Bob Knowling.[13] In addition to Keyworth, Perkins, and Knowling, the investigation targeted the *Business Week* reporters who'd co-written the offending story, Ben Elgin and Peter Burrows, both of whom worked out of the magazine's San Mateo bureau in the heart of Silicon Valley.

In his written proposal to Dunn, which he also sent to HP General Counsel Ann Baskins, DeLia advocated "discreet limited background investigations" of all five men. With the board members, DeLia intended to focus on "travel habits, vacation properties, educational and employment background, family tree, etc." The reporters were tagged for extra scrutiny. "Ancillary investigative activity to include, but not limited to, discrete [sic] on-site inspections/pretext interviews of places of employment, vacation properties, restaurants, bars, etc. . . . Electronic surveillance of email and/or other communication accounts, where applicable."[14]

On-site inspections/pretext interviews? Electronic surveillance? Even allowing for the anesthetizing effect of DeLia's jargon, this note should have set off alarms in Dunn's brain. "The word pretext in particular should have grabbed me, but it didn't," she admitted. "The way I think I interpreted that is you go into a bar and say, 'Does Bob Knowling come in here very often? I thought I saw him in here with a reporter from the *Wall Street Journal*.' I mean, come on! It just seemed like gumshoe stuff."[15]

Dunn wasn't alone in failing to appreciate the potential for mischief inherent in DeLia's plan. As it happened, she received his proposal by email on April 19, 2005, just a few hours before her first extended meeting with Hurd since he'd become CEO. Baskins took notes as CEO and chairman discussed numerous issues relating to the board, including information security. According to Baskins, Hurd thought that "the leaks were outrageous."[16] Dunn recalled reading much of DeLia's proposal aloud to Hurd, who agreed that it should be implemented, as Baskins indicated in her notes from the meeting: "Media: Discussion and agreement regarding efforts to prevent unauthorized disclosure of board matters to media." Later, after Spygate broke, HP's official position was that Hurd had not even been aware of "Dunn's leak investigation" until July, three months after he and Dunn and discussed the DeLia proposal.

The DeLia investigation was much broader and more involved than the two that preceded it. Because the whole board had been privy to the information leaked to *Business Week*, DeLia made a case for searching the phone records of all of HP's directors. Dunn not only agreed, but was too willing by half to assist DeLia, providing phone numbers for all the board members, including no less than eight different numbers for herself (office, Orinda home, home fax, husband's home office, San Francisco home, San Francisco home office, mobile, and car phone).

Apparently, it never occurred to her to question why DeLia wanted private, non-HP phone numbers. "The clear impression I had from Mr. DeLia was that such records could be obtained from publicly available sources in a legal and appropriate manner, and that this was just one of several methods that would be pursued in the investigation," Dunn declared a year and a half later in testifying under oath before a Congressional committee.[17] According to various documents, Dunn's initial belief that phone records could be legally obtained from public sources was shared by Hurd, Wayman, Baskins, and Jim Fairbaugh, the head of HP security, among other HP insiders.

In her eagerness to help, Dunn went so far as to annotate
the list of phone numbers she provided to DeLia with personal
insights about her colleagues:

> Larry Babbio: LB is a senior executive at Verizon. He
> told me once that he/Verizon receive requests every day
> to produce cell phone records for various purposes, and
> that the general public would be surprised how easily
> and often they are produced.
> George (Jay) Keyworth: He has experience in top-
> secret government activities (directed Reagan's 'star wars'
> program) and understands more than other directors
> how confidential information can be both protected
> and traced.
> Tom Perkins: Tom claims not to carry a cell phone and
> I have reason to believe this is true. He spends several
> weeks a year at his home in England.
> Bob Wayman: I know Bob has other home phone num-
> bers. He was surprised that I had the one above; appar-
> ently it is not supposed to be known.[18]

Dunn made yet another dumb mistake in accepting DeLia's
invitation to name the investigation, thereby establishing ownership of it in a bureaucratic sense. She was about to fly to
Hawaii, where she and her husband owned a condominium in
the Kona district on the Big Island. "Let's call this Project Kona,"
she suggested.[19]

How could someone who in most circumstances was careful
and methodical to a fare-thee-well have acted as rashly as Dunn
did in authorizing, assisting in, and naming Project Kona? No
one who started as a secretary and climbed to the top a large,

complex organization like BGI could be completely devoid of guile any more than of ambition, but the fact is that Dunn was essentially straightforward in manner and quite linear in her thinking. In the most fundamental sense, she was just not programmed to cope with the level of chicanery that she now encountered for the first time in her life.

"Pattie was always nice and upbeat even when things were getting ugly," recalled Sherbin, who would be in close contact with Dunn throughout the Spygate ordeal. "I think it was after she'd appeared on the cover of *Newsweek* in a horrifying picture and was being portrayed as the Leona Helmsley of the West Coast. She said without any irony at all, 'Bob, this is enough to make me lose my idealism.' I've dealt with a lot of people as a journalist and as an executive, or whatever I am, and she is just the finest person I have ever dealt with. I think she is a kind of purist who took a virtue and exaggerated it to the point where it became a vice, or at least a failing."[20]

But if Dunn was naïve in some respects, she also was actively manipulated by HP Global Security, a cliquish fraternity of ex-cops, former military men, and computer geeks whose chief, Fairbaugh, reported directly to Wayman and later to Hurd. Judging from their memos and emails, HP's spooks took themselves very seriously, communicating with one another in a semi-literate argot studded with code names. Tom Perkins was "Tango Papa," George Jay Keyworth was "Golf June Kilo," Pattie Dunn was "Papa Delta" and Carly Fiorina was "Charlie Foxtrot." Apparently, it was even thought necessary on occasion to mask the identity of Hewlett-Packard, aka "Hotel Papa."

In Global Security lingo, Dunn was a "client" or a "complainant"; in other words, she was an outsider who was to be respected for the power of her corporate position and placated if possible, but who was not to be allowed inside the investigation. DeLia took his instructions not from Dunn, but from the same person to whom he submitted his bills for services rendered: Anthony Gentilucci, who was director of investigations for HP Security. DeLia went way back with Gentilucci, who also was based in Boston. In claiming later that Gentilucci had no involvement in Kona until mid-July, HP overlooked an email in its files proving that in fact he was in the loop right from the start. DeLia sent the following email to Gentilucci on May 5: "A reminder to call your boss [Jim Fairbaugh] reference special projects work for PD."[21] HP's records show that as Kona progressed, DeLia and other security operatives briefed Dunn and Baskins at irregular intervals and occasionally requested their help, but told them only what they thought they needed to know, which wasn't nearly as much as they should have known.

In mid-June 2005, there was yet another leak to *Business Week* that again damaged Hurd personally, this time by impugning his integrity. Burrows and Elgin learned that the SEC had begun an inquiry into Hurd's sale of NCR stock just weeks before he had left the company to join HP. Between March 1 and 3, Hurd sold 36,000 NCR shares at $39 a share, netting $1.4 million. "If Hurd knew he was a candidate for the top job at HP at the time of the sales," the story noted, "the trades could constitute insider trading."[22] (In the end, the SEC took no action.) Hurd told Dunn that *Business Week* was working on the story shortly before it appeared, and the chairman relayed word to the other directors. "This information was closely held and thus reflects another breach of confidentiality," Dunn noted.[23]

The latest *Business Week* leak inspired Perkins to make two proposals to Dunn, the first of which struck her as bizarre and the second as transparently self-serving:

I don't know what to suggest, other than voluntary lie-detector tests for all involved. But, this is a huge deal, and if we did it, the act itself would become a major news story. Also, it would make the search for new Directors just about impossible. I wonder if the only solution is to create an Executive Committee of the Board, with full power to act, to deal with the most confidential matters?—and there will always be these matters. These committees can emasculate a board, and in general I am against them, but given the situation, and given all the confidential decisions which must be made in the next few months, I wonder if we have a choice? Perhaps the committee would consist of only Directors who take, or agree to take the test. . . . I wish I had a great solution to propose for the problem, which I think you could legitimately say has reached the crisis stage.[24]

Although Dunn shrugged off Perkins's suggestions, the new leak prompted her to ask DeLia for a written progress report on Kona. DeLia complied a few days later, sending a draft to Dunn, who in turn sent it to Baskins. DeLia hadn't much of anything to offer in the way of hard evidence. The report, which Baskins dismissed as "sophomoric" and "amateurish," was noteworthy only for the glimpse it provided into DeLia's investigative methods.[25] Somehow, he had gained access to the records of numerous telephone calls made away from HP premises, including 122 that Keyworth had made from his cell phone and 408 that Burrows made from his cell. "Telephone subscriber and call registers are obtained verbally from the various telephone carriers," the report noted.[26] Foolishly, neither Dunn nor Baskins thought to press

DeLia for details on exactly how he had obtained private phone records just by asking for them.

HP Security would produce a few more Kona reports over the next few months, each one longer than the last but no less inconclusive. By the fall of 2005, the investigation had petered out and HP had been leak free for several months. On September 10, DeLia sent an invoice to Gentilucci for $60,748.73, covering his work on Kona from May 16, 2005, to July 25, 2005. Dunn was not copied on this or any of DeLia's other invoices.

By the end of the year, though, Keyworth was again inflaming suspicions. Evidence belatedly surfaced that Pui-Wing Tam had in fact called Keyworth before writing the story that had precipitated Carly's ouster. In November 2005, Rosemary Ann Thomas, the senior secretary to the HP board, sent a confidential email to HP Security. Some weeks earlier, Keyworth had called from Italy with an odd request, Thomas reported. "He asked if there was some way messages could be taken off of his machine at home in Santa Fe. It seems that a reporter left several trying to reach him. He never returned the messages and in fact if I remember correctly he did not even go back to Santa Fe but saved them because of further discussions he had with Carly. Let me know if there is a secure way to do this and if they can be saved."[27]

Keyworth turned over the two voicemails Tam had left him in January to Gentilucci, HP Security's senior investigator. The voicemails sounded innocent enough. "We had spoken a couple of years ago—in 2002, actually, when I was writing about the HP/Compaq battle we had spoken," Tam said. "I don't know if you remember me. I wanted to get back in touch with you. There were a couple of things I was hoping to run by you."[28] Keyworth told Gentilucci that he hadn't listened to the messages until August and hadn't spoken to Tam for a couple of years. HP Security was unable to prove otherwise.

In December 2005, Keyworth was quoted by name in a Burrows story that credited Hurd's "shrewd refocusing and cost-cutting" for the 40 percent rise in HP's stock price since he had been named CEO.[29] Keyworth's quote was harmless—"Mark has been busy getting the engine tuned. Now, we're turning out attention to growth again"—but the issue in Dunn's mind was whether Keyworth had conformed to the board's confidentiality policy by clearing the interview with HP's press relations department in advance. "That Jay came out and cavalierly said whatever he felt like saying to Burrows with no clearance at all put me in a bad position with Larry Babbio because I was trying to be a peacemaker between the two of them," Dunn said later. "I was really ticked off!"[30]

Dunn emailed Sherbin: "Were you aware from Burrows that he was contacting Keyworth for the story or aware from Jay that Burrows had been in contact?"

"No on all counts," Sherbin replied. "Jay didn't contact me at all on this. Needless to say, this complicates things for us when we beg off all board interview requests with the rationale that the board doesn't speak to the media."

Dunn copied Hurd on her response to Sherbin: "This is disappointing. I will be contacting Jay to discuss."[31]

And then she sent what sounded like a wail in email form to Sonsini: "This is a smoking gun as far as I'm concerned. Talk me down."

CHAPTER EIGHT

THE POLITICS OF DILUTION

DURING MARK HURD'S third week as CEO, Tom Perkins flew with him on an HP corporate jet to Corvallis, Oregon, which was home to one of the company's most important operating hubs. "He all ready [sic] has his hands on the controls and is taking action. I am impressed! I am happy! (I have had a couple of drinks, too)," Perkins gushed in an email to Pattie Dunn and Jay Keyworth sent from Corvallis, where he and Hurd dined with the local managers and also fielded questions from a few hundred employees in the cafeteria. "Seriously, we have a terrific CEO now on the job. I think he will prove to be the right person at the right time."[1]

He would indeed, and as two-thirds of its filtering committee, Dunn and Perkins shared disproportionately in the credit due HP's board for making such an inspired, unconventional choice. In short order, the substitution of Hurd for Fiorina would shift the balance of power within HP's boardroom in ways that would strain and finally snap the makeshift alliance that had united Dunn and Perkins in the shared purpose of firing one CEO and hiring another. But at the dawn of HP's Hurd era, as Perkins's high-spirited email from Corvallis illustrated, these future archenemies basked together in the warm glow engendered by mutual accomplishment. "We were buddy-buddy," Perkins recalled.[2]

Dunn said later that she would have been willing to step down as chair at this juncture, but that Hurd asked her to remain in the post to shield him from the distractions and frustrations of having to manage so troublesome a board. He had grown accustomed to a similar arrangement at NCR, where his predecessor as CEO had stayed on as chair. Although Hurd wasn't a corporate-governance progressive per se, he accepted the concept of non-executive chairman and encouraged Dunn to literally write her own job description. She did, adopting a modest approach to the office. As chair, she would preside over board meetings, regulate the panel's internal affairs and, when necessary, convene it in executive session—that is, without management present. The idea was to hold Hurd to a high level of accountability to the board but not get in his way. Dunn would have no role in management of the company other than acting as a sounding board for Hurd. No one at HP reported to Dunn, who had no authority to hire or fire or incur corporate expenses. She didn't even have an office at headquarters, operating instead out of the study of her chalet-style home in the Orinda hills.

Hurd let Dunn know early on that he wanted her to play a role in helping steer HP that was more expansive in practice than on paper. The day before Hurd flew to Corvallis with Perkins, he set aside two hours for a wide-ranging telephone conversation with Dunn. "Mark wants to identify and prioritize a series of discretionary topics to include in agendas over a 12-month period," wrote Ann Baskins, who listened in on the meeting and took notes. "Examples include how we grow revenue, geographical reviews, cost cutting. He suggested that Pattie put together such a list for review."[3]

For the first time since Dunn joined the board, she felt that her quant-inspired views received a respectful, informed hearing from the corner office. The precision mathematics of business performance measurement was mother's milk to Hurd, who ordered up and memorized hundreds of metrics—prices, costs, margins, discounts, growth rates, and the like—during his first weeks on the job at HP.[4] Dunn also got Hurd's approval to hire David Nygren, the senior partner of Mercer Delta Consulting, to advise her and the board on how to update and improve HP's antiquated governance practices. Meanwhile, Dunn took herself to chairman's school, perusing the academic literature on corporate best practices and attending governance workshops at Stanford University, which was just down the street from HP. "My first thought was, 'How do I avoid screwing up?'" she recalled.[5]

Dunn and Hurd were similar in many ways—analytical, diligent, exacting, and yet personable. Hurd, a married father of three teenagers, was every bit as intense as Fiorina, but not nearly as haughty. He and Dunn established an easy rapport right from the start. Somehow, Hurd got hold of a photograph of a freckle-faced, gap-toothed Dunn at age seven, scanned it into his computer and emailed it to her. "What a cute little girl!" he exclaimed.[6] (Dunn knew the picture well: It hung on the wall of her home office.) Right up until their relationship abruptly ruptured in the fall of 2006, Hurd and Dunn dined together at least once a month, usually at Chantilly in Palo Alto, maintained frequent phone contact, and were just as likely to talk over personal matters as business issues as the new CEO and his wife struggled to transition from King and Queen of Dayton, Ohio, to Silicon Valley newbies.

At the same time, Perkins also saw Hurd as a boardroom comrade who would be much more receptive to his guidance than

Fiorina had been, and he continued to believe himself capable of dominating Dunn through sheer force of personality. He took it as nothing less than his due when Dunn nominated him to replace Bob Knowling, who resigned a few months after Fiorina's firing, as chair of the Nominating & Governance committee, the board's second most powerful post.

Actually, Perkins's appointment was hardly routine. Dunn recalled that Larry Babbio, who sat on the committee, had objected vehemently, telling her, "I don't think he's suited to the role. I think you're going to regret it." Dunn dismissed Babbio's opposition as the latest manifestation of the bad blood between him and Keyworth, still Perkins's main boardroom ally. In making Perkins N&G chair, Dunn was employing the same philosophy that had led her to put him on the CEO search committee. "There's an axiom on business that if someone's complaining about something, you give them the job of solving the problem," Dunn said. "Tom generally had a lot of ideas about governance. He told me many, many, many times that he'd been chairman of fifteen boards at the same time."[7]

It is also conceivable that Dunn was setting up Perkins for a fall by ushering him into a demanding position for which he was manifestly ill suited, just as Babbio had argued. As Dunn well knew, Perkins embraced a ruggedly Darwinian philosophy of capitalism and disdained the growing emphasis on corporate governance as a vogue of political correctness that was leaching business of its entrepreneurial vigor. He was particularly critical of Sarbanes-Oxley, or SOX. "Unfortunately, the compliance aspects of SOX can, if permitted, come to dominate everything that a board does," Perkins complained in his autobiography. "And at the end of the day compliance doesn't add to earnings per share and a rising stock price."[8]

Perkins told me that he was happy to occupy the N&G post even so, for he believed that he could use it to recruit the "right kind" of new directors. Hurd and Dunn had decided to add two new positions to the board, and Knowling's resignation, which came into effect in the fall of 2005, created a third vacancy. As it was, Perkins thought that he could count on the votes of Keyworth, Hackborn, and Salhany. If he could add a technology-savvy fellow traveler or two to the board and cultivate a close working relationship with Hurd, he could function as HP's chairman in all but name.

Not long after the Corvallis trip, Perkins invited Hurd and Dunn and their spouses to dinner at his Belvedere estate. "I had never met Paula Hurd and I wanted to try to build a rapport between the board and the CEO," Perkins explained. "It's the sort of stuff you do."[9] After dinner, Perkins and his guests retired to the living room, where Hurd and Dunn paired off on a couch for an intensive bout of Hewlett-Packard shop talk, which Perkins futilely tried to disrupt after a time by flying his remote-controlled, high-tech model helicopter around the high-ceilinged room. "I noticed it and I ignored it, and so did Mark," Dunn said. "It was like, how old are you, Tom, seventy-three or three?"[10] Hurd and Dunn did join the others in gathering around Perkins while he sat on the floor and played a video on his tablet PC about the designing of *The Maltese Falcon*.

Perkins took his charm offensive on the road a few months later. When he discovered that Dunn and Jahnke were planning to spend early July in England he invited them to celebrate American Independence Day at his English country manor house, Plumpton Place. Perkins rode out from London with his guests in a chauffeured limousine, entertaining them en route with tales of the *Falcon*, which was nearing completion in a Turkish shipyard.

Jahnke gave his host a gift meant to engage Perkins's intellect even as it flattered his ego: A copy of Benoît Mandelbrot's quant-intensive new book, *The Misbehavior of Markets: A Fractal View of Risk, Ruin & Reward*. The party arrived at Plumpton Place after dark, ruling out a tour of the world-class gardens that had been planted by Gerd, Perkins's late wife. No matter, Dunn was happy to hang by the fire. "There's something Goth about the house—it's a little spooky actually," she recalled.[11] The climax of the evening was an impressive fireworks display engineered by Richard, who was Perkins's major domo and an amateur pyrotechnician, which Dunn and Jahnke viewed from the front lawn with members of Perkins's domestic staff and a dozen of their friends who worked in neighboring houses.

What stood out in Perkins's recollection of the visit, oddly enough, was a comment that Dunn made about his shoes. "We were sitting there in this very nice house and she said, 'You're wearing rubber-soled shoes. I wouldn't let Bill wear them.' What's the difference?" Perkins grumbled. "Who notices and who cares?"

Perkins also recalled that Dunn raised the subject of the leaks in what he considered a suggestive way. "Here she was in my house talking about it, so I thought, 'She probably thinks it's me.' So I said, 'Hey, I'll take a lie detector test.' Which I would have."[12]

This was the second time that Perkins had suggested lie detector tests to Dunn, and he elaborated on the notion in an email he sent to her the very next day:

> I have been thinking about the Lie Detector Test (LDT) topic and want to let you know that I was serious about it. It could be a pilot of other tests at other times.
>
> I think that the following ground rules should apply:

1) The test should be strictly confidential, because of the explosive story that the media might make of it. Thus the administrative staff, setting it up, would not know the name of the individual taking the LDT.

2) Only you and the test taker would be given the results.

3) Great attention should be given to the preparation of the questions; the test should be exhaustive, so that the results would not be subject later to conjecture. The test should be administered by experts in the LDT field.

This would be an interesting experience (I might be able to use it in background for my next novel!) and thus not an imposition, at least in my case.

Dunn was instinctively opposed to lie detector tests, but did not know enough about them to make an informed counterargument. She asked Mercer Delta's Nygren to research the use of lie detectors in a corporate setting and to write a formal opinion letter. No expert himself, Nygren commissioned an analysis by Kroll Associates, which once had been owned by the same company that now owned Mercer Delta. "We did validation studies on lie detector tests and determined that it was not a reliable method," Nygren recalled.[13] Dunn presented Mercer's findings to Perkins, who flipped through the notebooks that Nygren had compiled and grudgingly agreed that LDTs were more trouble than they were worth.

The issue of the leaks and what to do about them would infuse growing tension into dealings between Dunn and Perkins, but their relationship started to unravel in the latter half of 2005 over two far more personal issues. The first was the size of Dunn's paycheck as chair. The compensation that HP provided its directors had doubled in 2004, reaching $200,000 a year. To Dunn, this sum seemed excessive, based on what she knew about what other companies were paying their board members. Not long after Hurd had become CEO, Dick Hackborn proposed that directors voluntarily reduce their board pay by as much as one-half in solidarity with the sacrifices being made by HP employees. Dunn liked the idea, as did Hurd. In the end, though, she heeded the advice of Nygren, who warned against fiddling with the directors' fees. "The trend in the US and Canada is toward increasing pay of directors," Nygren noted in an email. "As you search for new directors, you would hate for competitive pay to be the obstacle to recruitment."[14]

Perkins had a radically different take on the topic of pay, arguing that Dunn and Dunn alone should be paid an additional $100,000 a year as chairman. As he explained it, the extra money was not intended as a reward but as an inducement to approach the job of chairman the right way—*his* way, in other words: "Very foolishly, I think, I tried to make her into Tom Perkins. You know, this is what you should do. 'Pattie, go down there and do this.' I'll get you more money so it's worth your time to do all this. That was stupid." Perkins raised the matter at a board meeting and pushed back hard when a few of the other directors argued that $100,000 was too much. "Come on!" he said. "It's a big company and a big job."[15]

Dunn wanted no part of a Perkins-sponsored pay hike. "My view was either Tom thinks he can buy me for a hundred grand or he is demonstrating to one and all that he is going to decide who gets paid what—or both," Dunn recalled. "I just thought, 'Thanks but no thanks. I don't need this.'" Her objections softened when Babbio took it upon himself to push the $100,000 raise through the compensation committee, which he chaired. "It had a whole different slant coming from Larry," Dunn said.[16]

For his part, Perkins was offended by Dunn's approach to the issue of the board's mandatory retirement requirement. Perkins argued that the board should do away with an age maximum altogether, if only to spare him from the ritual embarrassment of what he described as the "annual is-Perkins-too old-to-be-on-the-board" debate. Dunn infuriated Perkins by taking the corporate-governance high road on what to him was an acutely personal matter. As she put it, "I wondered how this was being handled in other companies. Is it ageist? Or is it a good way to make room for a new generation of people? Shouldn't we know in advance whether we're doing something that governance watchers would consider a big black eye and bring accusations that we're entrenching our board?"[17] Dunn consulted Larry Sonsini, who advised her that expert opinion on mandatory retirement was divided and inconclusive.

Perkins put the mandatory retirement issue on the agenda of the N&G meeting that marked his debut as its chairman. Babbio was for keeping the age limit as strongly as Perkins wanted to get rid of it. (The committee's only other member, Salhany, lined up with Perkins.) Dunn, who attended most committee meetings on an ex officio basis, took the precaution of inviting Sonsini to this one. "I didn't want it to blow up, so I thought Larry could come in and sprinkle his holy water," Dunn recalled.[18] But when she announced that Sonsini was waiting outside, Perkins blew his top. "I know goddamn well we can do this if we want to! We don't need to talk to Larry or anybody else," he said and then put the issue to a vote. The margin was two to one, and full board approval was not required. "Next item," Perkins snapped.[19]

Dunn went out and told Sonsini that his services were not required after all. "Larry is a cool character and this was one of the few times I'd ever seen him fume," she recalled. "He sort of grimaced and said, 'Well, that's not right,' and he walked out."[20]

For some time, Hurd and other directors had been urging Dunn to officially take a seat on the N&G committee as its fourth member to avoid just this sort of tempest. She still thought it was a bad idea. "I didn't want to crowd Tom's space," she said. "I was already chairman of the board and I felt I had enough influence."[21]

Given time to reflect about his conduct at his first N&G meeting, Perkins was . . . completely unrepentant. "I embarrassed Pattie and pissed off Larry. But why did I do that?" he told me. "I did that because there were business problems we should have been addressing, instead of paying excruciating attention to all this governance crap."[22]

So much for the governance part of Perkins's brief as Nominating & Governance chair! If anything, the nominating aspect of the job would prove an even greater source of anger and frustration for Perkins, whose repeated attempts to recruit new directors that met his personal selection criteria failed utterly. "I never got anybody on the board that I wanted," he complained.[23] For this, he blamed Dunn at the time, acknowledging only belatedly that the insuperable obstacle to his ambition of recreating Hewlett-Packard's board in his own image had actually been Mark Hurd.

* * *

DUNN HAD RETURNED from the round of hometown director visits she had made shortly after becoming chairman stunned at the depth of the animus that existed among her colleagues. The bad feelings were so prevalent and ran so deep that even the board's conciliator despaired of ever closing its many fissures. Better to start over, Dunn reasoned, and reconstitute the board entirely—not through a mass purge, but gradually, through voluntary departures. "Ideally, everybody would write a letter of resignation that Ann Baskins would keep in her drawer until the appropriate time arrived," she said. "I thought it was a three-to five-year transition."[24] She discussed this approach with Hurd, who was all for it.

Even so, Dunn never did suggest to her colleagues that they put resignation letters on file, suspecting that none of them—with the possible exception of Hackborn—would ever agree to depart voluntarily and in fact would take great offense at the suggestion that HP would be better off without them. As for Hurd, it would have been impolitic in the extreme for a new CEO to advocate getting rid of the very board members who had just hired him. Together, Dunn and Hurd decided to at least begin diluting the poisoned well that was HP's board by adding two new directorships while trusting to attrition to work its subtractive magic over the long run.

Hurd required a great deal more of HP's board members than had Fiorina, who essentially resented the panel as a hindrance to her unfettered exercise of authority. At NCR, Hurd had grown accustomed to depending on the counsel and support of a handful of trusted directors a generation older than he was. "Mark told me, 'I'd like to know there are people on the board who had done difficult things, because I'm going to have to do some difficult things here and now,'" Dunn said.[25]

Hurd stuck with Fiorina's ambitious strategy of offering a wide array of digital products and computer services while returning

HP to what he called the basic "blocking and tackling" of getting products out on time, improving quality and service, and increasing profit margins.[26] Like an overgrown garden, though, HP had to be pruned before it could grow properly. Just four months into Hurd's tenure, HP disclosed plans to lay off 14,500 workers, or nearly 10 percent of its staff, and to stop contributing to the pension plan of its U.S. employees. "Our objective," Hurd said, "was to lay out a simpler, nimbler, more efficient HP."[27]

Like most CEOs, Hurd instinctively preferred to fill board vacancies with other sitting CEOs. In fact, he brought with him a couple of possibilities from his NCR days: James Cox of the cable TV giant Cox Communications; and James Hackett of Steelcase, a manufacturer of office furniture. Hewlett-Packard had a live CEO prospect of its own carried over from Fiorina's final weeks: John Hammergren of McKesson Corp., a large San Francisco–based health care systems provider.

Dunn was all for giving Hurd what he wanted, but she also insisted on bringing discipline and order to the search for new directors. At Dunn and Hurd's first big meeting, the new CEO assented to every proposal she put forward on the subject. "Agreement that we should shoot for the best candidates" to fill board vacancies, Baskins wrote in her notes from the meeting. "Also agreed that focus should be on addressing needed roles rather than seeking highly successful people who do not meet identified needs."[28]

Those needs were identified mostly by Dunn, who, with Nygren's help, wrote a "gap analysis" that showed that the board as currently constituted was far too U.S.-centric for a company that derived more than half its revenues from overseas and that it also lacked expertise in marketing and in consumer products.

Dunn and Nygren additionally concluded that the board could use additional technology expertise, but not necessarily of the Silicon Valley sort. Hurd ratified Dunn's composition guidelines, as did all the other directors. "We all bought into the idea that no one would be asked to join the board that Mark wasn't excited about," Dunn said.[29] This included Perkins, who, as chairman of the N&G committee, would lead the search, at least nominally, assisted by Andrea Redmond of Russell Reynolds.

As eager as Perkins was to cozy up to Hurd, he disregarded the CEO's marching orders in the belief that he knew best what sort of directors HP needed. In many key respects, HP had more in common with the other fifty largest U.S. corporations than with the smaller, younger technology companies that had sprung up around it. To Perkins, though, HP was still defined by its Silicon Valley address and history. "I started from the premise that the people on the board should have industry knowledge," Perkins said. "At HP, what is industry knowledge? Well, it's Silicon Valley—it's an entrepreneurial company with a product life cycle of eighteen months."[30]

Perkins objected vehemently to a candidate who could have added both marketing and consumer products expertise, an executive who was jointly interviewed by Dunn and Hurd and had impressed them both: Steven Reinemund, the chairman and CEO of PepsiCo. "I know that we want Directors who will 'wow' Wall St, but is a super star skilled at selling sugar water (Pepsie) [sic] going to bring much insight to HP?" Perkins declared in an email to Dunn. "I think we should take a strong look at Silicon Valley talent. A high tech CEO like T. J. Rogers, for example, Jeff Besos [sic] from Amazon, Eric Schmitt [sic] from Google, etc. Plus, I think a top venture capitalist should be considered."

Of the five VCs he mentioned by name, two were Kleiner Perkins partners: Brook Byers and John Doerr. "If we rebuild shareholder value, that's what will wow Wall St.," Perkins concluded.[31]

Dunn decided not to push back on Reinemund, who told Redmond that he was flattered by HP's interest but was too busy to join any board. Filling a board vacancy with a CEO is an odds-against enterprise, given the tendency of boards to monopolize the services of their own top executives. In HP's case, Fiorina's firing and the attendant furor over boardroom leaks only lengthened the odds. Mainly, though, Dunn and Hurd were willing to let Reinemund slide because Perkins deferred to their wishes in going along with the selection of Hammergren, who attended his first board meeting in September 2005. Keyworth, too, accommodated Hammergren, telling Dunn that the McKesson CEO would be "most welcome on the technology committee."[32]

Against his better judgment, Perkins also took an active part in recruiting Sari Baldauf, who had just retired at forty-nine as the second-ranking executive of the Finnish mobile phone giant Nokia. "The [*Financial Times*] named her the most powerful woman in Euro business earlier this year and she is considered the most sought after potential director in Europe now," Dunn advised Perkins. "There is reason to think she is interested in HP but we would have to move quickly."[33]

After meeting with Baldauf in London, Perkins sent a rave review back to the chairman and his other colleagues on the board:

> I think she would be an outstanding addition to our board. She is bright and totally fluent in English. Her [22 years] at Nokia, mostly in line management, is right on

the mark, and she has planning strategy background as well. Though not an engineer, she has good experience in managing big technical projects, both hardware and software—she says that she even likes engineers. Probably most important, her experience is world wide—her perspective on international markets would be very valuable to us. Plus, she is familiar in marketing high tech, high volume, low priced products.[34]

Yet, after Perkins had resigned from the HP board, he mocked Baldauf in an interview with a writer from *The New Yorker*. "An executive vice president of Nokia?" he exclaimed incredulously. "She's from Finland!"[35]

When I asked Perkins to explain his wildly contradictory comments about Baldauf, he replied, "My mission in London was to make the sale, so I gave her a good review. I went along for a couple reasons. First of all, she was a woman and that was politically correct and all that stuff. Secondly, she knew people in Europe that could be useful for the company. And she was willing to do it. But then I attended two board meetings with her and I thought, 'She brings nothing to the party.'"[36]

Perkins floated a lot of names, but there were three technology industry executives that he pushed hardest and longest. The first, Raymond Lane, was a partner in Kleiner Perkins but could not be fairly described as a Perkins crony, even so. As the long-time president and chief operating officer of the software giant Oracle Corporation, Lane for a time had brought focus and discipline to a company cast in the mercurial image of founder Larry Ellison. Some of HP's directors were well acquainted with Lane, who'd been a serious contender in the CEO search that resulted in Fiorina's hiring but had bowed out before its conclusion. He hadn't been with Kleiner Perkins long, joining in 2000 after he fell out with Ellison.

"Ray, in my opinion, is the PERFECT board prospect—Silicon Valley—top management experience—and venture capital," Perkins told Dunn and Hurd after arranging for them to have lunch with Lane at the Kleiner Perkins offices in Menlo Park. "He has serious insights into HP (not all of them positive) and I think he could be tremendously helpful." The Kleiner Perkins partners didn't much like the idea of Lane devoting a portion of his time to HP, but would let him decide for himself, Perkins added. "The fact that he is willing to meet with you both indicates that the door is slightly open. I give the odds at 50:50, perhaps a little better."[37]

Hurd was enthusiastic about Lane, whom he had known for years. On his rise to the top at NCR, Hurd had run a division that had competed with Oracle and had also rubbed shoulders with Lane on various software industry groups. At Perkins's suggestion, the CEO placed a courtesy call to Ellison to make sure he had no objections to Lane joining HP's board. He did not, as Hurd advised Perkins afterward: "I have talked to Larry E! He's O.K. with Ray. Proceeded to tell me his concerns with Ray. Long list."[38]

Lane met with Hurd alone for two hours and then returned to HP for an equally long second session with Hurd and Dunn. In the end, though, Lane decided in effect that joining the board of HP would not make him a better venture capitalist. "I just didn't see how being a director of a big public company had any relevance to what I was doing at Kleiner Perkins," he told me. Perkins reflexively blamed Dunn: "Part of her job was to close the deal, and she didn't close the deal," he said.[39] However, Lane said that Dunn didn't factor into his decision at all. "It was clearly Mark's job to convince me, but he did a horrible job of selling" he said. "Not that he was inept, but essentially he was telling me, 'I need a new board.' I stopped him and said, 'Why would I want to do this to my life?'"[40]

Perkins's second prime prospect, Stratton Sclavos, also was closely tied to Kleiner Perkins. Sclavos was chairman and CEO of VeriSign, an Internet security vendor that Kleiner Perkins had backed. (Ironically, by 2005 VeriSign's largest stockholder, with a bit more than 5 percent, was Barclays Global Investors.) Although Perkins barely knew Sclavos, the entrepreneur came highly recommended by the two Kleiner Perkins partners who had worked most closely with VeriSign. That was good enough for Perkins, who stopped by VeriSign one afternoon and spoke so glowingly of the opportunity that an HP board seat represented that Sclavos could have been forgiven for thinking that it was his for the asking—especially after Dunn went to the trouble of interviewing him.

Dunn later acknowledged that she had met with Sclavos only to placate Perkins and had erred in doing so because neither she nor Hurd ever considered the VeriSign CEO a serious candidate. Sclavos did not fit any of the board's agreed-upon search criteria except that he was a CEO. At $1.6 billion in sales, VeriSign was so small that if it had been part of HP, Sclavos would have reported to an executive three levels down from Hurd. When Perkins persisted even so, Dunn emailed Sonsini and asked him to set the VC straight: "Tom is not happy that neither Mark nor I considered Stratton the right fit. Would appreciate if you could talk through with him your views on the kind of person we need. Tom feels strongly that a Silicon Valley CEO is needed on the board, although when we went through the board composition exercise, we specified technology background without reference to location."[41]

Was Hurd slow to make his true views known to Perkins for fear of offending the venture capitalist or was Perkins so fixated on recruiting Silicon Valley directors that he was slow to get the message? A bit of both, it would seem. Hurd much preferred to let Dunn deal with Perkins; she was chair, after all. But Perkins was so dismissive of Dunn's authority that he tended to persist in an errant pursuit until Hurd finally called him off—if then. "I got your input about finding another CEO from a big complex company loud and clear and will make that my priority," Perkins acknowledged in an email to Hurd in February 2006, a full seven months into the hunt for new directors.[42] Yet a month later, Perkins was back where he had started, touting his Kleiner Perkins connections. "What about Jeff Bezos? He is young, entrepreneurial and hi-tech," Perkins suggested to Hurd. "My partner John Doerr is on the Amazon board and thus I might have some inside pull to bring him over to the HP board."[43]

Hurd was skeptical about Bezos. "Not known for ever running a company well," he replied. "Perhaps he's better than I've heard."[44] Hurd also forwarded Perkins's email to Dunn, who immediately chided the Nominating & Governance chair for circumventing her to take yet another tone-deaf recommendation to Hurd. "Weren't you and I going to talk first about who we thought looked interesting on the list?" Dunn demanded. "Thought this was how we left it on Monday—you were going to call me after you had the chance to look at the materials again." "Sure, please call me—this is just preliminary thinking on my part," Perkins replied.[45]

This perverse three-way dynamic came into play most egregiously with Perkins's third board candidate, Wilfred Corrigan.

The son of a Liverpool dockworker, Corrigan boasted an impressive Silicon Valley pedigree. At Fairchild Semiconductor, which, along with Hewlett-Packard, constituted the main stem of the Valley's corporate evolution, he had started as a chemical engineer and risen all the way to CEO. In 1981, Corrigan became CEO of LSI Logic, a manufacturer of custom-designed integrated circuits that he had co-founded. Kleiner Perkins had provided seed capital for LSI Logic and Perkins had acted as its lead director for years, with Corrigan occupying the chairman's post.

By the time Perkins approached him in early 2006, Corrigan was sixty-seven years old and about to retire at last from LSI Logic, which had performed dismally in the stock market for years. Dunn did her own research into LSI and was underwhelmed by what she found. "LSI's revenues are $2 billion, which is smaller than discussed at the Board meeting," she noted in a message that she sent to Perkins and Hurd the day before she was scheduled to meet Corrigan at HP headquarters.

"I couldn't remember their revenue," Perkins replied, "but I think $2 billion is plenty big enough to qualify Wilf as a success."

Hurd, who rarely communicated by email, did so now. "I was surprised at the revenue as well," he commented. "Regardless, let's see how the meeting goes."[46]

It went well enough that Perkins was able to persuade Hurd to meet with Corrigan, though not until the CEO had let six weeks pass. "I'd say Wilf is solid," Hurd told Perkins after sitting down with Corrigan. "We should discuss."[47]

With what he believed was Hurd's endorsement in hand, Perkins tried to stiff-arm Dunn into submission as he powered toward the goal line. "Mark had a good meeting with Wilf Corrigan on Sunday, and I have followed this up with a long conversation with Mark. The bottom line is that Mark thinks we should proceed to 'process' Wilf, with the view to inviting him to join the board at our meeting next week."[48]

Next week? Dunn's impression was that Hurd had no interest whatsoever in waiving the search criteria to permit Corrigan to join the board at any time, much less on so foreshortened a schedule. Dunn forwarded Perkins's full-speed-ahead email to Hurd along with a question. "Could you just confirm to me that you are in sync with this?" she asked.

"This is roughly right," Hurd replied. "I gave my view as solid. I do think it was to fit into our overall strategy of the development of the BOD."[49]

Dunn decided to counterattack Perkins on procedural grounds even so. "Please don't think me obstructionist, because I agree [Corrigan] can add value to the board, but I don't feel it is right that he would be waiting in the 'green room' while the Committee and the Board are discussing his appointment. They could well feel pushed to accept his appointment under these circumstances," Dunn told Perkins. "I can hear you saying 'there she goes again obsessing on process!' But I can't imagine Wilf would expect a board to appoint him on the spot."

In reply, Perkins seemed to blithely contradict his note to Hurd: "No, I had no thought of Wilf attending the May meeting. I really do want to follow the 'process' (see, you have influenced me for the better!) and let the board make the decision."[50]

Unwilling to take Perkins at his word, Dunn asked Baskins to intervene with Hurd. The CEO waited until the last minute to finally lay down the law to Perkins, who in truth had not given up on having Corrigan attend the meeting. "Mark persuaded Tom that inviting Wilf to tomorrow's meeting in anticipation of being elected was not prudent," Baskins informed Dunn. "However, I am not certain that they reached a meeting of the minds on a path forward."[51]

Corrigan thus was spared the humiliation of waiting outside the room where his hopes of joining HP's board were dashed. This was the first N&G meeting for John Hammergren, whose addition to the committee meant that Perkins could no longer be assured of winning votes by a two-to-one margin. Corrigan never even came to a vote. Hammergren questioned the propriety of nominating someone with ties to Kleiner Perkins, touching off a debate that Hurd effectively ended by shrugging his shoulders instead of endorsing Corrigan.

For a second time, Perkins had to issue what amounted to a disinvitation to join the HP board. "With Stratton it was especially embarrassing," he told me. "I'm a stranger and I call him up and talk him into coming on the board and then I have to say never mind. I knew Wilf much better, so at least I could say, 'Wilf, I'm sorry, but I've got this idiot chairman.'"[52]

* * *

RECRUITING BATTLES WERE only part of a pattern of steadily escalating conflict between Dunn and Perkins. The peculiar logic of HP's board dictated that the chairman spend far more time with Perkins, her nemesis, than any other director. Before every board meeting, Baskins and other members of HP's corporate staff drew up agendas, reviewed them with Dunn, and then conferred with the chairmen of each of the committees, except Perkins. Other people's agendas tended to make Perkins so irascible that the help refused to deal with him after a while, forcing Dunn to step into the breach. At each governance meeting,

Perkins would "blow his top" on the issue, Baskins said, adding that Perkins generally felt he could write the book on governance and did not need outside help.[53] Once a month at least, starting in July 2005, Dunn would meet privately with Perkins for an hour or more in his Kleiner Perkins office at the Embarcadero Center, turning familiarity into contempt in double time.

Although Dunn took more punishment than she delivered in these sessions, she did admit later to finding pleasure in occasionally "pushing Tom's buttons," as she put it. On her first visit, she teased him about his choice of office equipment. "Tom," she said, "it's not good when people come into your office and see a printer made by a competitor of HP." Perkins conceded the point, but complained that HP did not do what Compaq had done: provide a new computer setup for its directors every year. Later, Dunn mentioned to Hurd that Perkins's office printer was a Canon printer. "I did snitch," she admitted. "I didn't think it would matter much to Mark, but he went ballistic," Dunn said.[54] Perkins, too, would be angry—at Dunn—when Hurd needled him about his Canon heresy.

There was simply no way that Dunn could placate Perkins in his role as chairman of Nominating & Governance without fatally compromising her own authority and screwing up the board generally. To Perkins, the definitive purpose of the N&G panel was identical to that of the tech committee when he was its chairman: it was a vehicle for imposing his personal "guidance" on the full range of HP's activities. He was, in short, a usurper, as he candidly admitted later. "Where I first realized that Pattie and I were on divergent courses was over setting the agendas for board meetings," Perkins told me. "It really wasn't my business to do that, I grant you. It was her business, but I didn't like what she was doing. We had terrible board meetings under her regime. I'll say that without qualification. So I just said, 'Hey, it's well known that the governance committee opines on the whole agenda.'"[55]

On Dunn's second visit to Perkins's office, she was accompanied by Mercer Delta's Nygren, who had worked up a draft of proposed changes in HP's corporate-governance guidelines to bring them into line with regulatory requirements. Although company insiders tended to assume that HP was a paragon of corporate governance, in fact it had been negligent in adapting its old-fashioned founder's board to the stringent new realities. As written, the board's corporate-governance standards and code of conduct were rudimentary at best. The directors' names and affiliations weren't even listed on the HP corporate Web site. "HP was really behind the times," Nygren said. "Basically, they had no procedures in place to govern themselves."[56]

Nygren left the Embarcadero Center after that first meeting with Perkins's angry voice still ringing in his ears. The very subject of governance made the venture capitalist surly, not only because he considered fussing with corporate bylaws, committee charters, codes of conduct, and the like a ridiculous distraction from the real business of running the company, but also because he thought it bad policy for the HP board to lock itself into best-practice standards to which it could be held legally accountable in court. "I think Tom was right to say that we shouldn't put in writing what we couldn't live up to," Dunn said. "What I disagreed with was thinking that we couldn't live up to it."[57]

That HP's board in the end did adopt much-improved governance standards weakened only slightly by concessions extracted by Perkins was a testament to the chairman's tenacity. Much to Dunn's dismay, she generally would be portrayed later as an obsessive corporate-governance wonk. She did invest a lot of time and effort in the belief that a job that must be done was worth doing well, even if, in her view, a lot more of this particular job should have been done by HP's legal staff. To her, though, raising HP's governance game was not a labor of love, but an ordeal exacerbated by Perkins's ornery intransigence.

To mark the end of meetings, HP's board would gather for a lavish dinner, usually held on a patio at HP's home office. These tended to be convivial affairs, with cocktails to start and plenty of fine California wine during dinner. After dinner, Perkins invariably would apologize to Dunn for bullying her earlier in the day. "Tom would always promise, 'I'll never do it again,'" Dunn recalled. "Someone once told me that this was the same pattern as a wife beater: abuse, regret, apology, abuse."[58]

Perkins's temper spiked past the boiling point at the November 2005 board meeting. Mercer Delta had completed a six-month study of HP's governance practices and Nygren was to present its recommendations at an N&G committee meeting that began at 7:30 A.M. This ungodly starting time was a by-product of director scarcity; HP had to schedule committee meetings sequentially rather than simultaneously, because all ten directors had been pressed into service on multiple committees. It was N&G's turn to occupy the earliest time slot, much to the annoyance of Perkins, who arrived ten minutes late in a foul mood. "This is ridiculous," he said. "Who set the hell set up this meeting time?"

Before Nygren even had a chance to open his mouth, Perkins launched into an anti-governance diatribe that segued into a personal attack on Dunn, delivered at top volume and punctuated with the slamming of cups, pens, and other objects close at hand. Nygren was stunned. "For all of us, I think the reaction was, 'What the hell? We've never seen anything like this before,'" the consultant recalled.[59] In mid-tirade, Hurd muttered, "I can't take this shit," and fled from the room, leaving Hammergren and Babbio to try as best they could to shield Dunn from Perkins's anger.

Perkins erupted again during the January 2006 board meeting, which was held at the Esmeralda Resort & Spa in Indian Wells. The day after the Esmeralda event sputtered to a close, Dunn emailed Perkins with a suggested question for a director's survey that the N&G committee planned to conduct with Baskins' help as part of an annual board member evaluation required by regulators. Her question was: "Are you prepared to openly consider ideas put forth by every director, regardless of past disagreements?" she added, "It seems to me this gets at one of our core issues, which is, as Jay has put it, 'bad blood.'"

Perkins replied promptly, promising to include Dunn's question:

> Of course, everyone will give lip service to putting the 'bad blood' behind us. But, only time will tell if it will actually happen. There are some pretty ugly feelings in play. There is active lobbying going on among directors to get certain members off the board. You and I should talk about this, as (as far as I know) neither of us are involved in the lobbying. Isn't being chairman of HP fun? How ridiculous it is that as the company begins to thrive the board festers in petty, acrimonious interchanges. Fortunately, you and I are above all that. (!) (?) [This is a convoluted apology from me].[60]

Perkins also sent a post-Esmeralda email to Hurd, in which he held himself out, quite ludicrously, as a boardroom peacemaker:

It was a great meeting, but it was spoiled by the end of
the event exposure of frictions within the Board itself.
This is absolutely the last thing you need to have on your
plate. I am, and some others are, taking it as personal responsibility to solve what problems we have. Time and
the new members will help, but we will straighten all this
out among ourselves. As you know, I have started to work
with Ann Baskins to get to the root of residual tensions.
Please don't worry about your Board. The one thing we
have entirely in common is out [sic] faith in you and your
leadership.[61]

Dunn, whom Perkins had copied on his note to Hurd, responded to it in what she later described as "shameless ass-kissing"
mode tinged with sarcasm. "Tom," she wrote, "outstanding message. Thanks for sharing it. I am in full agreement with all your
points and Mark must really appreciate getting this from you."

Perkins sounded a bit plaintive in his reply: "Thanks Pattie.
I haven't heard from Mark—he may be on the road."[62]

In late January, just two weeks after the Esmeralda melt-
down, another board meeting degenerated into a donnybrook.
This was a conference call urgently organized by Hurd to discuss
HP's negotiations to acquire Computer Sciences Corp. The *Wall
Street Journal* had just run a story (co-authored by Pui-Wing
Tam) that revealed that HP was considering a buyout of CSC.
This was news even to most of HP's directors, but not, as it turned
out, to the members of the tech committee—Keyworth, Perkins,
and Hackborn—which already had vetted the deal. Hurd now
briefed the rest of the board in hopes of getting the conditional
approval he needed to move forward quickly with the deal
(which never did happen). But the CEO soon lost control of the

meeting, as heated arguments erupted over the peremptory role that the tech committee had played.

Mortified, Dunn took responsibility for this latest fiasco. "Given time pressures, I should have asked that summary rough draft of a few pages be sent to directors before the weekend to help get their heads around the matter," she wrote to Hurd. "I decided not to disturb you over the weekend with questions about whether there was anything I could do to facilitate things . . . that was a mistake." However, process improvements wouldn't fix the fundamental problem, she concluded. "I am very open to your thoughts about what I can do differently to help this board perform better. Having said this, I believe the only real solution is significant change in the players."

Hurd refused Dunn's apology. "This is my fault not yours," he replied. "I simply didn't lead the process very well."[63]

Late in 2005, Hurd had sent Dunn a number of emails and handwritten notes congratulating her on the job she was doing as chairman. "I needed to hear that," Dunn said. Hurd had been complimentary of Dunn's handling of the board throughout 2005, often taking her aside at the conclusion of meetings to thank her for a job well done. Other directors, too, had given the chairman the occasional stroke. To Dunn's surprise, after the blowup on the N&G committee over retirement age, Salhany had sent her a handwritten note saying, "You are doing a great job as chairman!"[64] Said Dunn, "I needed to know that I wasn't a crappy chairman because it allowed me to safely attribute what Tom was saying to his own weirdness."[65]

Perkins tried to turn the CSC incident to his political advantage by reviving his proposal that HP officially create a board within a board in the form of an executive committee that would "work with the CEO to get things done on a tight time scale."

Hurd was no keener than before about the prospect of a closer working relationship with Perkins, who undoubtedly would have volunteered to chair a new executive committee. "I think this is a bad idea," Dunn advised Hurd. "Why would directors rely on a small executive committee when they don't feel confident in relying on the work of today's committees?"[66]

However sincerely abashed Perkins may have been about his outburst at Esmeralda, he emerged from the meeting believing, or at least hoping, that the time had come to remove Dunn as chairman and install Hurd in the position. The hidden purpose of the director survey that Perkins had concocted in the name of good governance was to gather complaints against Dunn and compile them into a case for her ouster. "I drew up a list of twenty questions about the board, including, 'Is the chairman in the right job?' 'Is is she doing a good job?' and so on," Perkins said. "I couldn't go around asking questions like that so I thought it should be done like an attorney-client thing, with Ann Baskins going to each board member."[67]

Baskins understood what Perkins was up and tried to warn Dunn without overstepping her staff role into partisanship. "Ann said, 'Tom has asked me to sit down with every board member and find out what they think about how the board is working. I'm going to have to do it,'" Dunn said. "She was doing something funny with her eyes as if to say, 'Do you understand my meaning?'" Dunn did not take the hint. "Go ahead, Ann," she replied. "The more feedback we get from directors, the better."[68]

Well before Baskins completed her rounds, Perkins had decided that he had to make his move against Dunn at HP's annual meeting in mid-March 2006. He flew down to the meeting, which was held at the Hyatt Regency Century Plaza hotel in Los Angeles, on an HP corporate jet with Keyworth and Salhany. En route, Perkins told his travel companions that he planned to call for Dunn's removal as chairman at the conclusion of the annual agenda item on governance. Keyworth, too, had had his fill of Dunn, but he talked Perkins out of his planned "high-noon shootout" for purely expedient reasons.[69] "Getting people to throw somebody else out one year after we had this great turmoil with Carly to me just did not seem worth it," Keyworth said later, "But my real reason for saying no to Tom was that he was going to lose. He didn't have the votes."[70]

The HP plane was so late getting to Los Angeles that Perkins, Keyworth, and Salhany didn't take their places with the other directors in the front row of the Century Plaza ballroom until the annual meeting was almost over. "Tom was clearly agitated from the moment he walked in the room," said Dunn, who watched him from her vantage point onstage as he loped down the aisle to his seat with great, bounding strides. "You could just see the waves of anger coming off him."[71]

CHAPTER NINE

KONA II

FOUR DAYS AFTER the board meltdown at Esmeralda, Dawn Kawamoto took Jay Keyworth to lunch at Chez Panisse, the famous restaurant in Berkeley. Kawamoto covered Hewlett-Packard for CNET, an influential San Francisco–based technology Web site. Keyworth had known Kawamato since 2001, when Carly Fiorina had asked him to reach out to the reporter during the contentious campaign to acquire Compaq. He had maintained sporadic telephone contact with Kawamoto ever since. Until their lunch on January 19, 2006, though, the two had never met in person. Because Kawamoto didn't take notes or use a recorder, Keyworth naïvely assumed that he wasn't being interviewed. "I was just telling her how ticked off I was that Mark Hurd was being described all the time as a bean counter who didn't have any strategy capability," he said.[1]

On January 23, CNET ran a story about changes in HP strategy, co-written by Kawamoto and Tom Krazit, that referred explicitly to the board's "marathon sessions" at Esmeralda and was studded with numerous and occasionally idiosyncratic quotes from an unnamed "source within the company."[2] After HP's investigators had identified Keyworth as the source, he insisted that he had done nothing wrong because he'd only been trying to help Hurd and he hadn't provided the reporter with any proprietary information anyway. He hasn't changed his mind since. "The CNET thing was not a leak," he told me.[3]

Hurd and Dunn certainly did not see it that way. In their view, the CNET piece revealed confidential information about HP's most sensitive commercial relationships, its plans for acquiring infrastructure software companies, and its strategy for taking on a key competitor (mentioned by name) in the printing business. A separate article delved into HP's continuing discussions with Computer Sciences Corp. Hurd was incensed to see it all in print. "Simply ludicrous!" he exclaimed in an email to Dunn.[4]

Bob Sherbin, HP's communications chief, sounded the alarm about the CNET leak a good three days *before* the story was published, after receiving a phone call from Krazit. He took the news first to Hurd, conferring with the CEO in his office, and then alerted HP Security, which immediately launched an investigation that inevitably would come to be known as Kona II. "Mark believes the names worth looking at are Hackborn, Babbio, Salhany, Keyworth and Perkins," Sherbin advised in an email to Jim Fairbaugh, HP Security's chief, and Anthony Gentilucci, its director of investigations.[5]

Sherbin emailed Dunn to warn of the impending CNET leak a few hours after he'd met with Hurd and alerted HP Security. "I'm afraid it's my duty to tell you that there's been another leak around the board," wrote Sherbin, who did not share Hurd's suspicions about particular directors with the chairman.[6] Dunn waited until the CNET story had actually appeared to alert the board members by email from Hawaii. She also sent a separate, subtly sarcastic message to Perkins. "Tom," she wrote, "this will disturb you as much as it disturbs me. For our discussion. Break out the lie detectors!"[7]

Perkins did not rise to the bait, but instead responded with the latest in a series of emails focusing suspicion on others.

> This is incredible! I can't believe that this has happened again. But, in reading it, I don't think it damages the company too much—it's just that the news should come from us when we want it to, and not when it is leaked. I doubt if this came from a board member. Frankly, I don't think a board member would have remembered this much detail. It must be from one of the EC members, literally reading from the presentation booklet. [The EC, or Executive Council, consisted of HP's senior management executives.] I think Mark must put the fear of God (i.e., fear of Mark Hurd) into the EC members to stop this.[8]

In his first months as CEO, Hurd had asked HP Security to devise a more refined and comprehensive approach to investigating press leaks, even as Ron DeLia and Anthony Gentilucci were improvising their way to nowhere on Kona I. "Guys, I think everyone is aware that Kevin Huska and Jim Fairbaugh have been having discussions with the CEO on putting together a reactionary team for future events of 'Unauthorized Disclosures,'" Gentilucci explained in a memo to fellow investigators in mid-2005.[9] The mission of the Unauthorized Disclosures Team, he explained, was to "investigate, manage and/or consult on all significant cases of unauthorized disclosures whether they are caused by human, electronic or hardcopy transfer outside of the company."[10]

It appears that the very existence of the Unauthorized Disclosures Team was a closely guarded secret, even within HP Security. There was no telling where the company might next spring a leak, after all. Every board member, executive, and rank-and-file employee was potentially a suspect, including Dunn, who did not become aware of the UDT until long after she had left the board. She was neither surprised nor disheartened by the discovery. "Mark had an Attila the Hun approach to this whole issue," she said. "The fact that he put in motion a process to deal with leaks internally was to be expected and, I think, entirely appropriate."[11]

The CNET leak offered the Unauthorized Disclosures Team a golden opportunity to impress Hurd and justify its existence. Kona II's titular lead investigator was Vince Nye, an ex-cop who worked out of HP's Boise office and reported to Gentilucci in Boston. Gentilucci in turn reported to Kevin Hunsaker, a senior member of HP's legal staff. Under HP's new investigation methodology, the UDT was to shield its work behind attorney-client privilege. "To prevent the investigation documents and details from being discovered should there be litigation or some sort of SEC or other governmental inquiry, the investigation will need to be conducted at the direction of the Legal Department," Hunsaker explained in a memo to Gentilucci, Huska, and another team member. "This, as I believe you already know, does not mean that I will actually be conducting any of the investigation. (The actual investigating is your area of expertise, not mine.) But it does mean the investigation planning and any changes thereto will need to be done through me."[12]

Hunsaker, who reported directly to General Counsel Baskins, would make all the difference, bringing a drive and coherence to Kona II that had been missing from all of HP Security's earlier leak probes. However, Hunsaker, who specialized in the dry complexities of employment law in his day job, would get overly caught up in the excitement of the chase, authorizing investigative methods so ethically dubious that they would even unnerve a couple of HP Security's grizzled ex-cops.

When Baskins called her at her house in Kona to discuss the CNET leak, Dunn again made an argument for bringing in Kroll Associates to investigate. "We're really on this one. We now have more resources, more expertise," countered the general counsel in a subsequent email. "Mark has made it a priority that we be able to swing into action and do this right. It would be very demoralizing if we were to go outside." Dunn replied, "I don't have anything bad to say about the team. I just wonder if this is something we do particularly well."[13]

Perhaps because he was aware that Dunn had favored Kroll for the assignment that had come his way, Hunsaker seemed particularly eager to impress the chairman, though he managed to wait until the day she returned from Hawaii to introduce himself by email. "Good to hear from you," Dunn replied. "I put very high priority on the matter you are pursuing."[14]

That said, Hunsaker certainly did not recognize Dunn as the "business owner" of Kona II. As was to be expected, he mainly looked to Baskins, his boss, for help and advice as the investigation progressed. "I apologize for peppering you with 1000 questions, but we're trying to be as thorough as we possibly can," Hunsaker emailed Baskins a week into the probe.[15] Tellingly, it was at Baskins's suggestion that Hunsaker obtained the phone numbers of board members and other HP insiders not from Dunn, as DeLia had done in Kona I, but from Hurd's personal assistant.[16]

For his part, lead investigator Nye looked all the way up to Hurd for direction—or tried to anyway. "I think we have Mark's support, actually I know we do," Gentilucci reassured

Nye, mentioning that Hurd had just conferred with Fairbaugh, HP Security's head honcho. At the same time, Gentilucci tried to gently disabuse Nye of the notion that he was going to get to present his investigation plan to the CEO personally. "With his schedule, not likely to get on the agenda, but Kevin [Huska] can get his blessing."[17]

Nye defiantly attempted to arrange separate audiences with Hurd and with Dunn, and so informed Gentilucci in an angry email. "It's apparent that you want us to stay clear from Mark as you on two occasions have jumped in and said he is busy and we couldn't get on his calendar, so on and so forth. Let the dang investigation go forward," Nye wrote. "The man was at the meetings and I know had developed some of his own opinions and conclusions and shucks I'd like to personally hear them. . . . I am certainly not going to rely on Fairbaugh's input."[18] Clearly, Nye and team took its cues from Hurd's list of board suspects as relayed by Sherbin in focusing initially on Salhany and Babbio as well as Keyworth and Perkins. (Hackborn was quickly ruled out as a target.)

By January 30, 2006, the Unauthorized Disclosures Team was ready to put its investigation plan in writing in the form of a five-page progress report prepared by DeLia. According to the report, which was not circulated outside the UDT, investigators cast their net widely indeed, setting out to do all-encompassing background checks not only on Kawamoto and Krazit but also on a third CNET reporter, Stephen Shankland, who had contributed to the story. They planned to go so far as to attempt to "identify all relatives" of each of the three journalists "to determine whether there is a relationship to any member of the BOD, HP employees, other reporters and interested parties."[19]

The investigation plan also set forth a plethora of "covert operations" in various stages of implementation. The most important by far was obtaining cell and home phone records for the month of January for two board members (Keyworth and Perkins), all three CNET reporters, and two members of HP's communications staff who'd been in frequent contact with Kawamoto. In addition, the report noted,

> Pre-trash inspection survey is in progress for G. K., T. P., Kawamoto, Tam, Shankland and Krazit's residence.
>
> Pre-surveillance reconnaissance of Keyworth, Kawamoto, Tam, Shankland and Kranzit. Note: Due to T. P.'s travel schedule, which in part, is reported on in the press, may not allow for surveillance activity.
>
> Feasibility studies are in progress for undercover operations (clerical) in CNET and WSJ offices in SF, CA.
>
> Feasibility studies are in progress for undercover operations (cleaning company employees) for the buildings where the WSJ and CNET SF bureaus are located.

It was the disclosure of this covert agenda, which was only partially implemented, that would enflame the imaginations of reporters weaned on Watergate coverage and elevate HP's botched leak investigations into a scandal called Spygate. There would be outrage all around that a big, respectable company like Hewlett-Packard had stooped to this sort of invasive snooping, even if it happened to be legally permissible.

But Kona II was as flawed an enterprise judged by its efficacy as by its ethics. The absurdity of searching for a leaker in a haystack of relatives and household garbage and of putting undercover secretaries and janitors into news bureaus was underscored by a straightforward bit of detective work by Sherbin, a former reporter who'd spent enough time with Huska and other HP Security types to understand that they were clueless about the motives and methods of journalists. At his own initiative, Sherbin studied all of the HP stories over a period of four years in which Kawamoto had relied on anonymous sources. "While some of this smacks of efforts by the NSA [National Security Agency] to verify bin Laden's voice on scratchy tapes, I think there may be a pattern that emerges," Sherbin confided in an email to Dunn.[20]

Sherbin's project produced what as probably the most astute and useful analysis in the entire annals of the misbegotten Kona investigations. "Some of these stories appear to be repeats but they are, rather, slightly different version of the same piece," Sherbin noted, in a report he sent to Hunsaker and Dunn:

> A few observations:
>
>   She wheels out the source only for big stories, which means he's probably very senior because he's focused on the most key issues (the Board offsite, the July 19th announcement, Mark's appointment). Moreover, he's senior enough and reliable enough that she doesn't feel the need to square his information with a second source or even come to the company for official comments.
>
>   Given that she doesn't write about HP much and doesn't have time to cultivate sources a la Pui-Wing or Burrows, my guess is that this is one single source rather than several. While the descriptions of the source are vague, she gave herself away in the very first piece in which she describes the source as a director.[21]

Dunn was impressed. "There is a lot here that radically narrows the possible leakers," she told Sherbin. Hunsaker concurred and began describing Keyworth and Perkins as "main subjects" in his communications to HP investigators. Had Keyworth immediately been confronted with Sherbin's rigorous insight, it is entirely possible that he would have admitted to being Kawamoto's source, sparing HP from the later travails of Kona II and its explosive boardroom denouement.

Instead, HP persisted in its high-level game of cat and mouse, which gained added intrigue with the publication of Tam's latest scoop on January 31, the very day that Sherbin informed Dunn of his conclusions. This time, the *Wall Street Journal* reporter revealed that Bob Wayman soon would retire as chief financial officer and that the search for his replacement was already well advanced. Tam even identified the two leading contenders by name.[22] "There is information in the article that is both accurate and VERY non-public," Hunsaker advised his team. "Not many sources within HP had access to this info—the entire Board was well aware of it, though."[23]

Dunn struggled to keep her anger and frustration in check as she wrote the latest in a series of admonitory emails to her colleagues on the board:

> This is the second time in as many weeks that we've experienced potentially disruptive leaks. In this case, the information could have come from outside the company, but the reference to internal candidates points to highly placed sources inside the company.
>
> These leaks are unconscionable, as everyone will agree. Steps continue to be taken to try and identify their source.

We don't know that there is a board source in this instance. However, I will repeat what we already know: that every one of us has the duty of loyalty to HP, and we can't uphold that duty [when] we have unauthorized contact about HP with the press.[24]

Perkins was again quick to point the finger, this time at Wayman. "The source can ONLY be Bob himself," he told Dunn. "Where else would all that detail about Bob's early days come from?"[25] Dunn, who considered Perkins's accusation laughable, forwarded his latest email to Hurd along with a snarky note. "For your edification," she wrote. "Tom will have to play himself in the movie."[26]

* * *

AND SO NOW, inevitably, we come to the question that Watergate made a cliché: What did he know and when did he know it? There is no evidence that Hurd countenanced any of the covert tactics employed in the investigation or was even aware of their use until after the fact. However, the record indicates that it was Hurd, not Dunn, who initiated Kona II and who exercised ultimate managerial authority over the investigation through one reporting channel that ran down through Baskins to Hunsaker and another that extended from Wayman to Fairbaugh.

This doesn't mean, though, that Dunn shouldn't also be subjected in retrospect to Watergate's famous standard of culpability. Throughout Kona II, both Dunn and Baskins were kept apprised of the investigation's progress through a weekly conference call with Hunsaker. On February 2, about a week after her return from Hawaii, Dunn visited HP headquarters for an in-person debriefing on Kona II with Hunsaker and half a dozen investigators, including Gentilucci, Nye, and DeLia. In her sworn testimony before Congress, Dunn said that there was no discussion at this meeting of pretexting or other covert techniques, with one exception: the Jacob "sting."

A week after CNET ran Kawamoto's HP scoop, the reporter received an email via Hotmail from someone who identified himself only as Jacob.

> I am a senior level executive with a high tech firm in the valley and an avid reader of your columns. My real name is not used, you might understand why. Not quite sure how to approach you on this, but I'll attempt anyway. In short, tired of broken promises, misguided initiatives and generally bad treatment. Have some information that I would be interested in passing along. Felt it might be appropriate to contact you.

Kawamoto's prompt, noncommittal reply—she invited Jacob to call her—sent a wave of excitement through the UDT. The Kona II team had invented "Jacob" in hopes of tricking Kawamoto into unwittingly betraying her secret HP source. The basic idea was that Jacob would established his bona fides as a disgruntled HP executive by emailing Kawamato a tidbit of genuine inside information. Then Jacob would send a phony scoop to Kawamoto in an email outfitted with tracer software. The hope was that the CNET reporter would forward this email to her secret HP source for the confirmation she obviously could not obtain elsewhere, thus unmasking him. "We DEFINITELY need to get the approval of Ann, Mark and Pattie before doing it, but I think it's a very creative idea that just might work," Hunsaker told Gentilucci.[27]

Although the use of tracer software was legal, Hunsaker understood that the underhandedness of the tactic would not play well if HP's Kawamoto "sting" were somehow exposed to public view. "If/when we put the trace in an email and/or documents to the reporter, is there any chance it will be discovered? Is it something a firewall could pick up, or anti-virus," he asked two of HP Security's systems experts. "If CNET knows something like that was sent to them, and they ultimately trace it back to us somehow, we could end up with some seriously bad publicity."[28] Hunsaker was advised that the risk of detection could not be eliminated but that it could be reduced to a minimal level.

He decided to proceed, inspired in part by the belief that the list of suspects could now be narrowed to one. "I now strongly believe its Keyworth," he confided in an email to DeLia and Gentilucci on February 3, the day after the investigation team met with Dunn. "I also think Perkins is leaking info for personal reasons, but I think both January 23rd articles by Kawamoto were leaked by Keyworth."[29]

Although Hurd and Dunn did indeed approve the content of two emails sent to Kawamoto in Jacob's name, the documentary evidence suggests that neither Hunsaker nor anyone else told them about the tracer software. At a meeting at HP headquarters with Baskins and the team, Dunn recalled being told that investigators would be able to determine the postal zip code of anyone who opened Jacob's emails as forwarded by Kawamoto. In a later email to Baskins and Dunn, Hunsaker explained how the sting was supposed to unfold in another way, again without using the term "tracer software." The idea, he said, is that Kawamoto "would forward it to GK (or at least call him to tell him about it). Who would (hopefully) in turn would contact one of you, Mark, or Shane, or Randy etc. to see if it's true."[30] (Shane Robison and Randy Mott were two high-ranking executives who dealt frequently with Keyworth as chair of the tech committee.)

In phase one of the sting, Hunsaker got Dunn and Sherbin to help him identify a bit of confidential information that might appeal to Kawamoto and yet not damage HP by its premature disclosure. It was decided that Jacob would tip Kawamoto to the hiring of a Sun Microsystems executive to run a new hand-held computer group within HP. This was hardly earth-shattering stuff, but CNET covered HP closely enough to care.

As Hunsaker waited in his office for Dunn to secure Hurd's approval, his finger poised above the send button, Nye's excitement bubbled over into an all-caps email: "STRAP ON YOUR HELMETS FELLAS," he wrote, "WE'RE GOIN IN!!!"[31] Hurd's OK was relayed to Hunsaker by an email from Dunn. "I spoke with Mark and he is on board," Dunn advised.[32]

At 1:08 P.M. on February 6, DeLia sent out a general alert to the team: "The package has been launched."[33] And then . . . nothing. By the next morning, Kawamoto hadn't even opened Jacob's email. "This is like waiting for the Apollo 13 spacecraft to emerge from the dark side of the moon," Gentilucci complained to his colleagues at 9:32 A.M.[34] At 11:15, DeLia made a pretext call to CNET's San Francisco bureau to verify that Kawamoto had come into work. She had, but as it happened she'd turned Jacob's scoop over to Krazit, who wrote the story without forwarding the tracer email to anyone.

Hunsaker waited a week before having Jacob bait the hook for the second phase of HP's sting: the planting of faux inside information. "I saw the piece by Tom Krazit on the handheld news," Jacob wrote, "I should have something more in a week or so." Kawamoto bit. "Sounds good," she replied.[35]

That something would be an attachment designed to look like a slide purloined from an HP PowerPoint presentation. "Dawn," read the accompanying email, "HP has come up with the name for its next generation data center. Mark is meeting with the WSJ and maybe others on the 27th." The name was on the slide: "Infinity Data Centers." Hunsaker didn't consult Sherbin this time, but ran his concoction by Baskins and Dunn, adding in a playful aside, "I made [the name] up myself, and the rest of the stuff. I won't quit my day job yet."[36] "I think this is very clever," replied Dunn, who understood that Keyworth was fascinated by the next-generation data center project. Hunsaker basked in the chairman's approbation.[37] "By the way," he bragged to his new buddy Gentilucci, "Pattie D loved the slide on the new name."[38]

This time, Hunsaker went directly to Hurd for final approval, sending him an email that summarized Operation Jacob while omitting mention of the tracer software. "Pattie has seen the content and is fine with it," the lawyer wrote, "However, we will not send the message unless and until you are fine with the content of the message and the slide." Hurd replied by telephone and off went Jacob's final email. HP Security had posted surveillance teams outside the residences of Kawamoto and Keyworth in case she arranged to meet in person instead of communicating online.

DeLia's surveillance teams watched for most of a weekend before realizing nobody was home at either house. The UDT couldn't even be sure that Jacob's email made it through CNET's firewall to Kawamoto. In any event, she did not forward it to Keyworth. Nor did she or any other CNET reporter write a story about HP's phony data center breakthrough. She did not even bother to contact Sherbin, who, if given the chance, would have told Hunsaker that he really wasn't really so clever after all. "The idea of the WSJ having any interest in the name of the data center project was silly," Sherbin told me. "Second, the idea that CNET would have any interest in this was naïve. Finally, Dawn would have known that there was little chance that Mark, who rarely spoke to the media, would get involved in this slight a story."[39]

The Jacob sting was not the only dead-end path down which Hunsaker and team pursued Keyworth headlong. Shortly before Jacob sent his first email, a surveillance team shadowed Keyworth in Boulder, Colorado, where he had traveled to participate in a University of Colorado lecture series titled "Policy, Politics and Science in the White House: Conversations with Presidential Science Advisers." DeLia farmed this assignment out to his friends at Action Research, which employed investigators in Colorado. They attended Keyworth's lecture and later obtained a copy of a videotape of the event in hopes that it might show the HP director whispering conspiratorially into the ear of Kawamoto or another reporter. It did not.

A bit later, HP put Keyworth's house in Piedmont under surveillance in what proved to be a comically fruitless exercise. Mr. Keyworth was nowhere to be seen, so the agents instead tailed the missus, Marian Schwartz. "After lunch," they reported, "M. Schwartz was followed to a local community center where she played bingo. M. Schwartz was let go after watching her there for a time. At 8:30 P.M. Marion [sic] Keyworth was followed to the Oakland Airport and was lost in the vicinity of the private jet center."[40] Keyworth said his wife was outraged when she read this report later. "She actually was playing duplicate bridge," he said. "She's a serious bridge player who's never played bingo in her life."[41]

In the midst of the Jacob sting, Keyworth's laptop vanished from a restored farmhouse that he owned in rural Italy. Back in Palo Alto, Hunsaker turned cartwheels down the hallway at the news—or sounded like he might have, anyway, as he exulted in the possibility of finding a computer loaded with evidence of Keyworth's perfidy. "Let's get those guys in Italy to find that laptop!!!!" Hunsaker instructed Gentilucci and DeLia. "It could be the case breaker of all case breakers."[42]

After Keyworth returned to California, DeLia sent an investigator over to nose around Civitella di Val di Chiana, the small Tuscan town nearest to Keyworth's house, which was situated on an isolated hilltop next to an abandoned church and cemetery. HP's investigator obtained the police report of the incident and did "discreet pretext interviews" with Keyworth's gardener and maid, DeLia noted in the report he filed with the UDT. "Contact with local criminal elements was initiated and a 'no questions asked' cash reward was promised for any information leading to the return of the Compaq laptop. Owners of local bars that cater to questionable elements were also approached with the same offer."[43]

The laptop never was recovered, but it was no great loss, Keyworth said later. "If anyone had asked me for my computer, I would have given them a core dump of my disk," he said. "I didn't have anything in there that I gave a damn about."[44]

* * *

THE "SMOKING GUN" that enabled the Unauthorized Disclosures Team to finally get its man was a phone record that
linked Keyworth to Kawamoto. It was obtained by DeLia
through Action Research Group, the Melbourne, Florida–based
firm that performed various services for investigative firms and
law enforcement agencies. One of Action Research's specialties
was obtaining records from telephone carriers without benefit
of a subpoena, using one form of subterfuge or another—a practice generically known as "pretexting." Usually, pretexters posed
either as the person whose records they were seeking (often by
obtaining the person's Social Security number beforehand) or
as an employee of the target's phone company. The ultimate object was to gain online access to monthly billing records providing details of every call made or received.

As a rule, a corporation like HP could not legally gain access to private phone records without obtaining a subpoena.
But because pretexting had only recently had become rampant,
the federal government had yet to explicitly outlaw the invasive
practice (and would not until January 2007), and neither had
the vast majority of states. This created sufficient gray area for
some one hundred outfits like Action Research to openly ad-
vertise their services on the Internet. Founded in 1989 and run
by a father-and-son team, Action Research would later be identified by a Congressional subcommittee as "the biggest of the
big" among pretexting firms.[45] It would be shut down by federal court order in early 2007 at the request of the Federal
Trade Commission.[46]

DeLia was a devoted customer of Action Research on HP's
behalf, obtaining extensive phone records not only for Kona II
but also for Kona I and the Tam leak investigation that preceded it. For Kona II alone, Action Research ran the phone

numbers of twenty-four people, in most cases for a month. The
number of calls scrutinized totaled 1,750. After eliminating duplicate calls, Action Research obtained subscriber information
on 590 numbers: 413 land lines, 157 cell phones, and 20 toll-
free numbers.[47]

Hurd, Dunn, and Baskins all denied knowing of the pretexting while it was going on, and no documentary evidence to
the contrary has surfaced. Even some of members of the Unauthorized Disclosures Team were unaware of the extent to which
Action Research had been pretexting on HP's behalf until Kona
II kicked into high gear. They were, moreover, appalled by the
discovery. Even as UDT closed in on Keyworth, a debate over
the ethics and legality of pretexting erupted within its ranks,
pitting the Bostonian legatees of Digital Equipment Corp., Gentilucci and DeLia, against two West Coast Hewlett-Packard lifers,
Nye and Fred Adler.

Shortly after Hunsaker had been put in charge of the UDT,
Gentilucci sent him an email subtly disparaging his West Coast
rivals as "great investigators, old schoolers, by the numbers type
of guys, investigations 101. But in my view, [in] this case we need
to be flexible, multi-task, delegate, share, communicate. . . . We'll
get them there, but I think sharing my conversation with you
will assist in keeping us a cohesive team. We have a shot to break
this one."[48]

As the phone records obtained by DeLia through Action
Research began piling up in Hunsaker's inbox, he asked Gentilucci, "How does Ron get cell and home phone records? Is it
all above board?"

"The methodology utilized is social engineering," Gentilucci
replied:

He has investigators call operators under some ruse to obtain the call record over the phone. It's verbally communicated to the investigator, who has to write it down. In essence, the Operator shouldn't give it out, and that person is liable in some sense. Ron can describe the operation obviously better, as well as the fact that this technique since he, and others, have been using it, has not been challenged. I think it's on the edge, but above board. We used pretext interviews on a number of investigations to extract information and/or make covert purchases of stolen property, in a sense, all under cover operations.

"I shouldn't have asked," answered Hunsaker, who went online and did about an hour's worth of research into the legality of pretexting.[49] The lawyer didn't find a definitive court case or regulatory action, but what he did see persuaded him that pretexting was widely used and not unlawful, except when it involved financial companies.

On February 6, DeLia obtained a new set of phone logs from Action Research showing that Keyworth had called Kawamoto's cell phone fourteen times in 2005. What is more, Kawamoto had called a number registered to Marian Schwartz, Keyworth's wife, on January 18 (the day before the Chez Panisse lunch). "This is definitely great news," Hunsaker exclaimed. "May be the direct connection we've been looking for!"[50]

The breakthrough inspired a giddy, pun-filled email from Gentilucci: "Too close for comfort, appears to be a 'key' piece of the puzzle, 'worth' a lot of weight in this case. Sorry, couldn't help myself. . . . Good work team."[51]

Nye was not amused. In an email also sent to Hunsaker, he delivered what proved to be a prophetic warning:

Tony, I have serious reservations about what we are doing. As I understand Ron's methodology in obtaining this phone record information it leaves me with the opinion that it is very unethical at the least and probably illegal. If it is not totally illegal, then it is leaving HP in a position that could damage our reputation or worse. I am requesting that we cease this phone number gathering method immediately and discount any of its information. I think we need to refocus our strategy and proceed on the high ground course.

At the same time, Nye sent a private message to Adler: "This information is too detailed to obtain via voice over the phone by a pretense [sic] operator."

"Agreed," Adler replied. "I am VERY concerned about the legality of this information."[52]

Although Hunsaker did not respond to Nye (at least not by email), he did press DeLia to ask his contact at Action Research whether their methods were lawful. The firm sent the following message to DeLia, who forwarded it to Hunsaker: "As of right now there are no laws against pretexting. We are on top of everything going on regarding this issue and if any law were to pass we will be the first to let you know."[53]

On March 4, DeLia informed the team that he'd found gold while sifting through the latest batch of phone records: "We have a call from GK's cell to DK's office on 2/3." It had lasted ten minutes, signaling a substantive conversation.

Hunsaker snapped this crucial puzzle piece into place in an email that, tellingly, he sent only to Gentilucci:

I think the call to DK was simply him calling her to say he is not longer able to be her source. I would bet that Perkins insisted that he promise not to leak any more info—that way, even if we are able to show that GK was the source for DK's previous articles, Perkins would argue that GK should not be kicked off because he is a valuable contributor and has promised never to leak again. In any event, I think the call to DK from his cell phone is a HUGE piece of the puzzle for us—it clearly shows that he reached out for her, which is much, much bigger than a one minute call from her to him. I think we're pretty damned close to having everything we need."[54]

Any doubt that Hunsaker had landed with both feet on Gentilucci's side of the divide over pretexting was obliterated by the following exchange of emails two weeks later:

Hunsaker: When you get a chance tomorrow, give me a call—I've got a bit of a wild idea to get the clincher against GK.
Gentilucci: OK, sounds interesting. Does it have to do with DK/Jacob?
Hunsaker: Something totally new. It involves pretexting GK or his wife at their house.
Gentilucci: OK, I'll look forward to hearing it.
Hunsaker: It's probably too far fetched, but you never know.

Gentilucci: Just don't tell Fred and Vince.
Hunsaker: No kidding.[55]

* * *

A FEW DAYS before HP's March board meeting in Los Angeles
(the same meeting through which Perkins fumed after being
talked out of trying to topple Dunn), Hunsaker marshaled the
case against Keyworth in a persuasive eighteen-page report.
The "overwhelming weight of evidence reviewed by the Investigation Team indicates the source of the leak is HP Board member George Keyworth II," Hunsaker declared. Indeed, he added,
Keyworth "is the only feasible source." The report concluded
that Kawamoto's January 23 story was only the most recent of
seven stories she had written based on confidential information
fed her by Keyworth since March 2002.

Hunsaker sent the first draft of his report only to Baskins
and Dunn, who was again at her house in Hawaii. As she read,
Dunn felt nauseous. "It confirmed a strong hunch and yet it was
a hard situation," she told me. "If I had a magic wand, it would
be that Jay would serve until he reached a certain milestone age
and then move on. I thought that he was a source of disruption
to management and not the kind of person who used his inside
knowledge to benefit the whole board. But I didn't like the idea
of him being summarily yanked from the board in a possibly hu-
miliating way. I think I also knew viscerally that he would never
leave the board easily, because it was his life."[56]

Dunn waited overnight before replying to Hunsaker by
email. "This is a thorough report and we should get it to Mark
ASAP," she advised. "The only concern I have with the work at
this point is its reliance on the views of unidentified people to

support its various hypotheses about why GAK is the suspect. It could be interpreted that there is a vendetta or prior belief that the investigation was out to prove."

Ironically, Action Research was pretexting Dunn at that very moment because Hunsaker shared the chairman's concern about the appearance of bias. The phone logs that had incriminated Keyworth showed that he had made repeated calls not only to Kawamoto, but also to Dunn, Wayman, and Shane Robison, HP's chief technology officer. Hunsaker told DeLia to pull their phone records, too. "The reason for this is not because I believe any of them are the source," he explained. "To maintain the integrity and completeness of the investigation we need to treat them the same as the other individuals whose names came up as possible sources." Action Research did a particularly thorough job on Dunn, sending DeLia a five-page, single-spaced list of every call she'd made from her cell phone from January 13 to February 11.[57]

As Dunn had urged, Hunsaker immediately emailed his eighteen-page report to Hurd, who would later claim in testifying before Congress that he had not bothered to read it. "I pick my spots where I dive for details," Hurd said. "This was not a place that was a priority for me. It was the day of our shareholder meeting."[58] Actually, Hunsaker sent Hurd the report on March 12, three days before the annual meeting. "I will send everything out to Mark within the next 30 minutes, and will copy both you and Ann, so all of you have the exact same set of documents," Hunsaker advised Dunn that morning.[59]

Although Perkins was not privy to progress reports on the investigation—he was a prime suspect, after all—he seemed to sense that HP Security was closing in on his friend and ally. Perkins's hawkish views on the pursuit of leakers softened

abruptly, as he told Dunn in early March during one of their regular meetings at Kleiner Perkins. "I clearly remember saying,
'Pattie, I don't want to know who it was,'" Perkins recalled.
"Her eyebrows went up; she couldn't imagine that I didn't want
to know. I told her it will hurt the working relationship irrevo-
cably and it doesn't matter anyway, because what we really want
is no more leaks. I said, 'If you finally find out, don't tell. Deal
with the person, or persons, one on one.' She didn't say, 'I'm not
going to do that.' She didn't say anything, but just sort of nod-
ded. I guess she was nodding because she was hearing me rather
than agreeing with me."[60]

She was indeed. "I said, 'We'll see. I'll make a note of it,'"
Dunn recalled. "I never promised anything. But Tom, being Tom,
couldn't tell the difference."[61]

Hunsaker later added the following snippet to his report, apparently based on input from Hurd: "It's also worth noting that
a few days before the March 2006 Board meeting Perkins called
Mark Hurd and asked him, among other things, about the status
of the investigation of the leaks. Hurd told Perkins the investigation team had assembled a significant amount of circumstantial
evidence but that he was not sure where it would ultimately lead."

On March 15, as the board gathered in a Los Angeles hotel
ballroom for HP's annual meeting, Hunsaker jointly briefed
Hurd, Dunn, and Baskins on his report. Afterward, Dunn sent
an email to Larry Sonsini. "Mark and I agreed that the next step
after that is for us to meet with you to get your input on where
we stand and alternatives for any action."[62]

During the board meeting that followed the annual shareholder gathering, UDT posted an operative just outside the
boardroom to tail Keyworth during meeting breaks. He reported
that Keyworth and Perkins engaged "in a spirited verbal ex-

change just outside the men's room. I recall seeing JK [Jay Keyworth] pointing his finger towards the chest area of TP several times. Most of this conversation was one way, in that JK was doing most of the talking." Later that afternoon, he reported Keyworth and Perkins continued their verbal jousting. "At the conclusion of the exchange, JK stated to TP, 'They don't have enough to go there,' or words very close to that."[63]

After the board meeting, Hurd, Dunn, and Baskins repaired to the lobby lounge at the Park Hyatt to have a drink and puzzle through the issue of what use to make of Hunsaker's damning report. When they noticed Keyworth having a drink at the bar, Hurd said, "I'll take care of this." The CEO guided the director to another table out of Dunn and Baskin's earshot and told him that the CNET leaker had been identified. Hurd waited for a confession that never came. "He looked me straight in the eye and didn't say a word," Hurd told Dunn and Baskins after returning to them at the bar.[64]

At a meeting in late April attended by Hurd, Dunn, Baskins, and Sonsini it was decided that the precepts of good corporate governance required that Keyworth's fate be decided in an open session of the full board, Perkins's preferences notwithstanding. The issue probably would have been routed to the full board through the Nominating & Governance committee, had not Perkins been its chairman. "There was no discussion as to whether it should be taken out of Tom's hands," Dunn said. "It was presumed by us all that it had to be, because of his relationship with Jay."[65] At Sonsini's suggestion, the audit committee was selected as an alternate pathway. After all, the unauthorized disclosure of proprietary information violated the company's Standards of Business Conduct, which was administered by the audit committee. Bob Ryan, the audit panel's chairman, read the Hunsaker report and agreed to present its findings in summary form at the board's next meeting, on May 18.

Two weeks before the meeting, Dunn sent a curtain-raising memo to her colleagues that gave no hint of the fireworks to come. On the contrary, under the heading "Atmospherics" Dunn observed: "As any of you who have contact with management will know, the atmosphere about the Company is very positive, with a combination of Mark's influence, competitor (especially Dell) difficulties and good performance combining to make people feel good. Mark, however, is far from feeling as though the Company should be taking any bows, and is now concerned about complacency."[66]

Bright and early on the morning of the May board meeting, Ryan met with Keyworth, told him that he was going to be identified as the source of the CNET leak at the meeting, and recounted the evidence against him. Keyworth acknowledged that he'd had lunch with Kawamoto but gave the impression of being bewildered at the lengths to which the company had gone to identify him as the source for so benign an article. "Good God, if anybody had just asked me about it, I'd have told them," Keyworth said. "It's a great article. What's wrong with it?" Ryan reminded him that he and the other board members had agreed not to give interviews. "Moot point perhaps, but I didn't think of it as an interview," Keyworth said.[67]

When Perkins arrived for the board meeting, Dunn asked him to step into a conference room next to the boardroom. Both directors were startled to find two men wearing headphones sitting at a table piled high with electronic equipment. "It was like out of a James Bond movie," Dunn said. But there was nothing glamorous about the explanation offered by the men working the equipment: They were HP Security employees charged with safeguarding board meetings against electronic eavesdroppers. As Dunn recalled it, the occasion otherwise was surprisingly devoid of drama. Dunn had fully expected Perkins to react angrily when she told him Keyworth had admitted being the source of the CNET leak. Instead, he was calm and composed, she recalled in her Congressional testimony. "I told him the full board needed to hear the results, and he said he understood."

Dunn called the meeting to order, announced that the leak investigation had concluded and quickly turned the floor over to Ryan, who summarized Hunsaker's evidence without identifying the leaker in an attempt to encourage the board to deliberate on facts, not personalities. After a lengthy discussion, Ryan said that Keyworth had admitted to being Kawamoto's source and invited HP's longest-serving director to address the board. According to the official notes of the board meeting,

> He described the circumstances under which he became acquainted with Dawn Kawamoto, explaining that he initially established contact with Kawamoto at the request of former CEO Carly Fiorina, who asked Keyworth to speak to certain members of the media in support of the Compaq merger. . . . He said that his intent in describing the January Board meeting to Kawamoto was to help the Company and in particular to convey that HP and the CEO were addressing key growth opportunities and other important strategies rather than narrowly focused on cost-cutting efforts. Dr. Keyworth assured the Board that he had not been the source of the other stories written by Pui-Wing Tam of the *Wall Street Journal*. He indicated that he would not make unauthorized disclosures to the media in the future.

However, Keyworth stopped well short of apologizing for talking out of school to Kawamoto. "I said something like, 'To the extent that this article strained relations between me and anyone else on this board, I apologize.'" Keyworth recalled. "But I couldn't bring myself to say much more. I didn't feel I'd done anything wrong." He left the room feeling confident that his twenty-year tenure on the board would continue. "I thought the worst that might happen would be that they'd slap my wrist," he said.[68]

Wayman led a discussion of Keyworth's merits and demerits, going around the table according to seating order. Perkins offered an impassioned defense of his friend's character and the inestimable value of his long service HP. "This is an outrage," he said. "We're taking the finest member of the board out for stupid reasons." After a motion was made to demand Keyworth's resignation, Perkins exploded. "Incandescent with anger," by his own description, he wheeled on Dunn, who was sitting near him.[69] "You betrayed me!" he shouted. "You said we would deal with this privately."

"Tom, we had no such agreement," Dunn insisted.

Again, Perkins yelled, "You betrayed me!"[70]

Perkins calmed down abruptly when Hurd made what he considered a shocking comment. John Hammergren asked Hurd, "If it had been someone from your management team who had talked to CNET, what would you do?"

"I would have no choice but to fire him," Hurd replied.

Perkins stared at the CEO in utter disbelief, convinced now that Keyworth's fate was sealed. "If Mark had just said, 'Let's wait to the next board meeting,'" Perkins said. "He could have given a lot of different answers that would have defused it. Instead, he gave the worst possible answer."[71]

By a margin of six to three, the board voted to demand Keyworth's resignation. Perkins stood up and snapped his briefcase shut. "I quit," he said and rushed out of the room, blowing past a startled Keyworth in the hallway.

Ryan asked Baskins, "Is that a legitimate resignation?"

"If the board votes to accept, it is," she replied.

Ryan's motion to accept Perkins's resignation was quickly seconded, according to the official minutes of the meeting. This time there was no discussion, and the vote was unanimous. Before Perkins hit the parking lot, he was persona non grata at the company that mattered more to him than any other. "I wouldn't say there was joy in the room, but there was definitely relief," Dunn said.

Later, while stuck in traffic on the Dumbarton Bridge on her drive home, Dunn called her sister Debbie, who lived in Colorado. "You wouldn't believe what happened at the meeting today," she exulted. "It was one for the books."[72]

Perkins retreated to his office in Embarcadero Center, where he answered a late afternoon call from Larry Sonsini. HP's outside counsel told Perkins that under recent reforms public companies now were required to report resignations by directors to the Securities and Exchange Commission and must disclose the reasons for the resignation if it was caused by disagreement with the company or the board. "If it's a personal matter, it doesn't need to be disclosed," Sonsini said. "How would you characterize this? Is this a dispute between you and the company?"

"No," Perkins replied. "It's between me and Pattie. I can't breathe the same air with that woman." Perkins requested that the press release HP planned to issue state only that he resigned. "Don't say I resigned to spend more time with my children."

Late that night, Perkins sent Dunn an email withdrawing her invitation to the party he was planning on the Italian Riviera for the launch of *The Maltese Falcon*. "In view of today's events at HP, I would appreciate your considering my boat party invitation as 'not sent,'" he wrote.

Dunn replied promptly: "Understood. This falls on my 25th wedding anniversary so I guess I no longer have a conflict."[73]

CHAPTER TEN

THE WRATH OF PERKINS

THE SUBTRACTION OF its two most divisive members—
Tom Perkins through resignation and Jay Keyworth through the
censure of his peers—appeared by the summer of 2006 to have
left Hewlett-Packard's board poised on the threshold of a bright
new era. Mark Hurd and Pattie Dunn seemed to have every reason
to think that their long-term plan to upgrade the company's governance was more or less on track, the recent turbulence notwithstanding. "I think everyone felt that the board would work better
without Tom," Dunn said. "I know that I personally was hugely
relieved that he was gone."[1]

Dunn's relief was premature, to put it mildly, for she had
made an enemy of a rich and powerful man who publicly glo-
ried in the power of his vindictiveness. Perkins might not have
hated Dunn as passionately as he hated Narinder Kapany. He
later claimed not to hate her at all, in fact. "We disagreed strongly
on just about everything, but I never disliked her personally,"
he told me. But Perkins complained that Dunn had wronged him
just as egregiously as Kapany had, and he left HP determined to
make her pay. "The leak investigation gave her the result she
wanted," he said. "I think her only regret was that it was just
Keyworth [who was implicated] and not me and Hackborn, as

well. Then she could have gotten rid of all of us. With hindsight, I think that was her goal all along: to use the investigation to get rid of the fuddy-duddies and cronies that she thought were really in the way."[2]

Perkins spent the weekend following his resignation in Daytona Beach, Florida, where his *Sex and the Single Zillionaire* was launched at the Romantic Times Booklovers annual convention. Perkins had agreed to be first prize in a "pick the next Mr. Romance" contest, in which women vied to win "a date with a zillionaire"—a group date, as it turned out, since Mr. Romance dined with all three finalists. "I was dreading it, but it was really very pleasant," said Perkins, whose sunny disposition throughout the convention recalled the opening line from a classic Smokey Robinson song: "Now if there's a smile on my face /It's only there trying to fool the public."[3]

From his Daytona Beach hotel, Perkins fired a first broadside at Dunn by email:

> As the, now defunct, chairman of the HP N&G committee, I offer you one last bit of advice. Given last Thursday's debacle, you should resign as chairman of the board. The board may chose to reelect you immediately, but you should give the directors that choice.
>
> Now that the dust has settled, I can only paraphrase Nathan Hale: I regret that I have but one HP board seat from which to resign.
>
> There are no copies of this memo to others, save Mark.[4]

Dunn's stiffly impersonal reply had been lawyered by Baskins, whom she copied along with Hurd:

Please rest assured that I am highly cognizant that the chairman serves at the pleasure of the board. I will continue to seek advice from counsel and the board regarding steps that are in the best interests of HP."[5]

Perkins flew from Florida to Turkey, where *The Maltese Falcon* was nearing completion in a shipyard on the Black Sea. He spent a week or so in Istanbul fussing over his super-yacht and stewing over his hasty departure from HP. Adding insult to injury, his resignation from the board had barely registered on the media Richter scale. The *Wall Street Journal* and a few other publications had essentially rewritten HP's press release and let it go at that. Perkins's anger and frustration boiled over in another email to Dunn, written in Istanbul.

For you to have, for months, used the most sophisticated electronics and the best possible technicians (at doubtless huge cost) to SECRETLY monitor all of the telephone and email contacts of all of the directors, to discover the source of a relatively benign leak many months old is itself appalling! (You had best hope that these actions do not, themselves, become public. At this moment, with the President, CIA and NSA up to their necks in a monitoring scandal, this news would be devastating to you personally. . . . You should prepare for a firestorm.)[6]

Perkins had severed his ties to HP, but retained a seat on the board of News Corporation, Rupert Murdoch's globe-girdling media empire. Perkins, who'd been a NewsCorp director since 1996, had first met Murdoch through a director of Tandem Computer who also sat on NewsCorp's board. Murdoch had been looking to restructure his board, which at the time was populated mainly by relatives and subordinates, and wanted to add an outside director with Silicon Valley roots. By his own estimation, Perkins made his biggest contribution to NewsCorp by talking Murdoch out of offering $3 billion to acquire Skype Ltd., developer of software that enabled free calls over the Internet, during the height of dot-com mania. "We've had a few disagreements," Perkins said, "but I have a lot of respect for Rupert."[7]

On May 29, eleven days after he'd stormed out of HP's boardroom, Perkins lobbed a grenade at Dunn in the form of a long email that he sent to his fellow board members at News Corp. and to his partners at Kleiner Perkins:

Last January there was a relatively benign leak, to CNET, with a very positive spin—designed to put the new CEO in a positive light—but it was unauthorized, and it almost certainly had to have come from some director. The chairman of the board, Pattie Dunn, became obsessed with finding the director or directors involved. A massive secret program, run by hired electronic security experts, was initiated. All telephone and email connections for all directors for the past two years, from all their phones and computer, were examined.

About a month ago Pattie told me (I was chair of the Nominating and Governance committee), 'I am getting close.' I told her that I didn't really want to know the source, as the leaks had stopped, but if she did find out, the two of us should handle the matter off-line. We would obtain an apology, and a guarantee of non-repetition, and move on. I believed that all the directors were too valuable to the company to be compromised with other members of the board. She agreed.

But that is not what happened. The board meeting opened with her review of the magnitude of her secret program (which shocked us all), and then she dumped the director's name on the table. . . . Finally, a motion was introduced to ask for the director's resignation. In this new era of Sarbanes-Oxley, it passed; the swing votes were from two very new directors. I resigned after the vote for two reasons: 1) I thought the secret spying (which involved a room-full of electronic gear) was a huge over-reaction, and 2) the chairman betrayed our agreement because, after all, this primarily was my responsibility as the N&G chair, and a very valuable director was being destroyed. . . .[8]

Perkins's email played fast and loose with the facts. The interception of the directors' communications was nowhere near as extensive as Perkins alleged, and the leak investigations had been managed by HP Security, not outsiders. Bob Ryan, not Dunn, had run the board meeting at which the results of leak investigation were presented to the board and he had identified Keyworth as the culprit. Finally, the electronic gear that Dunn and Perkins had stumbled across in a room next to the board-room was used to safeguard the directors from authorized snooping, not to spy on them.

Perkins blind-copied Mark Hurd, Jay Keyworth, and Lucie Salhany on his email and also forwarded it to Andrea Redmond, the Russell Reynolds recruiter. When I asked Perkins why he'd sent the email to Redmond, he claimed he had done so inadvertently, even though he attached a note clearly meant for her:

Andrea, here is a confidential memo of explanation which
I sent to NewsCorp directors. Keep it to yourself, please,
but it sure isn't going to be easy to attract strong directors
to the HP board. I struck out three times in getting a Silicon Valley entrepreneur, to try to keep the HP entrepreneurial tradition in place. Pattie wants only compliant
'Wall St. window dressing types,' and frankly, Mark will
not resist having a weak board (how many CEOs want
any extra challenge?) Anyway, I feel very badly about the
whole thing—but being me, couldn't do otherwise.[9]

Redmond was surprised to receive Perkins's "bizarre" message, which she dutifully forwarded to Dunn. "HP was my
client," Redmond said. "I felt like she needed to know and the
company needed to know what was being said."[10]

Perkins conceded later that he had greatly overstated the case
in charging that HP had intercepted two years' worth of email
and phone traffic for every director. "That's what I thought was
true," he admitted.[11] But on what basis? Although the evidence
against Keyworth had been presented in considerable detail at
the May board meeting, the issue of how it had been obtained
was barely broached. The "talking points" Ryan had prepared
for his presentation disclosed only that investigators had "obtained, reviewed, analyzed phone records to identify calls to/from
reporters" and "conducted e-mail and telephone search between
reporters and HP-related individuals." The word "pretexting"
was not uttered at the meeting. In Ryan's talking points, the following generic reference to the dubious technique was lifted ver-
batim from Hunsaker's report and relegated to a footnote: "With
respect to non-HP phone records, the investigation team utilized
a lawful investigative methodology commonly utilized by entities

such as law firm and licensed security firm in the United States to obtain such records."[12]

Dunn was both infuriated and alarmed by Perkins's attack. As she perused the list of NewsCorp directors who'd received his email, she was especially disheartened to see the name of John Thornton, a former president of Goldman Sachs Co. "I thought, 'Great, now the entire Goldman Sachs partnership is going to think I'm a female version of Howard Hunt or something,'" said Dunn, who'd done business with Thornton at BGI. Dunn was painfully aware of Perkins's temper, but now she began to worry that he was unhinged and potentially dangerous. "This memo is what made me see that he was a fantasist," Dunn said. "It also was clear that he was on a vendetta against me."[13]

Dunn, in turn, forwarded Perkins's email to Sonsini and Baskins. "I guess I could call all this revisionist history or a very tortured view of the series of events," Baskins replied. "It's also, of course, a complete breach of confidentiality . . . to a news organization, no less."[14] For his part, Sonsini advised Dunn and Hurd to expect trouble: "I think that Tom's message, although couched in confidential terms, is unfortunate and could create some fall out. We should be prepared for his message to become public."[15]

For Perkins, the June meeting of the NewsCorp board was uneventful until the directors relocated en masse from London to Rome to inspect the company's Italian operations. On the company plane, Perkins took a seat next to Viet Dinh, a fellow board member who was a lawyer and a professor of law at Georgetown Law School in Washington, D.C. "Did you get my email?" Perkins asked Dinh, who replied that he had and that he'd been appalled by what he'd read. As Dinh recalled, Perkins "laid out a rather dramatic tale about how he had just resigned from HP in protest over an investigation that Pattie Dunn had instigated in order to uncover contacts between her directors and reporters. My first reaction was that it was inconceivable for a board chairperson to spy on her directors."[16]

An aficionado of historical irony might have laughed out loud at Dinh's profession of outrage. As an assistant attorney general in the Bush administration, the thirty-eight-year-old Dinh had been one of the architects of the USA Patriot Act, which gave law enforcement vastly expanded post-9/11 powers to combat terrorism, including the right to intercept the telephone and email communications of U.S. citizens. A Vietnam-born refugee who landed in America at age ten, Dinh was a hero to the right and a villain to liberal activists, who had accused him of running roughshod over the Constitution of his adopted country. Dinh's professional résumé featured a degree from Harvard Law and a stint as clerk to U.S. Supreme Court Justice Sandra Day O'Connor, but it was as a sharp-elbowed, hyper-partisan political operative that he made his mark in Washington in the mid-1990s, serving as a Republican lawyer on the Senate's investigation of Whitewater and then on the impeachment of President Clinton. Dinh was tagged with the derisive nickname "Viet Spin" by his Democratic detractors on the Hill, who accused him of leaking confidential information to the press to damage Clinton.

Perkins shared Dinh's conservative views on many issues, notably Sarbanes-Oxley. In fact, Dinh had just joined Kenneth Starr, the famously straitlaced Clinton special prosecutor, in a legal challenge to the act's constitutionality. In short, Perkins was so enamored of Dinh that he put him on retainer. A conventional lawyer probably would have tried to persuade Perkins that he was not in fact the Nathan Hale of corporate America. But Dinh was at least as much an ideologue and political pit bull as he was a lawyer. As Perkins's principal adviser in all things HP, Dinh helped give shape and heft to his client's scattershot accusations against Dunn and HP by honing them and fitting them into a legal framework.

To this end, Perkins redirected his barrage of provocative email messages from Dunn to HP's lawyers—both lead outside counsel Sonsini and General Counsel Baskins—starting with this one sent to Sonsini June 19:

> Viet was shocked at the HP chairman's recording of board members telephone and computer inter-connections. I emphasized that no communications were actually transcribed. He said that even monitoring connections and/or email addresses requires a subpoena (which as far as I know was never obtained) but, with or without a subpoena, such monitoring was simply "unconscionable."
>
> Larry, was any of this cleared with you before the event?

Dunn thought that if anyone at HP was capable of backing Perkins down, it was HP's distinguished outside counsel. He was, after all, the Great Sonsini—consigliere to the Valley—and had three decades' worth of experience in dealing with Perkins. To Dunn's relief, Sonsini did indeed come out swinging in his reply to Perkins:

> Tom, be careful about your discussions about the inquiry and the HP board process and deliberations in that all of that is confidential and, as you know, you have the obligation to continue to respect that confidentiality. You do not want to be in breach of your duties inherited while you were an HP director. Those duties of confidentiality

continue. Also, remember that you did not have any disagreement with HP or the board as a whole (although
you did have issues with the Chairman). I recognize that
a duty of loyalty to the NewsCorp Board may present
some concerns for you, but in my opinion they do not,
and should not, require you to disclose the details of the
investigation.[17]

Perkins parried and counterpunched:

I value the reminder that my directors' responsibilities
continue after my resignation, which is why, in part, I
make the following suggestions: I think you, or someone
from your firm, should check into the sub-rosa investigation of the director's communications at HP. Larry, the
investigation was a Pattie Dunn program, 100 percent-
conceived and managed by her, and unknown to the
board, except perhaps in the most vague and imprecise
terms, with the possible exception of Mark, who she may
have briefed.[18]

Although neither Sonsini nor Baskins was inclined to commission a formal investigation of the board, as Perkins was demanding they do, the general counsel did instruct Kona II project
leader Kevin Hunsaker to analyze Perkins's allegations. That
Hunsaker's four-page memo authoritatively debunked each of
the ex-director's claims was no great achievement, since they
were mostly based on what Perkins hoped was true rather than
what he knew to be true. And yet Hunsaker would play into
Perkins's hands even so, by introducing the word "pretext"
into the discussion. Specifically, he acknowledged, that "to obtain

information on the phone calls of certain non-employee directors, [Ron] DeLia's company retained a third party company who obtains the phone information by making pretext calls to the phone service providers."[19]

On June 28, Sonsini sent Perkins a curt, point-by-point rebuttal based on Hunsaker's internal report:

> There was no recording, review or monitoring of director e-mail.
>
> There was no electronic surveillance to monitor director communications.
>
> There was no phone recording or eavesdropping.
>
> The investigating team did not attempt to obtain the phone records of non-employee directors.
>
> The investigating team did obtain information regarding phone calls made and received by the cell or home phones of directors. This was done through a third party that made pretext calls to phone service providers. Apparently a common investigatory method which was confirmed with experts. The legal team also checked with outside counsel as to the legality of this methodology.
>
> There was no "secret spying," i.e., no electronic gear, listening devices, etc., were used.

Sonsini had unwittingly supplied a live round for a gun that Perkins had hurriedly loaded with blanks. Perkins had only the vaguest idea of what a pretext call was, but Dinh certainly understood and recognized that HP's use of the tactic had left it more vulnerable to attack than even the company's own lawyers seemed to realize, given the casualness of Sonsini's reference to pretexting as, "Apparently a common investigatory method which was confirmed with experts." Hunsaker had depended mainly on Tony Gentilucci, HP Security's lead investigator, to collect expert advice on the legality of pretexting. The expert on whom Gentilucci, in turn, had relied, John Kiernan, was a partner in a small Boston law firm that shared a telephone number and an address with outside investigator Ron DeLia. After Spygate broke, DeLia hired Kiernan as his personal lawyer.

Despite this apparent conflict of interest, HP's essential problem wasn't defective legal advice (as Kiernan advised, pretexting was not "unlawful") but rather that Hunsaker and his superiors failed to recognize that the issue was as much political as legal. In May, a few weeks before the climactic HP board meeting, Baskins asked Hunsaker to write a short memo outlining the methods that Kona II investigators used to obtain phone recalls. After again affirming the legality of pretexting, Hunsaker acknowledged that a few states, including Florida, had just enacted laws that would prohibit the practice. HP's vendor, Action Research, had informed DeLia that it would no longer do pretexting as of July 1.[20] Apparently, it escaped Hunsaker's notice that these state actions, not to mention the anti-pretexting bills then pending in both houses of Congress, were products of a groundswell of popular revulsion that was fast turning these sorts of privacy-invading investigation techniques into public relations poison.

Hunsaker should have listened to Vince Nye, who got it exactly right in a mid-March email expressing his disgruntlement:

Although in the opinion of our legal staff the practice of obtaining cell phone call data is legal and therefore was used in the investigation we conducted, it still in my mind is an inappropriate investigative tactic and unethical. . . . If one had to hold his nose and then conduct a task, then it is logical to step back and consider if the task or activity is the right thing to do. In this matter, collecting cell phone call data in my opinion was a nose closer.[21]

At Dinh's urging, Perkins had his secretary call AT&T to find out if his account had been hacked. It had, and AT&T supplied Perkins with a letter confirming that he had been pretexted. In late January "mike@yahoo.com" had tried to gain access to the billing records for Perkins's home phone in Belvedere by opening two online accounts with AT&T, one for local calls and the other for long distance. When the second attempt failed, Mike called AT&T Customer Care, provided the last four digits of Perkins's Social Security number, succeeded in opening the account, and perused the billing records for the entire month of January. "Coincidentally, the firewall in my computer, which is on a Wi-Fi system at home, had been eliminated," Perkins said. "I can't prove HP did that, too, but I think it's very likely they did."[22]

Perkins's fury now was exacerbated by legitimate grievance. Although he certainly had grounds for an invasion of privacy suit, extracting a few million dollars in damages from HP would hardly satisfy his compulsion to recast his impulsive resignation as a principled act while taking revenge against Dunn. From this point on, Perkins rooted his pressure campaign against HP in two dubious assertions. The first was that HP's leak investigations were really Dunn's leak investigations. The second was that Perkins had resigned from the board in protest of Dunn's use of pretexting. In a formal letter to all of HP's board members written on Kleiner Perkins letterhead, Perkins seamlessly combined these two notions into a single-sentence declaration, "I resigned solely to protest the questionable ethics and the dubious legality of the chairman's methods."[23]

* * *

ONE EVENING IN early July 2006, Perkins was the guest of
honor at an opulent reception sponsored by the government
of Turkey outside the Cirgan Imperial Palace in Istanbul. Turkey's
prime minister had hoped to host the event, but instead had to
attend the funeral of his brother. Other government ministers
turned out in force, though, as did the nation's naval command-
ers. The construction of *The Maltese Falcon* had kept hundreds
of Turkish workers busy for five years and had conferred a new,
global visibility and glamour on Turkey's luxury-boat shipyards.
Even the leader of the opposition, a socialist, had come to toast
the ultra-capitalist American and his twenty-first-century clipper
ship, which was anchored a few hundred yards out from the
palace in the Straits of Bosporus.

The jet-black *Falcon* was the length of a football field and
had masts twenty stories high. Lit by halogen lights, the world's
biggest, fastest, and most expensive sailing craft appeared "sleek,
metallic and ultramodern to the point of seeming foreboding,"
one guest wrote later. "If Darth Vader had an intergalactic yacht
built for himself, this is what it would look like."[24] The *Falcon*
was festooned from bow to stern with dozens of brightly colored
flags spelling out an inside joke in the language of international
maritime signals: "Rarely does one have the privilege to witness
vulgar ostentation on such a scale." It was funny but true—and
a prime example of Perkins's skill at anticipating and co-opting
criticism by adopting a pose of self-deprecation.

After a score or more of laudatory speeches by the locals,
Perkins got up and made some brief remarks in which he first
praised and then insulted his hosts, throwing in a few well-
rehearsed Turkish sentences for good measure. "This yacht will

stand up against the craftsmanship of any of the great shipyards of Europe," he said. Had he built the boat in Italy instead, it still would be years from completion, given the Italians' insistence on a thirty-five-hour workweek, Perkins said. However, he complained, a shipment of fine china and linens for his yacht's staterooms had been held up for weeks by Turkish customs for trivial reasons. "This is what gives Turkey a 'Third World' reputation," he sneered. "There is no way this should be happening."[25]

Perkins's comments were rude but effective. Even before he'd finished speaking, embarrassed government officials were barking into cell phones. "He is an extraordinary gentlemen, isn't he?" observed a Turkish businessman amused by the frenzy. "But I guess you shouldn't screw with him."[26] At two o'clock in the morning, the embargoed goods were delivered by high-spend tender to the *Falcon*, which promptly pulled anchor and embarked on a ten-day, 1,600-mile maiden voyage to the Italian Riviera.

Aboard were Perkins, the sixteen members of his crew, and a special guest: David A. Kaplan, a *Newsweek* senior editor who was a year into the writing of a book about Perkins and his gargantuan yacht. In Kaplan's first book, a group portrait of Silicon Valley's venture capitalists called *The Silicon Boys* (published in 1999), he had written extensively and, in Perkins's judgment, favorably about Kleiner Perkins.

During the trip, Perkins invited Kaplan to look over some notes he'd jotted down in which he explained his resignation as a director of HP as a protest against boardroom espionage. Kaplan was intrigued, as his host hoped he would be. Perkins feared that his accusatory emails might provoke HP into planting unflattering stories in the press about him and the circumstances of his departure. To counter this potential threat, he wanted a way to quickly publicize his version of what had gone on at HP, if need be. "I told Viet Dinh that I had a friend, David Kaplan, who was at *Newsweek*," Perkins told me. "I said, 'I know him pretty well. What if I prime him but pledge him to silence until HP makes the first move?' Viet said, 'That'll be just fine.'"[27] It was fine, too, with Kaplan, who recognized a juicy story when he happened across one.

En route to Italy, Kaplan not only recorded Perkins's account of the events at HP but also witnessed his agitated, conflicted behavior. "When he wasn't in the wheelhouse of the *Maltese Falcon*, Perkins often retreated to the passage cabin to fire off rounds of emails to Dunn, other members of the HP board, the CEO Mark Hurd, and everybody's lawyers," Kaplan observed in *Mine's Bigger*, his book about Perkins and his yacht, which was published in 2007 by HarperCollins, a NewsCorp subsidiary. "Thus, in one room of his boat, Perkins sat at the helm of a magnificent sailing machine—the product of a lifetime of sailing passion and venture-capital booty. But in the room next door, he was being sucked back into the world that the boat was supposed to provide the ultimate escape from. Worst of all for Perkins, who understood and appreciated irony, it seemed that he might actually be enjoying the action in both rooms."[28]

* * *

IN DECLARING FLAT-OUT at the May board meeting that leaking was a firing offense, Hurd had shocked Perkins more than he had offended him. For one thing, Perkins had assumed that the CEO respected Keyworth and would want to keep him on the board. Even more to the point, he could not remember Hurd ever taking so emphatic a negative position on an internal board matter. Although Hurd often was definitive on business issues, when it came to HP's board he tended to hide behind Dunn's skirts. And why not? Dunn was chair, not him, and as CEO he had better things to do than to try to impose order on a divided, unruly board.

The problem was that Hurd's calculated passivity only made a bad board worse. He alone had the authority to rein in Perkins and Keyworth, because they respected him as much as they disrespected Dunn. Instead, the CEO indulged HP's rogue directors by sidling away from conflict with them until it could no longer be avoided and by encouraging them to believe that he sympathized and agreed with their opinions on all sorts of things, even when he actually did not. "Mark is somewhat shy, I think, but has terrific social skills and a great ability to get along with people even if he doesn't really think much of them," said Bob Sherbin, who was Hurd's chief media handler for four years. "Mark is essentially a sales guy."[29] It certainly made sense for Hurd to try to stay on the good side of combustible directors who had actively schemed to fire his predecessor. But his politicking had the effect of emboldening Perkins and Keyworth, both of whom looked upon the CEO as an ally in their struggles to free HP from Dunn's pernicious influence.

In April 2006, a few weeks before Keyworth's boardroom unmasking, Hurd mixed vitriol and flattery in his first-ever conversation with Carly Fiorina. "He spent most of our breakfast together complaining vehemently about the Board and the level of what he called their 'interference,'" Fiorina wrote in an addendum to her autobiography. "He said he didn't understand why I'd been fired, and couldn't get a clear answer from anyone about what had really happened. He didn't understand how, or when, Pattie Dunn became Chairman. He claimed to agree with the choices I'd made while CEO. And he confided that the only thing he wished I'd done differently was to replace the most troublesome Board members. Tom and Jay were at the top of his list."[30]

To this day, Keyworth does not seem to understand why Hurd sided with the majority of HP's directors in voting to demand his resignation. "That remains forever one of the big mysteries," he told me. The best he can come up with is that it really was Dunn's doing. "Tom and I were both stunned at the way that Mark did not handle things when they blew up in the boardroom. I think, above all, it was because Pattie had so much momentum in going after me that Mark didn't want to get involved in the whole thing. He didn't want to take any ownership for it."[31]

However, Perkins arrived at the conclusion that Hurd had manipulated him, that he was not really the friend and collaborator he had presumed him to be while he was a director. "It dawned on me finally, like Charley Brown going 'duuuuhh,' that Mark actually did not want the sort of strong guidance board that I thought HP should have," he said.[32] In effect, Perkins would make Hurd the instrument of his revenge against Dunn, thereby forcing the CEO to become in fact the ally he had only pretended to be. Perkins's co-optation of Hurd began subtly with two emails he sent on July 17, the day before the HP board was scheduled to meet for the first time since Perkins resigned.

In the first, which was addressed to Baskins, with copies to Hurd and Sonsini, Perkins temporarily shifted the focus of his tactical attack from Dunn to the minutes of the May board meeting. Baskins had sent Perkins a draft copy of the minutes, which would assume final form when approved by the full board. "I cannot accept the minutes as written," Perkins told Baskins. He demanded that the minutes be altered to say that he had questioned the legality of the leak investigation and also that he had accused Dunn of betraying him by taking the issue to the full board, and that he had asked the board to delay voting on Keyworth's fate to allow a cooling-off period.[33]

In the second message, addressed only to Hurd, Perkins carefully positioned the wedge that he hoped to drive between HP's CEO and its chairman:

> A while back I promised you that we directors would clean up our act, and free you from worries about the H-P board. I am really sorry that I didn't deliver on this, and I apologize for the necessity of raising the issue of illegal activity by the board chairman in today's email to the board. But, it's an extremely serious matter, and I have legal obligations.
>
> Aside from this, I worry that Pattie, as new chair of N&G, will 'pack' the board with the kind of directors she so admires—ciphers from high cap companies, with no fast-cycle technology background, and certainly no Valley entrepreneurial genes. I worry that you will wind up with a 'blue-ribbon' board that will be of zero, or even negative, value to you when the going gets tough. I don't wish you bad luck—but life eventually delivers tough scenarios to CEOs of big companies—and I doubt if H-P will prove to be the exception.
>
> Anyway, I am rooting for you still, and I hope everything works out as you wish.[34]

On the evening of July 17, Hurd dined with Dunn and Baskins on the patio outside the CEO's office. Perkins and what to do about him was the only topic of discussion. Dunn argued that it was time to return Perkins's fire with both barrels by threatening to sue him for violating his obligations of confidentiality to HP and by starting a press campaign to discredit the former director before he had a chance to air his accusations publicly. Hurd called Sonsini to ask his advice, putting the outside counsel on speakerphone. Sonsini disagreed with the approach Dunn favored, arguing that the best way to deal with Perkins was to ignore him. "Pattie," he chided, "you're taking this too personally."[35]

Dunn returned home from Palo Alto that night in a deep funk. "What Larry said really bothered me," she said. "I felt that Larry had undercut me with Mark and with Ann and put me in a position where I could not defend myself. How could I continue to argue without seeming to prove the point that I was taking it personally?"[36]

The July board meeting, which began the next morning, was haunted by the Ghost of Indiscretions Past. The board had demanded Keyworth's resignation, but he had refused to submit it, on the grounds that he had been elected by the shareholders and only the shareholders could remove him. His defiant argument had the virtue of being correct. In preparation for the next annual meeting, in March 2006, HP either would leave Keyworth's name off its slate of nominated directors or recommend that shareholders vote to remove him. Until then, the CNET leaker had a right to remain, just as his colleagues had a right to shun and ostracize him.

Much to Dunn's relief, HP's board refused at its July meeting to rewrite history to suit Perkins. According to the official meeting notes, the board rejected outright Perkins's claim that he had questioned the legality of the leak investigation. "The directors concluded that such concerns had not been articulated and accordingly could not be part of the record." Although the directors accepted Perkins's assertions that he had accused Dunn of betraying him and asked for a cooling-off period, they decided that the minutes were fine as written and that "additional details were not required."[37]

Ten days later, Perkins finally played the pretexting card that Sonsini had inadvertently dealt him. In an email sent to each director, Perkins described the technique as a "fraudulent practice" and demanded that HP investigate Kona I and II "via an independent committee of the board (not including the Chairman, who initiated the illegal behavior)." Perkins mentioned that he had hired Dinh and attached his lawyer's gilt-edged curriculum vitae for added intimidation. "I did not resign from the board for frivolous reasons," he declared, "but because HP was standing into [sic] dangerous waters—waters hazardous with both illegal and unconscionable governance practices—and because my advice was being ignored."[38]

It was this email that brought pretexting forcefully to the attention of Dunn and Hurd for the first time. Dunn was rattled. "We need to get back to the board with a response on Tom's allegations urgently. I am receiving inquiries on this," she opined in an email to Baskins and Hurd. "We were going to send something on the legality of the investigations several weeks ago which didn't get sent."[39]

Hurd replied, "I have been assured by Ann, who has had two separate opinions that this process was legal. Is there any opinion to the contrary? I have not even heard the slightest inference that there was any illegal activity whatsoever."[40] (Obviously, the CEO wasn't on Vince Nye's email list.)

Hurd joined Dunn, Bob Ryan, Baskins, and Sonsini in a conference call to figure out what to tell the other directors about Perkins's charges. It was decided that instead, Wilson Sonsini

Goodrich & Rosati would review Perkins's allegations of illegality and report to the Nominating & Governance panel. The assignment went to HP's outside counsel even though two N&G members—Larry Babbio and John Hammergren—questioned it on the grounds that Sonsini had played a central role in advising both HP's management and its board (a potential conflict of interest in itself) on the leak investigations and their aftermath. Most important, Sonsini had opined that HP had done nothing unlawful and thus appeared to have a vested interest in the probe's outcome.

What most concerned Dunn at the moment was not Sonsini's capacity for objectivity but her standing with Hurd. After the call, she promptly sought reassurance. "If at any point you think I'm taking things personally in a way that is not helpful to the company, I will take this input from you," she told him by email. "I am really sorry that you have had to spend any time on this. Yuck!" Hurd replied, "Absolutely no worries!"— a response that Dunn found reassuring at the time, but wondered about later.[41] "It's kind of a non-answer, isn't it?" she said. "Perhaps it was intended to be comforting, but it's a bit like a smiley face."[42]

On August 14, nearly a month after anyone at HP had last deigned to respond to him, Perkins signed his name to a long letter written on Kleiner Perkins stationery and mailed it to every HP board member. His attempts to pressure HP into giving up Dunn having failed for the moment, he broadened his declaration of war to include the company itself. "It appears that my disagreement is not only with the chair, as I initially thought, but also with the Company," he wrote. The letter coupled a precise, lawyerly argument with a vague but disconcerting threat. Perkins argued that the mere fact that he was contesting the accuracy of

HP's account of his resignation was a "material" event that required the company to file a document called an 8K with the Securities and Exchange Commission disclosing his claims, thus exposing HP's pretexting-marred leak investigations to public view. Or else: "Having given the Company several opportunities to correct the record, I am now legally obliged to disclose publicly the reasons for my resignation," Perkins wrote, closing with a crocodile tear. "This is a very sad duty."[43]

By this time, it seemed to Dunn that the tenacity of Perkins's assault was subtly undermining her standing with some of her fellow directors. "The more this could be characterized as a personal feud Tom had with me, the less they were responsible for anything bad that could happen," Dunn said. "I may have overreacted, but I objected viscerally to the prospect that my colleagues were going to tote all this up as 'two people with strong personalities' who just couldn't get along."[44]

On August 17, Dunn wrote a memo titled "Thoughts on the TJP Situation" and emailed it to all of HP's outside directors except Keyworth. It was a play for sympathy framed as an attempt to explain why Perkins was raising such a ruckus:

> I won't indulge in a chronology of the intimidation, pressure, rudeness and criticism that Tom directed at me, but will simply say that I have never had remotely similar experiences with any one. Having said that, I found it an interesting challenge to work with him, and tried hard to win his good opinion. Now that the proverbial sewage appears to be hitting the fan, that effort seems naïve and doomed from the start.
>
> The question is why has Tom taken such an aggressive, take-no-prisoners stance that will, if pursued, redound

negatively for everyone, not least himself, and hurting the company about which he professes to care so much?

I am convinced that the answer is founded upon temperament compounded by a fundamental difference in philosophy between me and Tom about the nature of the board and the conduct of its governance. . . .

Coming as I do from a background steeped in fiduciary management, believing fundamentally that, when it comes to board decisions, "all of us are smarter than any of us," I could never agree to Tom's approach to governance. His approach reflects his background in venture capital. Jay, with Tom, used to say when he and Tom wanted me to agree to something to which it was not clear the whole board would agree, that I was bending to the "tyranny of the minority." In Tom's governance world, the smartest make the important decisions offline and then "sell or tell" everyone else the answer. In my governance world, the best answers arise because the appropriate people deliberate, listen to others, influence and are influenced by others, ultimately—hopefully most of the time—agreeing or, if not, constructively dissenting. Tom's model of governance may be appropriate in the world of venture capital, but it is outmoded and inappropriate in the world of public company governance.

The issue of the legality of the [leak] investigation is a question of fact that must be and is being dealt with. But as the linchpin of his issue with me and the Board, it is a red herring that Tom has latched onto as a device for hitting back at the real infraction, which was that ultimately he didn't always get his way and in particular

didn't do so in a matter that involved the unfortunate
behavior of his friend and close colleague on the board.
In my view, the way we choose to deal with Tom will be
a good proof point of the board's philosophy and approach to governance.[45]

Dunn did not mention it in her note, but she was preparing
to again go under the knife at UCSF Medical Center the very
next day. In mid-June, not long after Perkins had begun his email
assault against her, doctors found that her ovarian cancer, which
had been in remission for more than two years, had recurred in
the form of a tumor on her liver. "Recurrence is a really big blow
to anybody," said Dr. Bethan Powell, Dunn's principal cancer
doctor. "I don't know about you, but with all that Pattie was
dealing with at HP at time, I personally might have shot myself
in the head. But there was no crying, no woe-be-me at all. Pattie
didn't flinch."[46]

* * *

ON AUGUST 18, as Dunn was in surgery, Sherbin got a call
from Alan Murray, a veteran *Wall Street Journal* reporter who
worked out of the newspaper's headquarters in New York as a
columnist and an assistant managing editor. Murray had heard
that Perkins had resigned from the HP board in a dispute over a
leak and asked Sherbin to set up an interview with Dunn. Sherbin
was well aware of the simmering dispute between the company
and Perkins, so he immediately headed over to Baskins's office.
With Sherbin at her side, the general counsel wrote an email
alerting Hurd, Dunn, and Sonsini to this potentially explosive

development. Murray was sure to call Perkins for comment; the question was whether the ex-director would accuse Dunn and HP of breaking the law. Sherbin "believes that we should amp up our preparations for a scorched-earth response, but not be the first mover," Baskins declared.[47]

Had Sherbin realized that David Kaplan was lurking, he would have tried to hurry Murray into print with all due speed. However, HP's communications chief had no idea that Perkins already had debriefed the *Newsweek* reporter at length. It was only a question of timing, for Sherbin did appreciate the opportunity that Murray's interest presented. "Murray is far too intrepid to let this go. And it's important that we maintain good relations with him, as he's potentially our best major ally in the media on this issue," Sherbin advised a few days after Murray had called. "This means not permanently deferring his requests."

Dunn also thought well of Murray, who in recent months had interviewed her extensively for a column about Carly and also for a book that he was writing on "the new rules of power in corporate America," as illustrated in part by the Hewlett-Packard board's revolt against Fiorina.[48]

On August 21, Murray returned to Sherbin:

Any luck reaching Patti [sic]? I'm certainly hoping to talk to her. Here's my understanding: A story on CNET News, published Jan. 23, quotes a "source" talking about the board of director's retreat at Esmeralda Resort and Spa. The source talked about areas in which the company might want to make some acquisitions. Subsequently, Patti read the board the riot act, and Perkins quit. Perkins apparently claims he is not the source, but was offended by Patti's reaction.[49]

On this same day, Perkins made good on his threat to go public with his accusations—not through the press, not yet anyway, but by alerting various state and federal agencies. Dinh forwarded Perkins's email exchanges with Sonsini, his confirmation letter from AT&T, and other documents to the U.S. Department of Justice and to the enforcement arms of both the Federal Trade Commission and the Federal Communications Commission. "He wrote everybody," Perkins said. "I remember at the time I said, 'Viet, you should also have written the FDA because she gave me a headache.'"[50] Dinh also notified the Office of the Attorney General for the state of California and urged it to begin a criminal investigation. "In a nutshell," Dinh wrote in his letter to Robert Morgester, California's chief criminal prosecutor, "we have uncovered facts indicating that one of the largest corporations in America, the Hewlett-Packard Company, at the direction of the chair of the board, has engaged the services of a pretexting firm to fraudulently obtain confidential records from a public utility and has committed identity theft in order to spy on its own directors."[51]

Dinh wasn't a well-connected Washington lawyer for nothing. Within hours of receiving Dinh's letter, Morgester called Baskins to inform her that he was beginning an investigation into the hacking of Perkins's personal phone records. A few days later, Baskins also received notice from the SEC giving HP ten days to justify its position that no changes were needed in the 8K it had filed about Perkins's resignation. "This is not unexpected, and the good news is that the letter came from the Corporate Finance Division rather than Enforcement," Baskins told Hurd and Dunn.[52]

At first, Sherbin had had to stall Murray because Dunn was in no condition to be interviewed, having just undergone a six-hour operation to remove the tumor from her liver. By August 24, though, she was sufficiently mended to try to rouse her colleagues into seizing the PR initiative against Perkins by leveling with Murray. "I propose we use this as our opportunity to get the HP side of the story out there first," she stated in an email to Hurd, Baskins, Sonsini, and Sherbin. "In speaking to most directors one-on-one, everyone is convinced the story will get out there and questions whether we should therefore seek 'first strike' advantage. My view is that Tom has already had the first strike by going to the AG, NewsCorp, etc., and that we have no good alternative to getting the story we hope to have told out there first."[53]

Dunn's proposal fell on deaf ears. "Pattie was ready to push forward, but she ran into resistance." Sherbin recalled. "Hurd was very cautious about this sort of thing."[54]

Meanwhile, Perkins was readying his own first-strike campaign. At Dinh's urging, he had retained Mark Corallo as his media adviser. A former U.S. Army infantry officer turned public relations operative, Corallo was the chief spokesman for the U.S. Department of Justice from 2002 until Attorney General John Ashcroft's resignation in 2005. At Justice, Corallo was Ashcroft's point man in a public relations campaign to defuse political opposition to Dinh's handiwork, the USA Patriot Act. After leaving the Justice department, Corallo set up his own Washington PR firm. His highest-profile client was Karl Rove, who hired Corallo to help stave off indictment for his part in organizing the politically motivated outing of covert CIA agent Valerie Plame and the smearing of her diplomat husband, Joseph Wilson.

Working with a handful of assistants, Dinh and Corallo would continually outmaneuver HP and its larger legal and PR cadres after the Spygate scandal broke. "This was playing in a whole new league with those guys," Sherbin said. "Dinh would make things happen like no one I ever saw."[55]

As for Dunn, she would find herself in the position of a pedestrian who carefully waits for the traffic light to turn to green only to be flattened in the crosswalk by a Hummer she never saw coming. "I bow to Tom," Dunn said later, in a concession barbed with bitterness. "He is a powerful man. He's far more powerful than I am."[56]

* * *

ON AUGUST 30, THE Nominating & Governance committee gathered to hear the result of Wilson Sonsini's investigation of Konas I and II. The report was hastily done, and it showed. It was evident from even a cursory comparison between transcripts of the firm's (often slipshod) interviews with key players and the conclusions drawn from them, as presented to the board by Sonsini himself in the form of a PowerPoint slide presentation with no supporting documentation whatsoever.

The Sonsini report contained two essential conclusions. The first was that HP's investigators probably broke the law. The misdeed was not pretexting per se: "The use of pretexting at the time of the Kona investigations was not generally unlawful (except with respect to financial institutions)," the report stated. However, "HP subcontractors may have used social security numbers (not provide by HP) while pretexting, which more likely than not violates federal law."

The second was this: "CEO Mark Hurd acted properly in all respects. Mr. Hurd [was] not involved in directing either Kona I or Kona II."[57]

If the CEO was not to blame for the potentially criminal acts that Sonsini and his colleagues had identified, then who was? The report left this crucial question hanging, extending a temporary reprieve to the Hurd underlings most vulnerable to being thrown under the bus: Hunsaker, Baskins, and Dunn. "While all the persons involved in the Kona investigations acted in good faith and with best of intentions, certain errors in judgment were made," the report noted. Hunsaker was faulted for not researching the legality of pretexting more definitively and Dunn for not "[involving] either HP legal or outside counsel at the start" of Kona I.[58]

For Dunn, the Wilson Sonsini report actually came as a relief because it affirmed that she had acted honorably. In Kona I, "Ms. Dunn continually and explicitly reminded investigation team of their duties to act lawfully and properly," and in Kona II, "Ms. Dunn reasonably relied on repeated assurance of legality by HP legal."[59] In her earnest way, she took Wilson Sonsini's minor criticism to heart, sending a mea culpa to her fellow directors by email: "I accept [the] finding that 'Kona I' was conducted with insufficient legal support or project infrastructure. In retrospect, I can explain why I chose not to utilize Wilson Sonsini in this matter, but I cannot explain why I did not turn to alternative counsel. It was partly out of ignorance for how to proceed in such circumstances, which I offer as a reason but not as an excuse."[60]

With the Wilson Sonsini report safely behind him, Hurd decided that the best way to deal with Perkins was not to ignore him, as Sonsini had recommended, but to set the record straight by having first Dunn and then audit chair Bob Ryan guide Murray through the maze of Kona I and II and, secondly, by issuing a new 8K describing the leak investigations and their outcome. (Up to this point, not a word about the Konas had appeared in print outside of HP's internal documents.)

The Murray interviews were the easy part. On September 2, a full fourteen days after Murray first contacted Sherbin, Dunn

talked to the *Journal* reporter over the phone, with Sherbin listening in and taking notes. Dunn "was highly successful at dis-
passionately and carefully setting out the chain of events, which
Murray fully took on board," Sherbin reported the next day in
an email to Hurd and the two lawyers, Baskins and Sonsini. "The
p-word, pretexting, never arose. Pattie made it clear that the investigation was led internally but involved outside parties, and
that various records were checked. He accepted this and didn't
ask at all about how [or] what investigative methods were utilized."[61] Murray's follow-up interview with Ryan also went well,
in Sherbin's estimation.

On the other hand, the new 8K proved a contentious issue.
Dunn objected strongly to the wording of the document which
took its cues from Wilson Sonsini in emphasizing her role in the
pretexting-marred leak investigations without any of the report's
offsetting positive findings. "It brings up Perkins' objections, but
never says that the Committee exonerated the Chairman (if that's
the right word). This concerns me," Dunn complained in an email
to Sonsini, Baskins, and others involved in drafting the 8K.[62]

She fired off a second email soon after: "Does anyone else
think that there is too much focus on pretexting in this draft, as
though it were the only investigative technique used? As I re-
read it, it seems to me it gives more solace to Perkins than we
should want."

Sherbin agreed. "If we cite pretexting, we should sandwich
it among other methods," he replied. "I even wonder if we can
use another word or phrase or description altogether instead of
the p-word."[63]

Sherbin ran the 8K by HP's chief outside public relations adviser, Paul Taaffe, the chairman and CEO of Hill & Knowlton.

"As currently drafted, the media casualties will be Keyworth and Pattie, not Perkins," Taaffe counseled. "Indeed you give him the validation with the text on pretexting and its future use to continue to wage war which is contrary to the objective of the exercise. You should perhaps give PD a heads up."[64]

"Paul Taaffe has pretty strong views on the 8K issue," Sherbin dutifully advised Dunn. He continued:

> His main concerns are as follows:
> 1. We should respond to the Perkins claim of pretexting in the media, not in the 8K. The reason for this is that including pretexting in the 8K will wave a red flag to the media.
> 2. He believes that we should keep the scope of the 8K narrowed to confirming that Perkins' reservations were subsequent to his departure.
> 3. Outing Keyworth.
> 4. Establishing the principle of board confidentiality and the voluntary nature of the investigation.
> Anything further, he believes would legitimize Perkins, with the day-two story becoming the witch hunt, in which Perkins could gain the moral ground.[65]

After reading this, Dunn tried to lure Sonsini out into the open by calling attention to a sentence in the 8K that pertained directly to his performance. It said that HP's outside counsel had advised the N&G committee that pretexting "was not generally unlawful." Dunn suggested changing this phrasing to "was generally lawful."

It took all of three minutes for Sonsini to send a reply worthy of Yoda at his most cryptic: "I would not this change."[66]

Hammergren, whom Dunn had copied on her message to Sonsini, took her side: "Agree. In fact what he said was that pretexting was legal period."

"Larry continues to backpedal on legality issue," Dunn replied. "Not having been in the room, neither Ann nor I are credible in pushing back on this. Ugghh."

"I'll push back," vowed Hammergren, who sat on the N&G committee. "Get him on the phone. He is either in the middle here or incompetent. This amazes me."[67] Babbio also weighed in, complaining in a phone call to Dunn that the outside counsel was hiding behind "weasel words."[68]

In the end, though, Hurd signed off on an 8K that was filed without any significant changes in wording to what Sonsini had wanted. Only in retrospect would Dunn grasp the full import of the 8K's deficiencies. "The language of the 8K was probably the first black and white evidence that my interests and the company's interests were diverging," Dunn told me. "Thoughtless would have been the kindest interpretation of how the 8K through its silence portrayed my role."[69]

In anticipation of the media onslaught that was sure to follow the filing of the 8K, Sherbin assembled a short Question & Answer guide for his staff, relying on the input of HP lawyers. "There is one in particular that I want you to see and amend the answer as you see fit," Sherbin advised Dunn by email.

At this point it reads:
   Q. Was HP's board aware that pretexting was used
      by its outside agency?
   A. HP's Chairman was aware of the investigative
      techniques used by the outside agency, and that
      using disguised identities to obtain phone record

information was among the potential techniques that could be utilized.

Dunn was shocked. Just a week earlier, the Wilson Sonsini report had reached the opposite conclusion: that she had known nothing about the use of pretexting and had properly relied on the legal advice of Baskins, Sonsini, and others. *What was going on here?* "Bob," Dunn replied:

> I was not aware of the details of the investigative techniques involving phone records to this extent. The word 'pretexting' was never used with me (the first time I heard the word was in Larry Sonsini's email to Tom Perkins). I was informed that it was possible to legally obtain phone records simply by requesting them. I was not aware that disguised identities were involved. I gave this same input to the 'investigation of the investigation' team at Wilson Sonsini.[70]

The question that unsettled Dunn's sleep on the night of September 5, 2006, was this: Was Tom Perkins the only one out to get her?

CHAPTER ELEVEN

FEAR AND LOATHING IN PALO ALTO

THE *WALL STREET Journal* planned to publish Alan Murray's story on the morning of September 6, a comfortable few hours before Hewlett-Packard was to expose its boardroom shenanigans to public view for the first time by filing its 8K with the Securities and Exchange Commission. Like any competitive reporter, Murray worried about getting aced out of his big scoop at the last minute. "You still think this will hold?" he asked Bob Sherbin on September 3.

"Rock solid for now," Sherbin replied. "The vulnerabilities are what happens when you speak to Keyworth/Perkins and how they choose to respond."[1]

Actually, Murray had been trying to get to Perkins to talk for weeks, working through Mark Corallo. "Perkins was stonewalling me completely, but Corallo never said Perkins was not going to cooperate," Murray recalled. "Afterward, I felt very much abused by Corallo."

Murray called Corallo for the last time early on September 5, the day before he was to go to press. The *Wall Street Journal* has a "no surprises" policy that requires reporters to give subjects ample time to respond before a story runs, if they so choose.

"I might even have faxed parts of the story to him," Murray said. "He certainly knew what we were doing."[2]

At about 2:45 that afternoon, Kaplan called Sherbin and left a message saying that he wanted to interview Pattie Dunn for an article about HP's leak investigation that the magazine was going to post on its Web site sometime after four o'clock Eastern that afternoon. (Perkins had made Kaplan promise to hold off until after the New York Stock Exchange shut down for the day to prevent disruption in the trading of HP's stock.) Kaplan, who hadn't checked Perkins's account with any other sources for fear of tipping other reporters to his scoop, also put in hurried calls to Larry Sonsini and to AT&T. Sherbin purposely did not return Kaplan's call until late in the day, but he did promptly warn Murray that *Newsweek* was now on the story.

Newsweek.com waited until about 6:15 before publishing Kaplan's "Intrigue in High Places." The subtitle said it all: "To catch a leaker, Hewlett Packard's chairman spied on the home-phone records of its board of directors." That is, Kaplan took at face value Perkins's claims that HP's leak investigation was entirely Dunn's doing and that he had resigned in protest over her conduct of the probe. Dunn "took the extraordinary step of authorizing a team of independent electronic-security experts to spy on the January 2006 communications of the other 10 directors," Kaplan wrote, adding that she "acted without informing the rest of the board." Kaplan's account of the climactic May board showdown failed to mention Bob Ryan, who'd actually run the meeting. "Dunn laid out the surveillance scheme and pointed out the offending director." Perkins "was the only director who rose to take Dunn on directly," the story continued. "Perkins says he was enraged at the surveillance, which he called illegal, unethical and a misplaced corporate priority on Dunn's part."[3]

"Intrigue in High Places" quickly made the rounds at HP Security, to generally cynical reviews, as illustrated by the following email exchange between Tony Gentilucci and a colleague named Peter Hunt:

> Gentilucci: Not quite accurate, but we are being hung out to dry; the politics, smoke, mirrors are high. I have lost a lot of respect for a lot of people. Amazing really. If I am still here next week, we can discuss over a beer. Hunt: I don't believe half of what I read in the mags and rags . . . neither does anybody else. This is no negative reflection on the investigative acts, rather the senior mgmt that 'directed' it.[4]

Kaplan's story touched off the firestorm that Perkins had prophesied in the email he had written to Dunn shortly after his resignation. PR man Corallo was not just peddling the accusations of a disgruntled former director: He had "documents." Never mind that most of them had been written by Perkins himself and were rife with dubious assertions. The act of filing Perkins's correspondence with the SEC and other government agencies went a long way toward seeming to validate his audacious assertions, at least by the debased standards of journalism practiced at Internet speed.

It took all of an hour after "Intrigue in High Places" popped up on the Web for Paul Kedrosky to call for Dunn's resignation on his blog, Infectious Greed:

> This story of HP's chair, Patricia Dunn, and her alleged role in an investigation into HP's own board's 'leaking' is astonishing. Read the letter from ex-HP director Tom

Perkins (who resigned over the issue) to the HP board, as well as the attached document describing how someone in HP's employ hacked Perkins's residential phone line. Perkins walked out of a board meeting last May when Dunn announced what she had done, but that didn't embolden his fellow directors to call Ms. Dunn on her complicity in the investigation. It's time HP shareholders did what HP's board lacked the balls to do: Call for Ms. Dunn's resignation.[5]

To be fair, the documents that told the real story of what had transpired lay buried deep within HP and would only be extracted by subpoena (only to be ignored anyway). And, as Paul Taaffe of Hill & Knowlton had predicted, the lone document that HP did now contribute to the public record—the 8K—lent a measure of credibility to Perkins's allegations at Dunn's expense while leaving way too much unsaid.

The *Journal* put up Murray's HP story on its Web site late on Tuesday and on page one of the newspaper the following morning under the headline, "Directors Cut: H-P Board Clash Over Leaks Triggers Angry Resignation." Murray's carefully reported piece was more thorough and broadly sourced than Kaplan's. However, the *Journal* badly underplayed the crucial issue of HP's investigation methods; the "p-word"—pretexting—was conspicuous by its absence from the story. Murray did note that Perkins had made accusations of "illegal surveillance," but he dismissed them, in effect. "Board members acknowledge some discomfort with the methods used by the private investigator who obtained the phone records," he wrote, "but H-P says it was assured by the investigators that the methods were legal."[6]

Late Tuesday night, Taaffe emailed Sherbin after reading Murray's story. "Good play, but we need the 8K to carry some of the weight since it will be the reference for how this story rolls out," the Hill & Knowlton CEO advised.[7]

Actually, the tone of future coverage had been set by "Intrigue in High Places," and the story was already a freight train that rolled right over Sherbin when he arrived for work on Wednesday morning. "We weren't used to having stories appear that weren't really what we were hoping for, and here were two in quick succession," Sherbin said. "It was like getting a huge punching bag flown at you, reeling from one and then reeling from the other."[8] It was all he could do to keep track of who was writing what; by midday, he had collected some thirty-five stories, almost all of which took Perkins's assertions as fact while pointing the finger of blame at Dunn and Dunn alone. The filing of HP's 8K later in the day only added to the media frenzy. The company's admission that it had pretexted its own directors, and its outing of Keyworth as a boardroom leaker lifted the breaking story out of the realm of accusation and rumor and enthroned it as a first-rate corporate scandal: Hewlett-Packard's very own Spygate.

A representative second-day story by the Associated Press declared that Dunn had overseen "an invasive and possibly illegal effort to snoop into the home phone calls of fellow [directors]" and now was coming under the scrutiny of "business and ethics experts" who'd already concluded from afar that she had behaved disgracefully. As a professor at the University of Maryland's business school put it, "When you start spying on your own board, you darn well better have probable cause. If the chairman thinks that this is the way business ought to be conducted, maybe it's time for her to take a sabbatical. It's arrogant and inappropriate."[9] Conversely, the San Jose *Mercury News*, which considers itself Silicon Valley's daily newspaper, stopped just short of canonizing Perkins in its early Spygate coverage. "He's an icon in the valley for a reason," a Kleiner Perkins partner named Kevin Compton told the paper. "If something has rankled his sense of principles, he will make an issue of it." For good measure, the *Mercury News* also quoted John Doerr, who'd succeeded Perkins as the VC firm's managing partner and who praised Perkins as "ruthlessly, intellectually honest, with impeccable integrity."[10]

Dunn, who had grown accustomed at BGI to getting the benefit of the doubt from the press, was stunned to see herself portrayed now as a devious corporate spymaster and leak-obsessed process freak. "I must say it is an out-of-body experience to see oneself portrayed so publicly and negatively (and with ugly pictures to boot)," she confessed in an email to her fellow directors. "It can't be easy for any of you, either, to read and have to respond to people who are understandably dismayed by this spectacle."[11] Dunn also wrote a politely defiant three-page memo summarizing the chronology of the leak investigation. She sent it to Sherbin and Taaffe, with a copy to Hurd, and appended a note. "For what it's worth," she stated. "I wrote this for my own sanity."

> Tom wants to make the investigation itself the main story. His objective is to tarnish my reputation as completely as that of the leaker because I thwarted his desire to keep the matter a secret from the rest of the Board. His rewriting of the history of his reasons for resigning from the HP board indicate that he is prepared to bring embarrassment on HP in retaliation for my not having agreed to pro-

tect his friend from the Board's ultimate judgment. . . .
Having a seriously rich, very angry adversary may be my
undoing, but I know that HP's board processes will have
been immeasurably strengthened whatever the outcome
of this matter.[12]

Sherbin sympathized, but he had his hands full with Kaplan.
The *Newsweek* reporter wrote an email to Hurd and Dunn accusing HP's media relations department of disrespecting him by
ignoring his last-minute interview request. "I do believe in courtesy and in transparency and in more than 20 years of doing
journalism I'm not used to the kind of treatment I received yes-
terday, all the more so from a Fortune 500 company," Kaplan
complained.[13]

"Thanks for sending this to me," Hurd replied. "I'll certainly
look into it."

What Kaplan wanted was an interview, and he took encouragement in Hurd's response, replying promptly: "I understand
what they were trying to accomplish—I live in the real world—
but I thought, and think, it was cheesy. In any event, and more
important, I'd be eager to talk to you about all this—off the
record or on, or any other basis you can think of, though it's
too late to fly to Italy to race aboard Tom's boat tomorrow—if
you're so inclined."[14]

Meanwhile, Sherbin defended himself in an email to Hurd:

This guy had his story already written and was coming
to us at the final moment for comment, demanding to
speak to Pattie. He is writing a book on Perkins and his
sailing exploits and Perkins had been feeding him material,
for a long, long time, when he never came to us. In any

event, we had promised exclusivity to Murray. We played for time and I gave him a no comment but it was too late for his story.[15]

Although Sherbin didn't care for Kaplan's attitude, he supported the reporter's request for high-level access. "In terms of moving forward, I think at this point we need to have someone speak to him," he advised. "I don't think it should be Mark, at least initially. Best to be Pattie on a background basis, if she believes this makes sense."[16]

In other words, Sherbin advocated continuing the same strategy that had guided the writing of the 8K: keeping Hurd safely above the fray. Certainly this was the expedient approach, Perkins already having set up Dunn to take the fall for HP's misdeeds. And HP could better afford to lose its chairman than its CEO, if it came to that. On the other hand, Hurd had set Kona II in motion and had defined its parameters, if not the investigative methods employed. The morally correct thing to do would have been for Hurd to accept responsibility for the errant leak investigation and let the chips fall where they may. At a minimum, the CEO should have defended his chairman from false accusations. Instead, Hurd would hide and let Dunn assume the entire burden of trying to defend herself—and HP, for that matter— against the lynch mob Perkins had incited.

That said, Dunn could have played it a lot smarter. She didn't have to collaborate so dutifully in her own scapegoating. "Ready and willing, if not able," she replied to Sherbin's suggestion that she be the one to talk to Kaplan.[17]

Recognizing a populist bandwagon when he saw one, California Attorney General Bill Lockyer lost no time in clambering aboard with what were astoundingly precipitous comments, considering that his office had just begun investigating HP. The following quote from Lockyer appeared in the *Mercury News* on September 6, less than twenty-four hours after Kaplan's story appeared: "I have no settled view as to whether or not the chairwoman's acts were illegal, but I do think they were colossally stupid. We'll have to wait until the investigation concludes to determine whether they were felony stupid or not."[18] By the time Lockyer talked to a *New York Times* reporter the very next day, his views had hardened considerably. "A crime was committed. . . ." he said, though "Who is charged and for what is still an open question."[19]

The publicity alone was horrendous, but jail time? On HP's executive floor in Palo Alto, the dread was palpable. "The fact that the attorney general had weighed in was a whole new story," Dunn recalled. "The fear factor at HP went through the roof."[20]

On Wednesday evening, Sherbin alerted Dunn to another alarming development involving Lockyer: The Attorney General's office had begun telephoning journalists to tell them that HP had pretexted them, too. In all, nine reporters had had their private phone records purloined by Action Research: Peter Burrows, Ben Elgin, and Roger Crockett of *Business Week*; Dawn Kawamoto, Tom Krazit, and Stephen Shankland of CNET News; Pui-Wing Tam and George Anders of the *Wall Street Journal*; and John Markoff of the *New York Times*. "This one's not likely to earn us many points with the journos," Sherbin commented wryly.[21]

Not until Thursday, September 7—day three of Spygate—did Hurd, Dunn, Sonsini, and the rest of the HP brain trust attempt to craft a response to the rapidly unfolding public relations disaster that went beyond referring reporters to the 8K and refusing to comment further. "We need to act quickly to reclaim the high moral ground which we have lost," Taaffe urged.[22] It was decided that Bob Ryan would issue the following statement on behalf of the whole board:

> When Pattie Dunn was asked to serve as Chairman of HP it was with the clear expectation that board governance practices would be upgraded. One of her top priorities was to restore the confidentiality to board meetings where leaks had become a major problem for the board and management.
>
> An investigation was commissioned but the details remained unknown given that it involved all of the board members, including the chairman. The board was informed that the probe was ongoing and received assurances that it was legal.
>
> Once completed, the Nominating and Governance Committee with the assistance of outside counsel, Wilson Sonsini, conducted a review of the investigation. While it was found to have complied with all aspects of the law, the Committee was troubled by the serious ethical questions raised by some of the techniques employed that emerged in the review of the probe and recommended to the board and HP that this type of investigation not be used in the future.
>
> We want to be very clear. The board was not aware of the details of the investigation and the use of pretexting until after the probe was concluded. The board is troubled that such methods were used in its name and will not engage firms that employ them should the need arise again for outside inquiry.

The board's sole intention through the leak investigation was to ensure strict adherence to a code of conduct and accountability to operate as effectively as possible for the benefit of the company's stakeholders. Pretexting is not a practice that we endorse and we apologize for those affected outside of the board.[23]

Although Ryan's statement was far from definitive, it no doubt would have slowed the media's rush to judgment by forcing journalists to reexamine some of their assumptions, notably that Dunn was a "rogue" chairman who'd acted alone. In the end, though, Ryan's statement was quashed and the board chose to remain silent. The part that Hurd played in this abrupt change of plan is not clear. Of course, as CEO he could have issued his own statement, which would have carried even more weight than a board declaration.

Late Thursday night, Taaffe offered Dunn his sympathy and some grim advice:

I have just learned of the Board's failure to support you on a collective issuing of a statement. This must be distressing and hugely frustrating for you who bear the burden of the defense.

The media has moved to where we predicted it would move and right now they see you as guilty of deploying a technique which is to them, the victim, indefensible.

There can be no offense as for now we can only mitigate the reputational damage. The only new information, which will be cynically met with but is your only course, is plausible deniability on authorizing the investigation or understanding that these techniques were being used AND deep remorse that they were used.

If the Board is still sorting through the legal niceties then you need to determine your risk and advance that case in your own right by morning west coast time. Ideally several other directors would be available to support you in the media or be available to speak to media.

How you go out is dependent on legal counsel you personally receive. If we assume that the legal support is forthcoming and quick (neither of which I have seen so far) then you should issue your own statement followed by one on ones with the most important media with an option for a CNBC interview by the pm.

I see no other course. No journalist, even the contrarian ones, will be receptive of any other story. My colleagues who are very connected to the broadest media pool have fed back to me that the universal horror about pretexting and the need to understand who is responsible are barriers to advancing any other story.[24]

Dunn would not or could not read between the lines of Taaffe's message, which was a thinly veiled warning that Hurd and the board had decided to feed her to the wolves. Dunn still believed in Hurd, who called frequently to offer sympathy and talk over the latest turn of the Spygate screw. Much as she wished that Hurd would have come to her defense publicly, she did not consider his reticence a betrayal. In fact, she shared the belief that it was in HP's best interests to shield its emerging executive-suite star from the taint of scandal. "I think there is a deep instinct to protect the CEO in a situation like that," said Dunn, who actually felt a bit sorry for Hurd. "There was a lot of focus on Kona I," she said, "Mark wasn't there for the start of it, so I felt kind of bad for him that he'd inherited this situation, which wasn't of his own doing."[25]

Instead of heeding Taaffe's advice to hire her own lawyer, Dunn obligingly followed a script relayed to her by Sherbin from Hurd. On Thursday night, the chairman told her fellow directors that she was prepared "to go on the record tomorrow with a number of reporters emphasizing why the investigation had to be done, emphasizing that the direction given and assurances received throughout were that it be done legally, and clarifying that any problems with subcontractors are unfortunate but do not overcome the imperative of having come to grips with the leaks. Mark and Bob Sherbin have been closely involved in this decision."[26]

On Thursday, Dunn also traded emails with Andrea Redmond, the executive recruiter and fellow cancer survivor:

Redmond: Hang in there. This too will pass and quickly. In the meantime, get a punching bag. I am!

Dunn: Thank you! This makes cancer look easy!

Redmond: So the cancer was just to toughen you up! Try to keep this in perspective. I know this hurts like hell and it's all because of one guy with a lot of money who is holding a grudge. He's crazy. But all of this is not really about you—the person who you are in your heart and soul and nobody can touch or tarnish that. . . . Screw Tom Perkins and the press!

Dunn: I will be rereading this message all day today. Thank you, thank you. I really need this today.[27]

Early Friday morning, September 8, Sherbin telephoned Dunn at her apartment in downtown San Francisco and said he had lined up back-to-back interviews with Kaplan and five other key reporters, starting in one hour. Dunn felt woefully unprepared. "I had no materials to work from," she said. "It was just whatever I could remember." Even so, she never even considered not playing along. "I'd been pounding the table for a new strategy with the press for so long that I did not feel like I was in a good position to say no," Dunn said. "I guess if I'd had a lawyer then, I probably would have been told not to do it."[28]

With her husband listening in on a second phone line, Dunn ran the media gauntlet as best she could. In truth, it didn't much matter what she told the reporters as long as she could avoid making a horrendous gaffe (mission accomplished). In stepping forward solo to take the heat, Dunn seemed to be validating the underlying premise that it was her investigation to explain and justify: Defend it, you own it.

Dunn reinforced her ownership by signing her name to a form letter of apology to the pretexted reporters that had been written for her by HP's public relations and legal departments and approved by Hurd. In this instance, Dunn did act against her better judgment. "I didn't like it, but by then I'd gotten reluctantly used to the personalization of the whole thing," she said.[29] The letter read in part: "I want to write to you directly to offer my deepest, unreserved apologies that your phone records were obtained without your knowledge as part of the Board's investigation into breaches of confidentiality. I am very sorry that these activities occurred and am particularly regretful that members of the media, including you, were subjected to this."[30]

Although Dunn remained severely on the defensive, the apologies and the interviews did make a difference in the next round of Spygate coverage. Certainly, Kaplan's follow-up, a *Newsweek* cover story titled "The Boss Who Spied on Her Board," was far more thoroughly reported than his conflagration-igniting online piece. The reporter backed off from his initial assertion that HP's leak investigations were entirely the chairman's doing, concluding judiciously, "It remains unclear exactly what Dunn knew and when she knew it." Kaplan even allowed Dunn to get in a few shots at Perkins, as in this quote: "He's angry that I stood in his way to cover up the results of our investigation and the identity of the leaker."[31]

Dunn could live with Kaplan's latest story, but she deeply resented *Newsweek*'s choice of cover art, a paparazzi-style photo of her looking hard-bitten and haggard in pearls and power suit. Sherbin winced when he saw it. "In that unforgettable *Newsweek* cover, she was the Leona Helmsley of the West Coast," he said. "I think that was seared in people's consciousness at that point."[32]

Dunn did object to the way Kaplan had opened his cover story with an anecdote supplied by Perkins about the dinner party at his house in Belvedere to which he had invited Hurd, Dunn, and their spouses early in the CEO's tenure. After the meal, the group retired to the living room, where Dunn and Hurd talked HP shop while sitting together on a couch. Bored, Perkins fetched his radio-controlled toy helicopter and swooped it low, just over Dunn's head. "The spouses were in stitches," Kaplan wrote. "Perkins circled the toy helicopter for another mischievous pass. Dunn just kept on talking about regulatory issues and other arcana of management. 'Pattie!' Perkins asked: 'Didn't you just hear something zooming over your head?' Her answer: 'I just thought it was the dishwasher running.'"

Bill Jahnke, Dunn's husband, told me that Perkins's toy helicopter never came anywhere his wife's head, but that if it had, he would have been more inclined to take a swing at Perkins than to laugh with him.[34]

It would appear that Perkins had embroidered reality to support his assertion that Dunn was a humorless, clueless governance wonk undeserving of the HP chairmanship. Viet Dinh admired his client's media touch. "Kaplan's piece was perfect," Dinh wrote in a congratulatory email to Perkins. "Tom, loved the helicopter story—perfect color."[35]

Perkins forwarded Dinh's message to two dozen people, including several fellow NewsCorp directors, two partners at Kleiner Perkins and at least four HP board members, including Dick Hackborn and a very surprised Sari Baldauf, who barely knew Perkins, and certainly was not an admirer of the ex-director. "This all looks very strange to a newcomer—there sure is a need for trust building," Baldauf noted in forwarding Perkins's email to fellow directors (except Keyworth). "If I have an issue, I tell so, directly. And expect and appreciate the same from other people."[36]

Even Hackborn, Perkins's longtime colleague on the technology committee, took exception, informing his board colleagues that he just "put Tom's email address in my email host's spam filter to prevent his emails from reaching my PC in the future."[37]

* * *

BRIGHT AND EARLY on Sunday, September 10, HP's board convened by telephone in emergency session. Dunn opened the meeting but quickly gave way to Sonsini, who informed the directors that he had received a "settlement" proposal from lawyers representing Perkins and Keyworth. Sonsini ticked off the terms:

Dunn resigns immediately as chairman;

Keyworth resigns immediately as director;

HP pays Keyworth's foundation $2 million;

HP grants Keyworth a three-year consulting contract
  with Hurd;

HP thanks Keyworth for his service;

HP thanks Perkins and invites him back to the Board;

HP pays Perkins $1.5 million to cover his expenses;

HP agrees not to sue Perkins and Keyworth and
  vice versa.

Listening in from her home office, Dunn was flabbergasted by Sonsini's recitation. "I remember thinking, 'What do you mean a settlement agreement?'" Dunn recalled. "I couldn't believe that Perkins and Keyworth were somehow in a position to dictate terms upon which they would go away."[38] After Sonsini finished, Dunn composed herself and spoke for a few minutes, expressing a desire to remain as chairman and work through the crisis with her fellow directors. At Sonsini's urging, Dunn then recused herself by hanging up the receiver.

As the board deliberated, Dunn acted on advice she'd received the previous night over dinner with a friend and put in an SOS call to Mike Sitrick in Los Angeles. Sitrick, who ran his own eponymous PR firm, was one of America's foremost practitioners of publicity as high-stakes combat. Although best known as the go-to PR guy for Hollywood celebrities in crisis— think Michael Jackson, Rush Limbaugh, Paris Hilton—Sitrick's true forte was corporate scandal. At $695 an hour, he did not come cheap, but Sitrick embodied two traits rarely found in combination: an understanding both deep and nuanced of how the media works and a relentless pugnacity. As a profile in *Los*

Angeles magazine put it, "Sitrick's effectiveness is inextricably linked to his tough-mindedness, to a desire not only to engage in battle but to annihilate opponents."[39]

It was almost as if Sitrick had been waiting for Dunn's call. He told her that he knew exactly who she was and had been following Spygate with growing astonishment at the ineptitude of HP's public relations. Dunn said that she was going to recommend to Sherbin that HP hire him to simultaneously advise the company and her as its chair. Sitrick consented to this two-track approach but reserved the right to choose to represent her alone if it seemed that HP was not acting in her best interests.

"That could be kind of tricky, but OK," Dunn said.

"So who's your lawyer?" Sitrick asked.

"I don't have one," Dunn replied. "I think my interests and the company's interests are aligned pretty closely here."

"Lady, you really do need help," replied Sitrick, whose advice for the moment was to route all interview requests to him and avoid all contact with the press.[40] He also urged Dunn to hire James Brosnahan, a prominent Bay Area trial lawyer. Although Dunn initially blanched at hiring a criminal lawyer, she eventually did retain Brosnahan.

Dunn then called Sherbin, who was a bit offended at the implication that he, Taaffe, and their staffs needed crisis-management help. He also balked at Sitrick's hourly rate. As a concession to Dunn, though, Sherbin agreed to put Sitrick on retainer and immediately put him to work trying to extinguish media fires. He immediately regretted bringing Sitrick in. "Boy, was he unpleasant to deal with!" Sherbin said. "Within 24 hours, he just injected himself into our media relations."[41]

At noon, Sonsini and Bob Ryan called Dunn with a split decision. The board had not removed her as chairman; in fact, the matter had not even been put to a vote. For the moment anyway, the directors' resentment of Perkins's bullying and of Keyworth's defiance overwhelmed their discomfort at the pounding that HP was taking in the media. Although Dunn's colleagues were not prepared to oust her, they did want her to ease their burden by voluntarily stepping down as chair (while remaining as a director). "It's your decision, but we feel that this would take the heat off both you and the company," said Sonsini, adding that the board was planning to reconvene at six o'clock the following evening, Monday, and would expect her decision then.[42]

Dunn disagreed with Sonsini: Her resignation as chairman might or might not ease the pressure on the company, but it would definitely be interpreted as an admission of guilt; to her, this was not only unwarranted but also would make her an even more inviting target for reporters and prosecutors alike. If the board demanded her resignation, she would offer it up. Otherwise, the chairman intended to make a last-ditch effort to stiffen the backbones of her colleagues and convince them to join her in defying Perkins.

On Sunday afternoon, Dunn called two top-tier corporate governance experts whom she considered allies—Richard Breeden and Jeffrey Sonnenfeld—and persuaded them to address the board during its Monday meeting. Breeden was a former SEC chairman who had served as the court-appointed monitor of WorldCom, which had imploded under the weight of one of the biggest corporate frauds in U.S. history. Outspoken and oft-quoted, Sonnenfeld was a business professor at Yale University and the founder of Yale's Chief Executive Leadership Institute.

On Monday morning, Dunn emailed every board member a just-published op-ed piece by a third governance luminary, Nell Minow of the Corporate Library. Minow is "considered the most independent and outspoken in that crowd," Dunn wrote in the note she attached. "She voted all of BGI's shares against the HP board in 2005—she is not in my pocket."[43]

But Minow was on Dunn's side. "The first wave of reporting about the Hewlett-Packard board's 'pretexting' scandal completely missed the point," she argued.

> The story hit the media square in its biggest blind spot. They hear 'leak' and they assume that there is some Daniel Ellsberg–type hero who must be protected. And they bought without question the spin of an aggrieved director who quit in a huff. They were distracted by the issue of the legality of the investigative techniques and bypassed entirely the real issue and the real culprit. . . .
>
> What is of interest here is how a board still reeling from a series of major mistakes handles a profound betrayal of trust in the context of Sarbanes-Oxley and heightened scrutiny from regulators and investors. . . .
>
> It is a shame that the steps this board took to begin to repair its dysfunction have created another public mess. But now is when we see whether this board is ready to earn shareholders' trust. It would be a mistake to ask Dunn to resign until the full story is on the record. The board should retain outside counsel to prepare a full report, including the name of the firm that did the investigation and the level of supervision they were operating under.[44]

Just hours before the board was to meet, HP disclosed that the office of Kevin Ryan, the U.S. Attorney for Northern California, was "requesting information similar to that sought by the California Attorney General."[45] In other words, the federal authorities also had begun a criminal investigation, significantly ratcheting up the legal threat to HP.

On Monday, too, Spygate graduated to a full-fledged national political issue as Congress launched yet another investigation. In a letter addressed to Dunn as chairman, the ranking members of the House of Representatives' Energy and Commerce Committee declared that they were especially troubled by reports that HP, "one of America's corporate icons," had obtained the telephone records of journalists. The committee gave HP one week to turn over all sorts of documents pertaining to Kona I and Kona II, including "a list of all individuals that were part of or knew of the investigation."[46]

Although the board was to gather by teleconference for its Monday meeting, Dunn drove to Palo Alto from her home in Orinda so that she could sit in the boardroom with Hurd, Bob Wayman, and Ann Baskins while the meeting was going on. She showed up at HP headquarters a few hours early because she also wanted some time alone with Hurd.

Even in the happiest times, Hurd gave off nervous energy like a furnace generates heat. During meetings, he often paced around a room, gesticulating as he spoke. One first-time visitor to Hurd's office recalled that the CEO orbited his desk continually throughout an hour-long meeting, a human satellite on short tether. *Is he dissing me*, this fellow wondered, *or is this what attention-deficit-disorder looks like in a CEO?* Hurd did have a bad back that discomfited him at times. For her part, though, Dunn was convinced that Hurd's agitated affect was purposeful. "I think it's intended to motivate people, to get them to act," she said. "I don't know how calculated it is, but I suspect it's quite calculated."[47]

Even so, when Dunn met with Hurd in his office before the board meeting, he was fairly bouncing off the walls. Dunn had never seen him so agitated. Having come in search of reassurance, she instead found herself dispensing it. "I thought Mark was overreacting," he recalled. "But he may have been privy to communications that I wasn't privy to between the company and its lawyers and the legal authorities."[48]

After calling the board meeting to order, Dunn made a case for remaining as chairman and urged the board to wait until it could meet face-to-face to decide on her status or the Perkins-Keyworth settlement. Breeden and Sonnenfeld joined in by telephone with commentary that was generally supportive of Dunn's position but was impatiently received by the directors. After a brief and tepid discussion, the chairman recused herself and walked down the hall to wait in Hurd's office.

An hour later, Hurd came and told her that the board wanted her to remain a director but resign as chairman at its January 18 meeting. Masking her disappointment as best she could, Dunn agreed to step down, but asked to remain in the post until March. Her request was denied. Had the board not felt so pressed for time it probably would have preserved the non-executive chairman's position it had created at the same time it appointed Dunn to fill it and gone outside the company to find a replacement. As it was, though, the directors decided to anoint Hurd their next chairman and tried to offset this governance retrogression by slipping Hackborn into the new role of lead independent director. The board delayed the vote required to make these leadership changes official, to give Sonsini a bit more time to come to terms with Perkins and Keyworth. The board would reconvene the next morning at the ungodly hour of five o'clock so that it could wrap up its business in time to issue a press release before the stock market opened in New York.

After the meeting adjourned at 9:20 P.M., Dunn retired with Hurd to his office, where they remained talking into the wee hours. There was some transition-smoothing business to attend to: Hurd wanted Dunn to join him in making a statement to the press the next morning and a podcast to HP employees later in the day. Mostly, though, the CEO vented. Although the board meeting had gone as scripted, Hurd was just as agitated as he had been before the session. "Mostly, it was me trying to calm him down," said Dunn, who sat while the CEO paced. "He was distraught."[49]

Even if Sonsini succeeded in neutralizing Perkins, the state, federal, and Congressional investigations into Spygate were certain to continue. Documents that would confirm Hurd's central involvement in Kona II soon would be winging their way by special courier to Sacramento, San Francisco, and Washington, D.C. Although Hurd was accustomed to tough decisions, having laid off workers by the thousands at both NCR and HP, never before had his own neck been as close to the chopping block as it was now. "I wish I'd never left Dayton," he told Dunn. "We are all going down."[50]

Dunn spent nearly five hours with Hurd, finally making it back home at about 3:00 A.M. She set her alarm for 4:45 A.M. and blearily called the board to order at 5:02. This time Dunn did not have to recuse herself, though she had little to contribute to a session mainly devoted to fine-tuning the press releases that were about to commemorate her removal as chairman and HP's capitulation to Perkins. "I was horrified," Dunn said. "All the talk was, 'Would this satisfy Jay and Tom?'"[51]

HP put out a first press release announcing the tripartite Dunn-Hurd-Hackborn job shuffle at 6:00 A.M., a good twenty minutes before the board adjourned. A few minutes later, the company issued a second release announcing Keyworth's immediate resignation from the board. In his heavily lawyered statement, Keyworth offered the same sort of grudging mea culpa he had at the May board meeting:

> I acknowledge that I was a source for a CNET article that appeared in January 2006. I was frequently asked by HP corporate communications officials to speak with reporters—both on the record and on background—in an effort to provide the perspective of a longstanding board member with continuity over much of the company's history. My comments were always praised by senior company officials as helpful to the company—which has always been my intention. The comments I made to the CNET reporter were, I believed, in the best interest of the company and also did not involve the disclosure of confidential or damaging information.[52]

In this same release, Hurd supplied the public flattery required under the settlement agreement. "On behalf of HP, I apologize to Tom Perkins for the intrusion into his privacy," Hurd said. "I thank Tom for his contributions, his principles and his help in getting HP past this episode." This was about as ludicrous as corporate flackery gets, but at least Hurd drew the line at apologizing to Keyworth. HP used Dunn for that, noting in the press release that "HP board chairman Patricia Dunn expressed regret for the intrusion into his privacy."[53] According to Dunn, this sentence was not in the draft version presented to the board for its review. She was incensed at this bit of trickery, believing that if anything, Keyworth should apologize to her.

HP at least had succeeded in paring back Perkins's original wish list, mostly to Keyworth's detriment. All Keyworth got for leaving the board and publicly admitting to the CNET leak was a pat on the back from Hurd. "I appreciate his long and distinguished service to HP," the CEO said in his statement. "I have personally valued his experienced counsel and hope that he will continue to provide me with his advice in the future"—gratis, that is, because Hurd did not give Keyworth that three-year consulting contract.[54] Nor did HP put $2 million into his foundation. These were not minor disappointments for Keyworth, whose main source of income was the $200,000 in director's fees he'd just relinquished in resigning from the board. "Keyworth got screwed," Perkins said later. "He got no money."[55]

By his own account, Perkins had initially demanded that HP allow Keyworth to keep his seat on the board. However, this possibility was closed out once Keyworth was publicly outed as a leaker—a disclosure that was a byproduct of the pressure that Perkins himself applied on HP. "Once it blew up, HP had to make him evil, evil, evil," said Perkins, who added that Keyworth might have extracted some money from HP even so, if he'd employed a better lawyer. "I think Jay got terrible legal advice," he said.[56]

For his part, Perkins didn't care about the fees to which he would have been entitled had he rejoined the HP board or even the damages he could have collected by suing the company for hacking into his phone records. What mattered to the ex-director was not having to pay Dinh from his own pocket, largely because he considered the lawyer's $1.5 million bill excessive. "I was a little surprised at what Viet charged," Perkins said. "If I'd had to pay it myself, I think it would have been a different bill. Or I wouldn't have paid it at all."[57]

After settling with HP, Perkins took a celebratory sail on *The Maltese Falcon*. When Kaplan telephoned looking for a fresh quote or two, the mega-yacht was nearing the island of Minorca in the Mediterranean. Perkins "told *Newsweek* press reports that he wanted to return to the board were wrong," Kaplan wrote. "And he says he has no interest in pursuing any possible lawsuits against HP for hacking his personal phone records or for any compensation he lost by resigning in May. 'My No. 1 thing was to get Pattie out as chairman, and I got that,' he says. 'So I'm happy.'"[58]

Keyworth, by contrast, was miserable, and the sharp reduction in his income and the termination of his access to the HP's corporate jet fleet wasn't nearly the half of it. Dunn may have been cast as Spygate's principal villain, but Keyworth's reputation had been sullied, too. Former General Electric CEO Jack Welch, whom Keyworth greatly admired, went so far as to brand him "an ethical criminal."[59] For HP's unrepentant leaker, the bottom-line reality was that he had been forced to resign in disgrace from a company that had become a cornerstone of his identity for twenty years. "It was the second worst thing that ever happened to me in my life," Keyworth told me (the worst being his wife's death).[60]

CHAPTER TWELVE

DUNN AND DUSTED

THE IMPUGNING OF Pattie Dunn's integrity had incapacitated her as chairman well before she was removed from the position. Leaderless and demoralized, HP's board somehow never got around to authorizing a truly independent investigation of Kona I or Kona II. In the end, it was not the board but Mark Hurd who "lawyered up," hiring the Philadelphia-based firm of Morgan Lewis & Bockius on September 8, a few days before he replaced Dunn as chairman. As Hurd told reporters, "Morgan Lewis reports to me, not to the HP board."[1] The hiring of Morgan Lewis marked an unceremonious end to Larry Sonsini's long and lucrative tenure as HP's chief outside counsel.

Hurd gave Morgan Lewis a week and a half to do what Wilson Sonsini had failed to: investigate the investigations in a way that would quiet the din of outside criticism. What did Morgan Lewis do that Wilson Sonsini hadn't already done? It's impossible to say, given that HP never did release the Philly firm's report. One thing its lawyers did *not* do was interview Pattie Dunn. After Hurd called in a Morgan Lewis team headed by partner Michael Holston, Dunn was entirely excluded from the flow of communications between the board and HP management. "Morgan Lewis was directing things, and they weren't talking

to me after Holston showed up," Dunn recalled. "I was really
out in the cold."[2]

By this time, Hurd needed all the help he could get in hanging
on to his own job. Dunn's demotion had not blunted the media's
determination to break through HP's silence and trace its leak
investigations in their every errant particular. On the contrary,
now that Dunn was "done and dusted," as Viet Dinh boasted,
reporters naturally shifted focus from her to other players, just
as Congressional investigators began leaking potentially incrim-
inating HP documents. In the week after Dunn stepped down
as chairman, the names of Ron DeLia, Action Research, Kevin
Hunsaker, and Anthony Gentilucci all surfaced in print for the
first time. But the new prime suspect was Hurd, whose claims
of non-involvement were cast into doubt by a burst of skeptical
news articles on September 21, illustrated by this sampling of
headlines: "H-P CEO Hurd Might Have Had Bigger Probe Role"
(*Wall Street Journal*); "HP CEO Allowed 'Sting' of Reporter"
(*Washington Post*); "Hurd Was Briefed During HP Probe" (San
Jose *Mercury News*); and "HP CEO Mark Hurd linked to 'dirty
tricks'" (ZDNet). "Pressure is mounting on [Hurd] to what explain what appears to have been a greater role in the company's
spying operation than was initially indicated," the *New York
Times* reported.[3]

Meanwhile, California Attorney General Lockyer went on
PBS's *NewsHour with Jim Lehrer* and again rattled HP's cage.
"We currently have sufficient evidence to indict people both
within HP as well as contractors on the outside," said Lockyer,
who after two terms as attorney general was now campaigning
for state treasurer. "People's identities were taken falsely, and
it's a crime."[4] Lockyer's comments earned the Democrat a rebuke
from the editorial page of the *Wall Street Journal*, which accused

him of emulating his New York counterpart, Eliot Spitzer, by "using the airwaves to poison public opinion against future defendants and make it easier to intimidate them into settling."[5]

Perkins sent a reassuring email to Hurd a few days after Lockyer's television appearance. "I am continuing to try to take the steam out of the boiler as it pertains to you," Perkins advised the CEO. "John Doerr had a very good conversation with Bill Lockyer about the situation based upon my assessment (i.e., you are one of the victims). It can't hurt."[6] Doerr, of course, was Kleiner Perkins's managing partner, but he also wielded influence as Silicon Valley's preeminent Democratic fundraiser and in that capacity had become acquainted with Lockyer.

Actually, Perkins's string pulling could indeed have hurt Hurd if his intervention was seen as interfering with a criminal investigation. Perkins told me that Doerr did nothing more than take a phone call from Lockyer after Congress held its Spygate hearing. "Pattie testified and, in my view, outright lied, and also in Bill Lockyer's view outright lied," Perkins said. "So he got very angry at HP and at Mark and everybody. He called John to find out what really happened and John said, 'It wasn't Mark Hurd,' basically. And then I talked to him—Lockyer called me—and I said the same thing."[7]

Lockyer took issue with Perkins's account, albeit gingerly. "I've sort of learned not to argue with billionaires," he told me, 'but I don't recall it that way at all." Lockyer said that that he did indeed call Doerr, but only to ask him how to contact Perkins, who was off somewhere on *The Maltese Falcon*. "We'd had letters from Perkins and his lawyer, and I wanted to talk to him myself," Lockyer said. "I believe Doerr said, 'I know he'd be happy to talk. You should call him.' That was the extent of it."[8] What is more, Lockyer did reach Perkins by telephone, but the AG said that this conversation occurred in mid-September, well before before Dunn testified before Congress.

Was Perkins trying to curry favor with Hurd by exaggerating his steam-reduction efforts on the CEO's behalf? It's possible, though Perkins denied it. Certainly Perkins, in his comments to David Kaplan, and Dinh, in speaking to other reporters on Perkins's behalf, made a point of praising Hurd even as they were trashing Dunn. As Dinh told a reporter from the Associated Press, "Despite this current disagreement, Tom Perkins has a warm place in his heart for HP and believe in the prospects and performance of HP under the leadership of Mark Hurd."[9]

Hurd's annexation of the chairman's post put him uncomfortably on the spot in the sense that he could no longer rely on Dunn to take the lead in dealing with the media. In Sherbin's opinion, it was past time for Hurd to step forward and comment publicly about Spygate. All in all, Hurd had kept a much lower profile than had Carly Fiorina, consenting only to the occasional one-on-one interview with key HP beat reporters. His last press conference had been eighteen months earlier, on the day he was introduced as HP's new CEO. At Sherbin's suggestion, though, Hurd agreed to make a public statement at a press conference after the next regularly scheduled board meeting ended on September 22. Sherbin had taken the idea to Hurd without getting the approval of his boss, Cathy Lyons, who had just returned from Europe and was tied up in a daylong staff meeting. "When I told Cathy about the press conference, she swore at me like I'd never been sworn at before," Sherbin said. "To be honest, I was feeling so much stress by this time that I just broke down and cried."[10]

Early on the morning of September 21, just hours before the board meeting began, Dunn received an email warning from her lawyer, Jim Brosnahan. A source within Morgan Lewis "advises that the Board may terminate you today on some basis and that Hurd supports this reluctantly," Brosnahan wrote. "I am doing everything I can to stop it including explaining that it is very dumb. . . . They are going to do it on the grounds that your public statements do not comport with their documents"—specifically, that Dunn's denials that she was aware of HP's pretexting while it was taking place were contradicted by a PowerPoint presentation made by Ron DeLia on February 6, 2006.[11] However, the slide in question referred merely to "Phone Records" and said nothing about how investigators had obtained them.

Dunn arrived in Palo Alto for the board meeting expecting the worst, but not yet resigned to her fate. She was asked to leave the room shortly after the session began, without being given a chance to speak. However, the directors were disinclined to rubberstamp Dunn's removal. Larry Babbio, John Hammergren, and Bob Ryan were particularly emphatic in arguing that Hurd and HP should honor the agreement reached just nine days earlier, allowing Dunn to remain as chairman until January and as a director indefinitely. By some accounts, Hurd had prevailed only by threatening to resign as CEO. "There was a rumor that I walked out of the board meeting on Thursday and that I wasn't coming back," Hurd acknowledged later in an interview with *Business Week*'s Peter Burrows. "I don't know where it comes from. I'm not walking—on my own, anyway."[12]

This time, it was Lucie Salhany, the newly installed chair of the Nominating & Governance committee, who emerged from a board meeting to deliver the bad news to Dunn. "We're going to ask you to resign, but you have a chance to talk to us and tell us whatever you want to tell us," Salhany said.[13]

Dunn took a seat in HP's boardroom for the last time and told her colleagues how disappointed she was that they had lacked the strength of character to resist Perkins's bullying and do right by her and by HP. This was a Dunn that her colleagues hadn't seen before, confrontational and more than a bit pissed off. Dunn said she would do what Keyworth had refused to do and resign as requested, but also insisted on going around the table and asked every board member, "Why do *you* think I should resign?" Not every director responded, but those who did said that she'd become a distraction and should resign for the good of the company. (The consensus was most succinctly expressed in an email Dunn received the next day from Sari Baldauf: "This all is terrible, but the company has to get back to business.")[14] Hurd said nothing. What Dunn considered the kindest comment came from Hammergren, who said, "This is liberating for you. Think of it as granting you the option to go off and defend yourself."[15]

The meeting ended with a rush of feeling, as most of the directors hugged Dunn and murmured thanks for her contribution over the years and regret over what had happened. There were tears, but none from Dunn. "I wasn't feeling too sentimental at that moment," Dunn recalled. "Disgusted and angry was more like it."[16] (Later, though, Dunn was touched to receive farewell messages from several directors, notably Hackborn. "It is sad to note that with your and Jay's departure, I am the only one left from the original pre-merger HP Board," Hackborn wrote).[17]

The plan was for HP to announce Dunn's departure during a press conference the next day at which Hurd would offer his first extensive public comments about Spygate. Dunn said that she wanted to join in and explain her departure in her own words, but that Hurd's lawyers refused to allow it. Even so, Dunn agreed to return to Palo Alto the next morning with Brosnahan to negotiate the wording of the press release and the accompanying 8K.

Immediately after the board meeting adjourned, Dunn met with Hurd and Holston in the CEO's office to discuss the mechanics of her resignation. Dunn brought Brosnahan along as an improbable goodwill gesture. "Believe it or not, I was still in the frame of mind that I didn't want to see the ultimate divergence of interests between me and HP," Dunn said. "I'd heard from a couple of people at HP that Jim was considered difficult and divisive and so I thought if he and Mark could look one another in the eye and see that neither of them have antlers or whatever, we could have a nice adult conversation."[18]

It didn't exactly work out that way. According to Brosnahan, the exchange of perfunctory pleasantries had barely been completed when he looked Hurd in the eye and declared, "A crime has been committed"—that is, the lawyer claimed, HP had obstructed justice in agreeing to make payments to a potential witness—Perkins—in the midst of a criminal investigation. "That agreement is a terrible problem for Hewlett-Packard. Whoever did that shouldn't be in your company," said Brosnahan, not knowing that Hurd had approved the settlement with Perkins and Keyworth.[19]

Brosnahan recalled that Hurd shot him a look of disbelief over the reading glasses perched on the end of his nose. "This meeting is over," the CEO said and stormed out of the room, followed closely by Holston. Dunn was chagrined by her lawyer's effrontery, but Brosnahan laughed it off. "It was a comfortable chair and I was enjoying the moment in a way because I'd never kicked a CEO out of his own office," he recalled.[20] Brosnahan spent a few minutes consoling Dunn over the fact that the meeting had not gone as anticipated, and then they made their way to the parking lot without seeing Hurd.

Early the next morning Dunn returned to Palo Alto with her husband and lawyer to work out the terms of her departure in advance of a press conference that HP had scheduled for 1:30 P.M. She, Jahnke, and Brosnahan sat in a conference room and communicated with Hurd and Babbio, who was representing the board, through handwritten notes conveyed back and forth by messengers. Dunn did not ask for much—no golden parachute, consulting contract, or multimillion-dollar foundation contribution. As she remembered it, there was not even any discussion of a mutual non-disparagement and hold-harmless agreement of the sort HP had just signed with Perkins and Keyworth. What Dunn cared about most was that her part in the leak investigation be accurately described in the press release announcing her resignation. Also, she did not want the company to tie her resignation to Hurd's roughly simultaneous decision to fire Kevin Hunsaker and Anthony Gentilucci.

By the time it was all down in writing, the press conference was about to start. Dozens of journalists were milling about downstairs, and television reporters already were broadcasting live from the parking lot. Babbio walked into the conference room and shook Dunn's hand. "Come and say goodbye to everyone," he urged. As Dunn approached the boardroom, the door burst open and out came Hurd. "He kind of rushed up and threw his arms around me," Dunn said. "He gave me this huge bear hug and then straightened his tie and went off to the press conference."[21] Dunn left by the back gate to avoid the camera crews that lined the headquarters entrance on Page Mill Road and went off to have lunch with her husband and her lawyer at a Palo Alto restaurant.

The wording of the press release HP issued was exactly as had been negotiated. It included a brief statement from Dunn in which she conceded nothing and, at Brosnahan's insistence, apologized for nothing:

> I followed the proper processes by seeking the assistance of HP security personnel. I did not select the people who conducted the investigation, which was undertaken after consultation with board members. I accepted the responsibility to identify the sources of those leaks but I did not propose the specific methods of the investigation. I was a full subject of the investigation myself and my phone records were examined along with others. Unfortunately, the people HP relied upon to conduct this type of investigation let me and the company down. I continue to have the best interests of HP at heart and thus I have accepted the board's request to resign.[22]

HP attached a laudatory statement by Hurd in which he thanked Dunn "for her eight years of service on HP's board and the actions she has taken to strengthen its composition and governance capabilities. There is no doubt in my mind that she had the best interests of HP in mind throughout her time on our board."[23] However, at the press conference Hurd read a statement in which he pointed the finger right at Dunn. "It was the responsibility of the HP Chairman to pursue the leak situation," he said. The CEO did admit to approving the sending of phony emails to CNET's Dawn Kawamoto in the name of the fictional "Jacob Goldfarb," but otherwise accepted blame only in the most general sense. "While many of the right processes were in place, they unfortunately broke down, and no one in the management chain, including me, caught them," said Hurd, who claimed not to have read Hunsaker's climactic eighteen-page report detailing the case against Keyworth—the same report that HP's own documents show that he had discussed at length in meetings with Dunn, Baskins, and Sonsini. "I understand there was a written report of the investigation addressed to me and others, but I did not read it," he said. "I could have, and I should have."[24] After Hurd finished, he declined to take questions.

The CEO was followed to the podium by Holston of Morgan Lewis, who read a prepared statement that was a bit longer than Hurd's and consisted mainly of an analysis of the techniques used to investigate the leaks, including the Goldfarb "sting." Holston said that Social Security numbers had been used to obtain through pretexting the phone records of four journalists, three HP board members, and one HP employee. Holston, a former federal prosecutor, did not opine on the legality of what had transpired, at least not publicly.

Holston did not explicitly raise the question of culpability, but implied that Dunn had taken a much larger role in managing the leak investigations than had Hurd. Kona I had begun when Dunn contacted Security Outsourcing Solutions, Ron DeLia's firm, said Holston, who made no mention of the two previous leak investigations that HP Security had conducted without Dunn's participation. For the first month or so of the investigation, "Ms. Dunn worked directly with Ron Delia," Holston added, but failed to note that DeLia's primary reporting responsibility was to his HP Security boss, Gentilucci. Nor did Holston mention the part Hurd had played in the formation of the Unauthorized Disclosures Team or in initiating Kona II with the list of suspects forwarded to HP Security. Rather, Hurd was "made aware that the Kona II team was assembled and was beginning to identify the source of the leaks," Holston said. "Over the next three months, regular updates were provided by members of the investigation team to Ms. Dunn and, to a lesser extent, to Ann Baskins." The Morgan Lewis lawyer did find that Hunsaker's report identifying Keyworth as the leaker had been "addressed" to Hurd, but did not say whether the CEO had read it. Like Hurd before him, Holston refused to take reporters' questions after he finished reading his statement.[25]

CNBC televised HP's press conference live and followed with the usual postmortem from a panel of experts. Among them was Viet Dinh, who lived up to his Viet Spin moniker by first hailing Dunn for doing "a courageous and graceful thing" in resigning from the HP board and then praising her extravagantly for what she most emphatically had not done—that is, "taking responsibility for the investigation that she initiated, conducted, and supervised." Sticking to the Perkins playbook, he also praised Hurd. "I believe Mark Hurd when he says that his involvement was tangential and indirect in investigations; I think it is right for him to take the helm at this time in order to right the course of HP. Tom Perkins believes in HP. He definitely believes in the leadership of Mark Hurd."[26]

The confluence of Dunn's resignation and the double-barreled public statements of Hurd and Holston cinched the outside world's assumption that Dunn was the mastermind of Konas I and II, but it did not eliminate suspicions that Hurd was a lot more involved that he had admitted. For one thing, his demeanor at the press conference hardly inspired confidence. "Hurd is being very, very careful, with lots of use of weasel words like 'I recall,' 'I think,' 'I understand,' etc." blogged Paul Kedrosky, who covered the event live. Hurd was "uneasy through and through, lacking confidence, ill-at-ease, not clear on his own

participation, and generally sounds like he is on a short leash."[27]
More important, Hurd's self-portrait in passivity did not fit at
all with HP beat reporters' understanding of the CEO's fundamental identity as "an operations expert who asks a lot of questions," in the description of Damon Darlin of the *New York
Times*. "As shocking as it has been to hear the methods used—
obtaining private phone records, or trying to plant tracking software on a journalist's computer—it is almost as surprising that
Mr. Hurd sat on the sidelines while the company's Clouseaus
drew up plans to infiltrate newsrooms with spies masquerading
as secretaries or janitors."[28]

* * *

PATTIE DUNN WAS hardly Jim Brosnahan's most infamous
client. This distinction went to John Walker Lindh, a twenty-
year-old American convert to Islam who joined the Taliban in
Afghanistan and was wounded and captured just six weeks
after the 9/11 attacks. Brosnahan agreed to defend Lindh, aka
the "American Taliban," fully expecting that he would become
the country's most reviled lawyer. "I was absolutely sure that
this case could kill my career," recalled Brosnahan, who also had
reason to fear for his life.[29] Death threats poured in by telephone,
email, and the U.S. mail, forcing the lawyer to hire bodyguards
for round-the-clock protection. In the end, Brosnahan negotiated a deal with the Justice Department under which Lindh
pleaded guilty to two of the lesser charges in a ten-count indictment and received a twenty-year prison term instead of the death
sentence that many commentators had advocated.

Brosnahan had accepted Lindh as a client only after the boy's
parents assured him that they were hiring him to defend their

son, not the Taliban. "I represent individuals, not movements," Brosnahan recalled. "I told them that if I ever got the feeling that I was being used for the purpose of a movement, then I was off the case."[30] Brosnahan, who had spent much of his career as a partner in Morrison & Foerster, San Francisco's largest law firm, was a dyed-in-the-wool civil libertarian who always carried a copy of the United States Constitution and Bill of Rights in his shirt pocket. A friend had given it to him as a present after Lindh's sentencing.

Brosnahan, who was seventy-two years old when Dunn hired him, had represented a wide range of defendants during a prolific career in which he had taken nearly 140 cases all the way to a verdict. A bit more than half of them were criminal cases. Brosnahan, a towering presence in the courtroom at six foot five, belonged to the legal profession's upper tier—nationally prominent trial lawyers—but disdained its trend toward specialization by type of case; he was a proud generalist. Although Brosnahan had successfully represented white-collar defendants right from the start of his career, he distrusted corporate executives on general principle. "Jim is a very liberal Democrat with visceral suspicions of business people," Dunn said. "Just the word CEO raises his hackles." And the word chairman? "He had some idea, but I think he came to really understand the difference between a CEO and a chairman from representing me."[31]

The more that Brosnahan learned about the facts of the matter, the more he felt justified in his reflexive dislike of Mark Hurd. "I formed the view early on that Mr. Hurd had made the decision that he wasn't going to support Pattie Dunn. More than that, he was going to hang her out to dry," Brosnahan said. However, it was also apparent to the lawyer that his client "had bonded so tightly with Hurd in a corporate sense that she was not prepared psychologically for the idea that he actually was not on her side."[32]

Realizing that it was pointless for him to continue disparaging Hurd to Dunn, Brosnahan told his client the old story about the two prisoners who had spent so much time in a jail cell together that they knew one other's repertoire of jokes by heart. They assigned each joke a number and no longer bothered with set-ups and punch lines. One prisoner would say, "number 16" or "number 43," and the other guy would crack up. "I'm not going to tell you each time that Mr. Hurd is not supporting you," Brosnahan informed Dunn. "I'm just going to say, 'number 23.'"

Dunn was predictably surprised when Hurd failed to attend her induction into the Bay Area Council's Business Hall of Fame on September 20, the day before she was booted off the HP board. On balance, though, the dinner was a morale booster for Dunn, who had feared that the council, perhaps San Francisco's preeminent business group, would withdraw an honor it had bestowed on dozens of luminaries over the preceding sixty years, including Dave Packard and Tom Perkins. In her first public appearance since the advent of Spygate, Dunn received a standing ovation from the crowd of nine hundred before and after her speech, in which she mentioned the scandal only in passing: "All I will say about the maelstrom is that I look forward eagerly, in the near future, to the time when I can set the record straight and go back to leading my life as discreetly as possible."[33]

Even after Hurd and Holston had effectively trashed her two days later at HP's September 22 press conference, Dunn still could not bring herself to repudiate the CEO. Hurd called her at home at 8:30 the next morning to make nice and downplay the previous day's verbal assault. ("I take your point that anyone involved only hears the bad stuff relevant to them," Dunn later noted in an email to Hurd thanking him for his call, "but I had taken assurance that the kind of language that was in the press release would find its way into your comments or the lawyers, and that just didn't happen. . . . I would like to think that you will tell your daughters they will be disinherited if they become *lawyers*!!")[34] According to her husband, Dunn rolled her eyes in disbelief while speaking to Hurd—and yet the dime still did not drop. "My hypothesis at the time was that he had gone along with a dastardly plan this lawyer cooked up," she said.[35]

Brosnahan sounded like a quarterback repeatedly calling the same signal—"23, 23, 23"—as he prepped Dunn to testify before the Oversight and Investigations Subcommittee of the House Energy and Commerce Committee on September 28. Dunn was reminded of a song she'd often heard in the Las Vegas of her youth: "Between the Devil and the Deep Blue Sea." Brosnanhan advised her that she could invoke her Fifth Amendment right against self-incrimination and say nothing, as would have been customary for a witness under criminal investigation. "If you take the Fifth, you are ruined as far as your reputation is concerned," he added. "But if you go and testify and there are any punctuation marks that aren't properly made, they can get you for perjury. Even if you are testifying to the best of your memory and knowledge and you make a mistake, they can use it as a basis for perjury."[36]

Brosnahan left this critical decision up to Dunn, who never considered taking the Fifth, even though she had been placed at a serious disadvantage by HP's refusal to give her copies of any of the more than 5,000 emails and other documents it had turned over to Congress. On September 24, a Morgan Lewis partner named John Hemann called Raj Chatterjee, Brosnahan's associate, and offered to provide access to the documents—at a price. "HP 'strongly' wants to participate in preparing Pattie,"

Chatterjee explained in a memo. "He said Pattie is free to use HP's jet, and can review documents on the jet. He would then like Pattie to sit with Ann and Mark together to go over their statements. He wants to avoid inconsistencies and having Mark, Ann and Pattie cross each other." Chatterjee added that based on conversations with the staff of the subcommittee HP had compiled a list of questions likely to be asked at the hearing. "I asked for a copy, but Hemann avoided responding."[37]

Brosnahan was aghast at the suggestion. "The first thing you learn in Criminal 1 is that you don't get all the witnesses together in a meeting to decide what it is they're going to say," he said. "The truth as we saw it was breathtakingly straightforward: Pattie wasn't in charge of this thing at all and other people were. She was she going to go to Congress and tell them what she knew."[38]

On September 26, two days before the hearing, Dunn caught a commercial flight to Washington with her husband. In the taxi on the way into the city from Dulles Airport, Dunn was leafing through the *Wall Street Journal* when she came across a piece by Dinh entitled "Dunn and Dusted," on its opinion page. Dinh praised HP for "its decision to come clean with the available facts about Chairman Patricia Dunn's ill-advised investigation," while portraying his client as a heroic Everyman: "What happened to Tom Perkins is unique only because of the players involved. Thousands have had their phone records illegally accessed." With a master's flourish, Dinh even tried to rehabilitate Keyworth's reputation by dismissing the CNET story that prompted Kona II as a harmless "puff piece." Last but not least, the lawer applied a spit shine to Hurd's tarnished image on the eve of a hearing at which the CEO also was to testify.

"Like any good scandal, Kona has sucked everything and everyone, however peripheral, into its vortex," Dinh wrote.

> But based on all available information, I believe that [Hurd's] knowledge was tangential and his involvement indirect. It would be surprising—and much more disturbing—if Mr. Hurd had zero knowledge of, or involvement in, actions of H-P employees and contractors under the direction of the board chairman. One may well ask whether Mr. Hurd should have done less to help or could have done more to stop the investigation. But here, too, I think he should get the benefit of any doubt. As CEO, Mr. Hurd was charged with the management and operations of H-P, in the process engineering one of the most remarkable turnarounds in recent corporate history. Even if he had the will, he did not have the unilateral authority to challenge Ms. Dunn's management of the board.[39]

The main political object of the hearings on "The HP Pretexting Scandal," as it was officially billed, was to focus national attention on the threat to personal privacy posed by the pretexting of telephone phone records. A couple of bills outlawing the practice already had been introduced in both houses of Congress but had stalled out short of the floor. For Joe Barton, the Texas conservative who chaired the House Energy and Commerce Committee, the issue was unavoidably personal; his first wife recently had been victimized by identity theft. The highly publicized hearing, which was held on the last day the 109th Congress was in session, also gave Republicans a chance to deflect attention from the war in Iraq and the many other issues that would turn

the upcoming 2006 midterm elections into a disaster for the em-
battled party of George W. Bush.

HP did not have a particularly well-connected Washington
office, but Hurd was well served in his dealings with the House
committee by some high-powered help, most notably Hill &
Knowlton and Mark Menenzes, a partner in the law firm of
Hunton & Williams. HP's outside advisers took the lead in persuading Hurd that it was better to take the initiative and volun-
teer to testify before the committee than to hang back in the hope
that he would not be subpoenaed. Menenzes was particularly
well qualified to negotiate with the Energy and Commerce Committee on Hurd's behalf, having served as its chief counsel for
energy and environment from 2003 into 2006.

On the morning before the hearing, Dunn met individually
with four Republican members of the subcommittee in their offices. She was accompanied by her lawyer and Drew Maloney,
a veteran lobbyist and former Republican committee staffer
whom Brosnahan had hired as a Capitol Hill fixer. These were
brief meet-and-greets most memorable to Dunn for the conversation she had with Marsha Blackburn, a Republican from Ten-
nessee who was dazzlingly decked out in gold jewelry. Afterward,
the second-term Congresswoman called Maloney with a bit of
advice. "I think the meeting went well," she said. "But tell her
not to wear so much jewelry tomorrow." Dunn did shed her $200
"lucky" necklace for the hearing but defiantly sported her wedding ring, which a reporter for *The Times* of London once described as "the biggest rock I've ever seen on a finger."[40]

Dunn also had a very different sort of pre-hearing meeting
with Mark Paoletta, who was directing the HP investigation as
the Energy and Commerce Committee's chief counsel for oversight and investigations. Paoletta had worked for the committee

for a decade, an eternity in the revolving-door realm of Congress, and had amassed a great deal of power in managing two hundred investigations, including the subcommittee's probes of corporate corruption at Enron, Global Crossing, Qwest, and Health South. "I could literally open up the newspaper, read about something and say, 'Let's look at that,'" Paoletta mused after he had left the Hill for private practice. "I went through three chairmen and four subcommittee chairmen. I was sort of an institutional rock there. New chairman comes in. 'How do we do institutional oversight?' They're looking to you."[41]

Paoletta was a diligent and ambitious movement conservative of the same generation as Dinh and Corallo. As a young White House lawyer in the administration of George H. W. Bush, Paoletta had played a key role in the hugely contentious but ultimately successful nomination of Clarence Thomas to the U.S. Supreme Court. In his book *Blinded by the Right: The Conscience of an Ex-Conservative,* journalist David Brock accused Paoletta of supplying him with derogatory information that he used to discredit a woman who had made damaging statements about Thomas.[42] (Paoletta told the *Washington Post* that Brock's account was "simply not true.") Not long after Paoletta had left the Hill to go into private practice, he volunteered to serve as one of three leaders of the "truth squad" formed late in the 2008 presidential campaign to fend off "liberal elite" criticism of Sarah Palin.

Dunn walked into a conference room in one of the Congressional office buildings to find Paoletta sitting at the end of a long table flanked by three other lawyers for the committee. "They all looked mad, like they had personally been violated," Dunn said. "Paoletta in particular really kept needling me. His approach was along the lines of 'Everybody knows you are guilty.

I just want to know what the hell were you thinking when you committed this crime?'"

During the afternoon of the day before the hearing, the sub-committee issued a memorandum summarizing the findings of the staff investigation headed by Paoletta. To support the memo, the staff prepared two thick binders of documents that had been submitted by HP, Dunn, Sonsini, DeLia, and Action Research. The memorandum's recitation of the facts of the case echoed in every vital particular the version of events that HP had presented at its press conference in emphasizing the culpability of Dunn, Baskins, and Hunsaker while skating lightly over the involvement of Hurd, Sonsini, and HP Security. To wit:

> At the urging of Patricia Dunn, the Non-executive Chairman of the Board, H-P began an intensive investigation into Board leaks, which was run through H-P's General Counsel's Office and E-mails obtained by the Committee show that Dunn and Baskins were aware of and approved various aspects of both the Kona I and Kona II investigations. The day-to-day control of the investigation was headed up by Mr. Kevin Hunsaker, an in-house H-P lawyer and head of the company's ethics department. . . .
>
> While the CEO, Mark Hurd, was provided either briefings or reports on both the Kona and Kona II investigations, it is not clear what level of knowledge he had about the various aspects of both Kona I and Kona II.

Conspicuous by their absence from the briefing books compiled by the staff for committee members were any of the multitudinous emails showing that HP Security was already two months into a leak investigation before Dunn got into the act with Kona I and documenting Hurd's leadership in establishing the Unauthorized Disclosures Team and initiating Kona II. Tellingly, the second document in the bundle was the email in which a vacationing Dunn casually suggested the name Project Kona to DeLia.

Like many Capitol Hill hearings, this one was not an inquiry, but a kind of show trial designed for bipartisan grandstanding. "I have to ask our witnesses, what were you thinking?" thundered John Dingell, Democrat of Michigan, who accused HP of running "a plumbers' operation that would make Richard Nixon blush if he were still alive."[43]

There were fourteen witnesses, ten of whom appeared together and took the Fifth one by one. They included the owner and four employees of Action Research Group, plus Baskins, Hunsaker, DeLia, and Gentilucci. Dunn, who was sitting in the first row behind the witness table, was shocked at Baskins's appearance. Ashen and dressed entirely in black, HP's former general counsel looked like a mourner at a funeral—her own. Brosnahan had expected Baskins to testify and considered her potentially the most useful witness of all for Dunn's defense. As the managerial link between Hurd and Hunsaker, she probably knew more about the extent of the CEO's involement in Kona II than any other HP insider. Late on the night before the hearing, Hurd fired Baskins, terminating her twenty-four-year career at the company. "Stepping down was a very hard decision for her, but by doing so she has put the interests of HP ahead of her own," said Hurd in the press release HP issued announcing Baskins's departure, which was officially billed as a resignation.[44]

Nearly five hours into the hearing, reporter Peter Lattman posted the following item on the *Wall Street Journal*'s law blog as part of his live coverage:

> All day long there has been this mysterious, rather strapping man roaming back and forth from committee member to committee member, whispering in their ears, handing them papers, and looking pretty powerful. Picture a square-jawed hockey coach pacing back and forth along the bench, barking at his players from time to time—except this guy's wearing a suit and, well, whispering. Who is this guy? Turns out it's Mark Paoletta.[45]

Dunn was sworn in sitting alongside Sonsini and Fred Adler of HP Security in a second panel of witnesses, none of whom took the Fifth. She began to testify with Brosnahan's final instructions still ringing in her ears. "Under no circumstances are you to take responsibility for anything that happened," Brosnhan told her. "If anyone uses the words culpability, responsibility, accountability, do not go there."[46] While Dunn maintained her composure during four hours of questioning, she occasionally allowed her anger and frustration to show through in the form of sarcasm, most notably in the following exchange with Rep. Cliff Stearns, a Florida Republican, who was determined to get her to do what her lawyer had ordered her not to do. As Stearns persisted, Dunn could hear Brosnahan loudly and repeatedly clearing his throat behind her.

> Stearns: Is it just possible you could say yes or no, that you feel you have some culpability?
> Dunn: If I knew then what I know now, I would have

done things very differently and there are some specific
things I would have done very differently.
Stearns: I am interpreting that—
Dunn: It is a foundational component of corporate governance that directors must rely on the reasonable rep-
resentations of management.
Stearns: But—
Dunn: And those I did have.
Stearns: I am interpreting what you say is that knowing
what you know today it was wrong?
Dunn: Absolutely.
Stearns: And knowing what you do today that you have
to accept responsibility, you have to accept personal responsibility for what happened. That is my interpretation of what you are telling me. Is that a correct
interpretation?
Dunn: Sir, I do not accept personal responsibility for
what happened.
Stearns: Okay, okay. Mr. Chairman, I think she is basically saying she is not culpable here, and she accepts no
responsibilities for what occurred. I understand. Now,
under the circumstances, considering how you feel,
wouldn't it, at this point, occur to you that you might
want to resign because of all these problems?
Dunn: I have done so, sir.
Stearns: Okay. Okay. Okay.
Dunn: I will do so again, if you like.[47]

Dunn drew a second, ill-advised guffaw from the packed
hearing room in an exchange with committee chairman Barton,
who, like many members, questioned her claim that she believed

HP's investigators had been able to obtain private phone records simply by asking carriers to provide them:

> Barton: If I called you up, Ms. Dunn, and said, I'd like your phone records for the last six months. I'm Chairman Barton of the Energy and Commerce Committee, but I'd like to look at your phone log, would you give me that?
> Dunn: If I understood why you wanted it. . . .
> Burton: No. I call you up; would you give me it, your phone records?
> Dunn: In your position? I would give you my phone records.
> Barton: Praise the Lord. I wouldn't give you mine.
> Dunn: I hope that doesn't mean you have something to hide.

Sherbin, who listened to Dunn's testimony from a seat in the hearing room gallery, was distracted by the sight of Mark Corallo in the corner furiously working his BlackBerry. Afterward, Sherbin contrived to bump into Corallo. Sherbin said that Corallo told him that during the hearing he had texted questions to Paoletta, who in turn had relayed some of them to committee members. One of the low points of Dunn's testimony had come when she was asked to explain why the leak investigations had been code-named Kona. "That was my question," Corallo told Sherbin.[48]

Dunn did not stick around after she had finished testifying to hear Hurd, who had been granted the tactical advantage of going last and appearing alone, thus sparing him the prospect of getting into a he-said, she-said confrontation with his predecessor as HP chairman live on C-SPAN. For the most part, committee members treated Hurd with deference, in part because he was deferential himself, apologizing for what he termed a "rogue investigation" even as he accepted personal responsibility only for making sure that it never happened again. "Members of the committee, I want you to know that I am not putting myself above the breakdown that occurred," Hurd said. "I wish I had asked more questions. There are signs which I wish I had caught. I am responsible for the company, which means I am responsible for fixing it and leading it forward through this hard time."[49]

That Hurd offered what he called a "heartfelt apology" to everyone HP had pretexted was only to be expected of a corporate leader in his position, and yet initially he had balked at expressing deep regret, according to one HP insider. "This was totally alien to Hurd," this source said. "It really stuck in his throat."

Asked by Republican Michael Burgess, of Texas, if he could restore integrity to HP, Hurd paused dramatically to remove his reading glasses and said, "I will." All in all, Hurd got off easy, especially compared to the grilling Dunn had endured.

A few hours after the hearing concluded, Dunn and her entourage—Jahnke, Brosnahan, and Chatterjee—met to dissect the day's events over dinner at the Hay-Adams. The consensus was that Dunn had acquitted herself pretty well, holding her ground in the face of unrelenting skepticism while avoiding perjury traps. For her part, all that Dunn knew for sure that was she was bone weary. "I didn't get the questions I wanted to get, not that I expected to. And I thought it was a pretty unfriendly crowd," she said. "I was afraid that I might have been a little sarcastic and that could come back to haunt me."[50]

An hour into the meal, Dunn's cell phone rang. It was Hurd. She put the CEO on speaker so her companions could listen in.

It seemed to one and all that Hurd was in a state of post-hearing euphoria, positively giddy with relief. "I love you," he told Dunn, who was briefly rendered speechless by surprise. She did not respond in kind, but changed the subject. Hurd went on to critique her performance at the hearing, saying that she'd handled herself admirably overall but had unnecessarily provoked the committee by refusing to take responsibility as Rep. Stearns and others had demanded she do. "On a scale of one to ten, I give you an eleven on execution," he said. "But on tactics I give you a three." Hurd said "I love you" two more times before he hung up and ended what for Dunn had been an extremely awkward conversation. Dunn got it at last: She now believed that Hurd had sold her out to save himself; Brosnahan had uttered his last "number 23."

A week after Dunn had returned home to San Francisco from Washington, Perkins hit the jackpot in his revenge campaign against her. Already Dunn had been stripped of her chairmanship, booted off HP's board, scapegoated by Hurd and his lawyers, vilified by columnists and bloggers galore, and pilloried by a Congressional committee before a live television audience. On October 4, Dunn was indicted by the state of California on four felony counts, each of which carried a maximum penalty of three years in prison: fraudulent wire communications, wrongful use of computer data, identity theft, and conspiracy. "We intend to aggressively prosecute this case," declared Attorney General Lockyer, who simultaneously filed criminal charges against Hunsaker, DeLia, and two employees of Action Research Group.[51] Baskins, who had prepared for the worst by hiring a big-time criminal lawyer, was not charged. As for Hurd, Lockyer all but issued him a get-out-of-jail-free card: "There currently is no evidence that Mark Hurd engaged in criminal conduct," he told reporters.

The next morning, Dunn and her husband walked hand in hand through a gauntlet of photographers and reporters into the Santa Clara County courthouse in San Jose. After she made a brief appearance before a judge, they made their way back through the throng and drove a few blocks to the sheriff's department, where Dunn was booked, fingerprinted, and photographed. She made a point of smiling as brightly as she could under the circumstances, in the expectation that her mug shot soon would be appearing in newspapers everywhere. Mercifully, the photo was not leaked.

Early the next morning some of the same news photographers were waiting outside the entryway to the UCSF Medical Center when Dunn arrived for a hurried consultation with Dr. Powell. Just a few days before, a PET scan had turned up a few new hot spots on her lungs, and Dunn had to decide whether to submit to another round of chemotherapy. This time, Dunn denied the paparazzi their money shot by walking into the clinic arm in arm with a fellow patient. Dr. Powell tried to lighten the mood with a quip. "It doesn't matter if they don't want you at HP," she said. "There is always a place for you here at the cancer center."[52] Dunn, now America's most notorious cancer patient, laughed long and hard. She had lived so long in the shadow of death that she no longer feared it. What Dunn did dread was that she would not live long enough to stand trial and clear her name.

* * *

THE COMBINATION OF Dunn's indictment and the one-sided Congressional hearings served to settle the matter of Spygate culpability in journalistic terms. Even the news outlets that in mid-September had begun to home in on Hurd and to raise pointed questions about his role in the leak investigations now moved on to other stories and other scandals, leaving the documents that would have blown holes in the narrative that Perkins had promoted and that Hurd had countenanced to gather dust in the Santa Clara County courthouse and in Congressional archives.

It did not help that several of the most experienced HP beat reporters were severely constrained by legal considerations. Peter Burrows and Ben Elgin of *Business Week* stopped covering HP altogether after they joined fellow BW reporter Roger Crockett, *New York Times* reporter John Markoff, and the *Times* itself in seeking financial compensation from Hewlett-Packard for having pretexted their telephone records. (*Business Week* did not participate.) HP settled with this group, averting a threatened lawsuit by coughing up an undisclosed sum thought to be considerably less than the several million dollars apiece that the reporters had sought.[53] CNET and its three pretexted reporters—Dawn Kawamoto, Tom Krazit, and Stephen Shankland—did sue HP, alleging invasion of privacy.[54] This suit is still pending.

HP also settled a civil suit brought against it by Attorney General Lockyer's office over the pretexting of phone records. The company paid $2,500 for each violation of California's unfair business practices law, or $14.5 million in total.[55] In return, the AG's office agreed not to pursue any more civil claims against HP or any of its officers or directors. As far as the state was concerned, Hurd and HP were home free.

HP also got off with a wrist slap from the Securities Exchange Commission. The SEC ruled that HP had violated federal law in failing to accurately disclose why Perkins had resigned from the board in May 2005. However, the agency merely issued a cease and desist order as part of an agreement in which HP promised not to do again what it did not have to admit having done in the first place. "HP acted in what it believed to be a proper manner," declared Michael Holston, who had replaced Baskins as general counsel.[56]

Meanwhile, as a defendant in a pending criminal case Dunn was unable to defend herself publicly even after Perkins denounced her anew in a speech at a San Francisco venture capital conference in February 2007, that marked the beginning of his advance publicity campaign for *Valley Boy*, which was due out in October. Brosnahan was livid and issued a statement that sounded more like an invitation to a duel than a typical lawyer's riposte. "I am sorry that Patricia Dunn must endure Mr. Perkins's cowardly attacks," he declared. "He is a bully, and he is bullying the wrong people."[57]

The state's criminal case against Dunn proved short-lived. A month after Lockyer brought charges against Dunn, he was elected California state treasurer and was replaced as attorney general by a nationally known Democrat, former governor and Oakland mayor Edmund "Jerry" Brown Jr. A few weeks after Brown took office, the AG's office offered to drop its felony charges against Dunn, Hunsaker, and DeLia if each pleaded guilty to a single misdemeanor charge.[58] Brosnahan refused to even discuss it. "We said, in the words of the song, 'take your misdemeanor and shove it,'" he recalled. "Our attitude was that there was going to be a trial and we were going to win."[59]

On March 14, 2007, Judge Ray Cunningham of the Santa Clara County Superior Court dismissed all charges against Dunn. In the judgment of the court, the state lacked sufficient evidence to even bring Dunn to trial. Judge Cunningham also agreed to dismiss a reduced misdemeanor charge against Hunsaker, DeLia, and Matthew DePante of Action Research after each of them had performed ninety-six hours of community service. (Dunn was not required to perform community service.) Judge Cunningham had proposed this resolution of the case to the AG's office, which had signed off on it.

Brosnahan was exultant at the outcome, though he did regret the lost opportunity to get Perkins on the stand. "When it comes to cross-examining Mr. Perkins, I had delusions of adequacy," Brosnahan said. "I don't know that Tom does all that well out in the open. I think he's good from behind trees."[60]

For her part, Dunn was hugely relieved yet did not find this a completely satisfying outcome. The dismissal of charges eliminated the threat of jail time, but it also deprived her of the uniquely potent remedial powers of a not-guilty verdict at what would have been a highly publicized trial. Dunn's disgrace was front-page news for days on end; her vindication was a one-day story buried inside. Dunn did continue with a highly selective public relations campaign that included a *60 Minutes* profile and a James Stewart article in *The New Yorker*, among other Sitrick-supervised initiatives. However, their cumulative impact fell far short of the hoped-for exoneration. In the court of popular opinion, Dunn was still the Chairman Who Spied on Her Board.

"I have resisted advice from many respected sources that I should 'go on offense' to reclaim my reputation regardless of any harm it might to do H-P to raise this issue in the public," Dunn wrote in September 2007, in an email to Hurd, Bob Ryan, Dick Hackborn, and the other members of HP's board. "I have turned down countless interview requests from the media. My response to these urgings has been to say that I simply want to move on, and that I continue to hope that in time the Company would do what it could to set the record straight about me."

What prompted Dunn to write this message to her former colleagues was the impending publication of *Valley Boy* and what she suspected were Perkins's renewed efforts to persuade federal prosecutors to indict her. "The scenario that has been described to me is that he is seeking to orchestrate a book launch with the filing of federal charges so that he can 'finish me off,'" Dunn wrote, adding that Hurd had told her recently that he would "try to persuade Tom that publishing the book with Chapter One as written was 'unacceptable.' I don't know what influence individually or collectively the Board may feel it has with Tom, but I urge you to use it, in the interests of the Company, to convince him that he should leave me alone."[61]

If Hurd did indeed try to get Perkins to back off, he failed; *Valley Boy* was published with only slight modifications. Its first chapter consisted of an account of the role Perkins had played in the ouster of first Carly Fiorina and then Pattie Dunn. In essence, Perkins repeated the various accusations against Dunn that he had first assayed in his post-resignation emails and letters, adding the occasional new dramatic flourish here and there. Perkins had not expected the May 2006 board meeting to be his last. "I arrived early and Pattie cornered me," he wrote.

> She said that she had the goods on the leaker. When I asked how, I couldn't believe her response. Over the past many months, HP had employed a team of security experts. She took me into their room, where a table was filled with electronic gear, unfamiliar to me. Pattie said that it could detect the presence of "bugs" over a wide area, and even suppress them. She said that these experts, or others, had otherwise obtained all of the personal telephone connections for target board members for the

period of the leak. They were tracing calls not just made
from HP, but from the directors' homes, cell phones, and
so forth. I was amazed![62]

Dunn was hurt less by what she characterized as Perkins's
"lies and distortions" than by the fact that they were swallowed
whole by the majority of the journalists who either reviewed the
book or interviewed its author on his victory lap of a book promotion tour. A piece in the *Mercury News* put it this way:

> Perkins makes it clear that he had considered Dunn un-
> worthy of HP long before he angrily resigned from HP's
> board. He did so after learning that she had authorized
> the clandestine investigations into the unauthorized dis-
> closure of boardroom discussions that finger his friend
> George Keyworth as 'the leaker.' Not one to go quietly,
> Perkins forced HP leaders to oh-so-gradually own up to
> the company's skullduggery and endure the world-class
> scandal they richly deserved.[63]

In 2008, the Australian technology magazine *PC Authority*
bent its own selection criteria in its eagerness to include Dunn,
HP's ex-chairman, on its list of the ten worst technology chief
executives, and to hail Perkins. "Dunn, of course, was the person
who masterminded HP's 2006 investigation over the scores of
boardroom leaks," the magazine explained. "The irony is that
it were not for the honorable nature of one HP director this story
would never have got out."[64]

* * *

WHEN I FIRST met with Perkins in his office in May 2009, the hero's mantle did not appear to be resting lightly on the Spygate whistleblower. Perkins not only sighed deeply but squirmed in his chair at my first mention of Dunn's name. "Pattie loathes and detests me," he said. "I mean, I've ruined her life in a way. I have. I know that. . . . I decided to focus my wrath 100 percent on Pattie Dunn and not even a little bit on Mark Hurd. OK, why? Because as bad as the whole thing was and as bad as losing Keyworth was and so on, it was not remotely as important as beating IBM and Dell and keeping Mark Hurd in the saddle—for the shareholders, including me as a shareholder. And so I did what I did."

That Hurd not only survived Spygate but also benefited from it—replacing Dunn as chairman and consolidating his control over HP's unruly board—was perhaps the truest measure of the brilliance of Perkins's stage management of the scandal. Hurd "is a good poker player and he played his cards pretty well," Perkins said. "He skated quite free of the whole spying thing, partly because I helped."[65]

For her part, Dunn was unwilling to either forgive or forget. "I think at the base of it all I wasn't impressed enough with Tom to make him happy," she said. "I know he's done some great things. But what I saw was an insecure, lonely old man who offended a lot of people without knowing it by pushing his greatness around. I tried at one level to humor Tom and to cater to Tom and to give him his way whenever I could—whenever it didn't matter. But I think he knew that at the bottom of it I wasn't going to give way when it did matter, and he just couldn't tolerate that."[66]

As much as Perkins hurt Dunn, Hurd wounded her just as deeply, because she admired the CEO and trusted him implicitly. "In every conversation I had with Mark he was as outraged as I was about Perkins's behavior," Dunn said. "On more than one occasion he said to me, 'You're going to beat this guy out of the bushes and I'm going to shoot him out of the sky.' I felt a lot of support from Mark, even past the point where everybody and his brother told me he'd thrown me under the bus. I do feel that if we had stood together, we could have faced Tom down. Mark had a tough set of circumstances to deal with, but in my mind it still comes back to, where was his spine?"[67]

In his five years as HP's chief executive, Hurd has ascended from semi-obscurity to stardom. His ability to bring focus and discipline to the management of the disheveled businesses that he inherited from his prima donna of a predecessor, Carly Fiorina, has won him as many admirers on Wall Street as in Silicon Valley. HP's confident, smoothly handled $13.9 billion acquisition of Electronic Data Services in 2008 cinched Hurd's climb into the executive-suite stratosphere. Over the last few years, his name has popped up on numerous lists of America's best CEOs.

However, the Hurd of Spygate was not the likable straight arrow whose forthright smile graces the cover of business magazines with increasing frequency. This Hurd was a dissembling corporate politician who nimbly dodged and weaved his way through a boardroom riven by personal animosities and philosophical differences. Dunn and Perkins were archenemies, but somehow each of them admired Hurd and counted him as an ally in their war for boardroom dominance. In the end, though, Perkins's pursuit of revenge forced Hurd to choose between publicly admitting his own culpability for HP's errant leak investigation or turning on Dunn. This was a high-order test of moral character, and Hurd flunked it big time, becoming the main instrument of Perkins's revenge scheme.

Not even Perkins had had the temerity to demand reinstatement to the HP board, but he did manage to arrange the next best thing in early 2008. Perkins, a longtime director of News Corp., turned Hurd into a big-game trophy of sorts by arranging for Rupert Murdoch to invite HP's CEO onto the board, as well. Or, as a Reuters headline put it, "HP Chief joins whistle blower on News Corp. board."[68]

Dunn's post-Spygate life was not without its consolations. Several of her former HP colleagues reached out to her behind the scenes to say that they regretted having allowed themselves to be stampeded by Hurd into forcing her off the board. Meanwhile, Stanford's Joseph Grundfest, Yale's Jeffrey Sonnenfeld, and other business "thought leaders" who had taken the time to research the goings-on at HP embraced Dunn as a kind of martyr of the corporate governance movement. As Sonnenfeld put it, "Pattie Dunn was practicing good governance by wanting to show the leak to the full board. The good ol' boy stuff had to end, and that was what Pattie was doing."[69] Dunn accepted invitations to make the keynote address at meetings organized by the Corporate Directors Forum and other prestigious governance groups, and she joined the board of directors at Stanford's new Arthur and Toni Rembe Rock Center for Corporate Governance.

Nor did Dunn emerge entirely the loser from the power struggle in which she represented the post–Sarbanes-Oxley world of accountability and governance and Perkins the chancy, ends-justify-the-means culture of Silicon Valley. A board that had been dominated by relatives and cronies of HP's founders at the time Dunn joined in 1998 now has turned over entirely. The directors who supplanted HP's old guard are not the sort of Silicon Valley luminaries that Perkins championed, but top executives from big, establishment companies like the one Dunn herself ran. Across the Valley, technology companies have followed HP's lead in adding seasoned governance experts to their boards, much to the disgust of Perkins, who has taken to railing in speeches and op-ed essays against "compliance" boards.

But Dunn must live with the bitter irony of knowing that what started out on her part as a quest to bring order and decorum to HP's board of directors ended as an out-of-control investigation that tarred her as a villain while ennobling her archenemy into a hero. Was Dunn overly confident of the corporate close-combat skills she had honed to a fine edge in her rise to the top of Barclays Global Investors? Was she too clever by half in hastening Perkins's self-destruction as an HP director? Was she altogether too willing to trust in the prophylactic powers of rules and procedures, not to mention the pro forma reassurances of lawyers? Yes on all counts. Dunn should have tried to call off HP's investigators the moment they strayed into accessing personal phone records. But the same could be said, and even more emphatically, of Hurd, a CEO revered on Wall Street for his mastery of operational detail.

In September 2007, a year almost to the day after Dunn was forced from HP's board, Hurd called her at home, ostensibly to update her on the company's progress in dealing with various Spygate-related lawsuits brought not only by pretexted reporters but also by disgruntled shareholders. "My takeaway at this point was that Mark was calling to let me know he and the company have kept a lot of potential suits out of my hair and I should therefore be grateful. I couldn't believe the gall here," Dunn reported in an email to Brosnahan. "I told him that as far as these suits go, 'bring 'em on—c'mon down—because none of this should have ever happened.' . . . I feel like suing Perkins AND

HP and getting the full story out."[70] Instead, Dunn chose to hold her legal fire and instead cooperate with the writing of this book, in hopes that it might spark a reappraisal of HP Spygate before the inexorable progress of cancer ended the threat that her stubborn survival poses to Hurd's reputation.

NOTES

In 2006, Hewlett-Packard turned over thousands of emails and other documents to the House Energy and Commerce Committee. These documents are listed below by the filing numbers assigned to them by House investigators, i.e., HP0019676 or PD00083.

CHAPTER ONE

1. Michael S. Malone, *Bill and Dave* (New York: Portfolio, 2007), p. 1.
2. Deloitte Inc., "Asset protection; defending against industrial espionage," 2007, www.deloitte.com/assets/Dcom-UnitedKingdom/Local%20Assets/Documents/UK_ERS_ElecEspionage.pdf.
3. Mark Landler, "Phone Giant in Germany Stirs a Furor," *New York Times*, May 27, 2008.
4. Spiegel staff, "Did Deutsche Telekom Spy on Journalists and Board Members," Spiegel Online International, May 26, 2008.
5. "Chairing the Board: The Case for Independent Leadership in Corporate North America," The Milstein Center for Corporate Governance and Performance, Yale School of Management, 2009, p. 11.
6. Ibid.
7. Anthony Bianco interview with George Keyworth.
8. David Kaplan, *Mine's Bigger* (New York: HarperCollins, 2007), p. 69.
9. Ibid.
10. Anthony Bianco interview with Tom Perkins.
11. Ibid.
12. Thomas J. Perkins, *Valley Boy* (New York: Gotham Books, 2007), p. 52.

CHAPTER TWO

1. Perkins, *Valley Boy*, p. 44.

2. Ibid., p. 45.

3. Anthony Bianco interview with Tom Perkins.

4. Perkins, *Valley Boy*, p. 49.

5. Ibid., p. 52.

6. Ibid., p. 54.

7. Ibid.

8. Anthony Bianco interview with Narinder Kapany.

9. Jeff Hecht, *City of Light: The Story of Fiber Optics* (Oxford: Oxford University Press, 2003), p. 59.

10. Ibid., p. 70.

11. Ibid., p. 69.

12. The first big-time laser-based product—the supermarket barcode scanner—would not debut until 1974, followed by the laserdisc player in 1978 and the compact disc player in 1982.

13. Bianco interview with Perkins.

14. Perkins, *Valley Boy*, p. 58.

15. Ibid., p. 57.

16. Bianco interview with Kapany.

17. Bianco interview with Perkins.

18. Perkins, *Valley Boy*, p. 61.

19. Bianco interview with Kapany.

20. Bianco interview with Perkins.

21. Anthony Bianco interview with Richard Jaenicke.

22. Joel Selvin, "For the unrepentant patriarch of LSD, long, strange trip winds back to the Bay Area," *San Francisco Chronicle*, July 12, 2007.

23. Bianco interview with Perkins.

24. Perkins, *Valley Boy*, p. 66.

25. Anthony Bianco interview with Herbert Dwight Jr.

26. Bianco interview with Jaenicke.

27. "Spectra-Physics Reported Paying $5 Million for U-Labs; Jaenicke Going to Mountain View," *Laser Focus*, February, 1970.

28. "Optics Technology Inc Picks Ralph Munziato [sic] as President," *Wall Street Journal*, October 2, 1972. (The correct spelling of the new president's surname is Nunziato.)

29. Bianco interview with Perkins.

30. Ibid.

31. Perkins, *Valley Boy*, p. 79.

32. Phyllis Louise Egan, "Hewlett Packard: From Instrumentation to Computers: A Study of Strategy and Structure," (Master of Business Administration thesis, San Francisco State University, 1984), p. 31.

33. Kip Crosby, "A Core Plane in Amber: An Interview with Barney Oliver, Part One," *The Analytical Engine, Journal of the Computer History Association of California*, Volume 2, Number 3, May, 1995, p. 18.

34. Bianco interview with Perkins.

35. Perkins, *Valley Boy*, p. 77.

36. Bianco interview with Perkins.

37. Anthony Bianco interview with Roy Clay.

38. Bianco interview with Perkins.

39. Anthony Bianco interview with William Terry.

40. Bianco interview with Perkins.

41. Perkins, *Valley Boy*, p. 79.

42. Bianco interview with Perkins.

43. David Packard, *The HP Way* (New York: HarperCollins, 1995), p. 102.

44. Arthur L. Norberg, "An Interview with Bernard More Oliver," Charles Babbage Institute for the History of Information Processing, August 9, 1985, and April 14, 1986, p. 79.

45. Perkins, *Valley Boy*, p. 81.

46. Ibid., p. 83.

47. Michael Malone, *Bill and Dave*, p. 179.

48. "Slower Growth is Smarter Management," *Business Week*, June 9, 1975.

49. Bianco interview with Perkins.

50. Perkins, *Valley Boy*, p. 143.

CHAPTER THREE

1. Anthony Bianco interview with Tom Perkins.

2. David A. Kaplan, *The Silicon Boys* (New York: William Morrow, 1999), p. 180.

3. Bianco interview with Perkins.

4. John W. Wilson, *The New Venturers* (Reading, MA; Addison-Wesley Publishing, 1985), p. 128.

5. Bianco interview with Perkins.

6. Ibid.

7. Ibid.

8. Anthony Bianco interview with Herb Dwight.

9. Perkins, *Valley Boy*, p. 109.

10. Bianco interview with Perkins.

11. Bianco interview with Dwight.

12. Bianco interview with Perkins.

13. Ibid.

14. Jim Hansell, *Money Is No Object* (Santa Clara, CA: MCD Publishing, 2009), p. 16.

15. Ibid., p. xvii.

16. Ibid., p. 43.

17. Bianco interview with Perkins.

18. Perkins, *Valley Boy*, p. 138. In his written account of the Focus fiasco, Perkins used "Tony" as a pseudonym for McNeilly.

19. McNeilly finally completed a drug treatment program and went on to found two more tech companies. He was laying plans for a third when he died of a heart attack in 2005 at age sixty-six. Not long after Focus Semiconductor failed, Jim Hansell had dinner with his old boss. McNeilly had completely lost interest in Focus but "wanted to know anything I could tell him about Perkins," Hansell recalled.

20. Bianco interview with Perkins.

21. Ibid.

22. Ibid.

23. Ibid.

24. Wilson, *The New Venturers*, p. 78.

25. Brian O'Reilly, "How Jimmy Treybig Turned Tough," *Fortune*, May 25, 1987.

26. Anthony Bianco interview with Jimmy Treybig.

27. Ibid.

28. Ibid.

29. Wilson, *The New Venturers*, p. 78.

30. Fred A. Middleton, "First Chief Financial Officer at Genentech, 1978–1984," an oral history conducted in 2001 by Glenn E. Bugos for the Regional Oral History Office, The Bancroft Library, University of California, Berkeley, 2002, p. 13.

31. Perkins, *Valley Boy*, p. 120.

32. Perkins, "Kleiner Perkins, Venture Capital, and the Chairmanship of Genentech," an oral history conducted in 2001 by Glenn E. Bugos for the Regional Oral History Office, The Bancroft Library, University of California, Berkeley, 2002, p. 6.

33. Wilson, *The New Venturers*, p. 80.

34. Middleton, "First Chief Financial Officer at Genentech," p. 13.

35. Ibid., pp. 28–29.

36. Perkins, *Valley Boy*, p. 124.

37. Perkins, "Kleiner Perkins, Venture Capital, and the Chairmanship of Genentech," p. 30.

38. Kaplan, *Mine's Bigger*, p. 79.

39. Perkins, *Valley Boy*, p. 113.

40. Bianco interview with Treybig.

41. Ibid.

42. Philip L. Zweig, *Wriston* (New York: Crown Publishers, 1995), p. 834.

43. Robert A. Swanson, "Co-founder, CEO, and Chairman of Genentech, Inc, 1976–1996," an oral history conducted in 1996 and 1997 by Sally Smith Hughes, Regional Oral History Office, Bancroft Library, University of California, Berkeley, 2001, p. 50.

44. Bianco interview with Perkins.

45. Ibid. While serving on the Corning board, Perkins again crossed paths with Narinder Kapany, who had submitted a request for funding to Corning's venture capital arm. Perkins was asked to review Kapany's proposal and happily obliged. "I shot that down," he said.

46. Perkins, "Kleiner Perkins, Venture Capital, and the Chairmanship of Genentech," pp. 16, 23.

47. Ibid., p. 16.

48. G. Kirk Raab, "CEO At Genentech, 1990–1995," an oral history conducted in 2002 by Glenn E. Bugos for the Regional Oral History Office, The Bancroft Library, University of California, Berkeley, 2003, p. 21.

49. Perkins, "Kleiner Perkins, Venture Capital, and the Chairmanship of Genentech," p.16.

50. Bianco interview with Perkins.

51. Perkins, "Kleiner Perkins, Venture Capital, and the Chairmanship of Genentech," p. 16.

52. Genentech continued to operate as a separate company, though Roche had an option to buy out the company entirely. Genentech still traded on the New York Stock Exchange, and Roche got only two seats on Genentech's thirteen-member board.

53. Perkins, "Kleiner Perkins, Venture Capital, and the Chairmanship of Genentech," p. 38.

54. Ibid., p. 41.

55. Ibid., p. 15.

56. Bianco interview with Treybig.

57. Ibid.

58. Middleton, "First Chief Financial Officer at Genentech," p. 13.

CHAPTER FOUR

1. Anthony Bianco interview with Tom Perkins.

2. Ibid.

3. Matt Marshall, "VC legend leads charge for HP-Compaq," San Jose *Mercury News*, December 23, 2001.

4. Dave Kirby, "VC's ego shows through," San Jose *Mercury News*, December 30, 2001.

5. Thomas J. Perkins, "Venture capitalist fires back on his HP role," San Jose *Mercury News*, January 5, 2002.

6. Bianco interview with Perkins.

7. George Anders, *Perfect Enough* (New York: Portfolio, 2003), p. 189.

8. Bianco interview with Perkins.

9. Anthony Bianco interview with Pattie Dunn.

10. Bianco interview with Perkins.

11. Anthony Bianco interview with Fred Grauer.

12. Bianco interview with Dunn.

13. Lucy Kellaway, "Soft skills, hard finance," *Financial Times*, May 21, 1999.

14. The New York Public Library for the Performing Arts, in Lincoln Center, has a folder of clippings about Cross and Dunn and also the duo that preceded it, Rome and Dunn.

15. "Henry Dunn Dies; Vaudevillian, 66," *New York Times*, February 13, 1966.

16. A transcript of Dunn's remarks can be found in "Guide to the Associated Actors and Artistes of America (Four A's) Records 1909–1995," Tamiment Library/Robert F. Wagner Labor Archives, Elmer Holmes Bobst Library, Box 8, Folder 3.

17. Patricia Sellers, "Behind Every Successful Woman There Is . . . A Woman," *Fortune*, October 25, 1999.

18. Anthony Bianco interview with Aileen Deborah (Dunn) Lammers.

19. Ibid.

20. Bianco interview with Dunn.

21. Bianco interview with Lammers.

22. Bianco interview with Dunn.

23. Ibid.

24. Anthony Bianco interview with Cary Zellerbach.

25. Anthony Bianco interview with John Casey.

26. Bianco interview with Dunn.

27. Anthony Bianco interview with William Jahnke.

28. Bianco interview with Lammers.

29. Anthony Bianco interview with William Fouse.

30. Bianco interview with Dunn.

31. Ibid.

32. Bianco interview with Grauer.

33. Julie Rohrer, "What went wrong at Wells Fargo?," *Institutional Investor*, January 1984.

34. Anthony Bianco interview with Donald Luskin.

35. Anthony Bianco interview with Martin Taylor.

36. Anthony Bianco interview with Jeffrey Skelton.

37. Ibid.

38. Bianco interview with Dunn.

39. Bianco interview with Taylor.

40. Ibid.

41. Bianco interview with Dunn.

42. Ibid.

43. Anthony Bianco interview with Andrea Redmond.

44. Peter Burrows Burrow, *Backfire* (Hoboken, NJ: John Wiley & Sons, 2003), p. 130.

45. Anders, *Perfect Enough*, p. 61.

46. Ibid.

47. Bianco interview with Dunn.

48. Anthony Bianco interview with Matthew Barger.

49. Bianco interview with Dunn.

50. Ibid.

51. Bianco interview with Barger.

52. Anthony Bianco with Dr. Bethan Powell.

53. Bianco interview with Dunn.

CHAPTER FIVE

1. Anthony Bianco interview with Jay Keyworth.

2. Dan Stober and Ian Hoffman, *A Convenient Spy* (New York: Simon & Schuster, 2001), p. 50.

3. Ibid., p. 50. CIA operatives presented Keyworth with a cobalt-blue toilet seat "as a jibe at his fastidiousness."

4. Ibid., p. 52.

5. Ibid., p. 55.

6. Ibid.

7. James Risen, "In China, Physicist Learns, He Tripped Between Useful Exchange and Security Breach," *New York Times*, August 1, 1999.

8. Martin Anderson, *Revolution* (Stanford, CA: Hoover Institution Press, Stanford University, 1990), p. 91.

9. Gregg Herken, *Cardinal Choices* (Stanford, CA: Stanford University Press, 2000), p. 201.

10. Anderson, *Revolution*, p. 91.

11. William J. Broad, *Teller's War* (New York: Simon & Schuster, 1992), p. 104.

12. Herken, *Cardinal Choices*, p. 201.

13. Ibid., p. 207.

14. Bianco interview with Keyworth.

15. Broad, *Teller's War*, p. 128.

16. Herkin, *Cardinal Choices*, p. 215.

17. "Reagan Adviser Accuses Media of Tearing Down U.S.," *Los Angeles Times*, February 23, 1985.

18. Bianco interview with Keyworth.

19. Ibid.

20. Ibid.

21. Ibid.

22. Ibid.

23. Carly Fiorina, *Tough Choices* (New York: Portfolio, 2006), p. 209.

24. Anthony Bianco interview with Tom Perkins.

25. Fiorina, *Tough Choices*, p. 280.

26. Bianco interview with Perkins.

27. Fiorina, *Tough Choices,* p. 190.

28. Ibid., p. 305.

29. Peter Burrows, "Ousting Carly Was Just the Start," *Business Week*, March 7, 2005.

30. Anthony Bianco interview with Pattie Dunn.

31. Fiorina, *Tough Choices*, pp. 280–281.

32. Bianco interview with Keyworth.

33. Fiorina, *Tough Choices*, p. 283.

34. Ibid.

35. Bianco interview with Dunn.

36. Fiorina, *Tough Choices*, p. 281.

37. Ibid.

38. Ibid.

39. Fiorina, *Tough Choices*, p. 190.

40. Bianco interview with Dunn.

41. Ibid.

42. Fiorina, *Tough Choices*, p. 294.

43. Keyworth email to Dunn, "Afterthought," January 6, 2005, provided to the author by Dunn.

44. Bianco interview with Dunn.

45. "Confidential to Independent Directors Only: Board Communication to the CEO," Final Draft, January 10, 2005, provided to the author by Dunn.

46. Fiorina, *Tough Choices*, p. 287.

47. Bianco interview with Keyworth.

48. Fiorina, *Tough Choices*, p. 287.

49. Dunn email to Knowling, "Quick update," January 11, 2005, and Knowling email to Dunn, January 11, 2005. Both provided to the author by Dunn.

50. Fiorina, *Tough Choices*, p. 290.

51. Anthony Bianco interview with Robert Sherbin.

52. Fiorina, *Tough Choices*, p. 249.

53. Anders, *Perfect Enough*, p. 196.

54. Anthony Bianco interview with Robert Sherbin.

55. James B. Stewart, "The Kona Files," *The New Yorker*, February 19, 2007.

56. Bianco interview with Perkins.

57. Perkins email to Dunn, "Telephone Call," January 29, 2005, provided to the author by Dunn.

58. Bianco interview with Dunn.

59. Ibid.

60. Ibid.

61. Bianco interview with Perkins.

62. Anthony Bianco interview with William Jahnke.

63. Patience Wheatcroft, "A stiletto heel is lodged in Fiorina's back," *The Times* of London, February 10, 2005.

64. The author obtained a copy of the letter from Dunn. Fiorina never answered the letter, but did reply in a fashion by portraying Dunn unflatteringly in *Tough Choices*. Before it was published, Fiorina sent a formal business letter to Dunn asking permission to reprint her farewell letter. Dunn responded that she would grant permission only if she was given an advance look at the pertinent part of Fiorina's manuscript. Carly complained but complied, merely mentioning Dunn's letter in her book.

CHAPTER SIX

1. Anthony Bianco interview with Jay Keyworth.

2. "HP Chairman and CEO Carly Fiorina Steps Down," HP press release, February 9, 2005, http://www.hp.com/hpinfo/newsroom/press/2005/050209a .html.

3. "PR Team Background Information for Directors," February 24, 2006, PDH00006546.

4. Eric Dash, "From a Woman in Front of the Curtain to One Preferring to Work Behind It," *New York Times*, February 11, 2005.

5. Dunn email to Knowling, "Update on Search Firm Selection Process," February 10, 2005, PDHM00008175.

6. Anthony Bianco interview with Pattie Dunn.

7. Bianco interview with Keyworth.

8. Ibid.

9. Fiorina, *Tough Choices*, p. 281.

10. Anthony Bianco interview with Tom Perkins.

11. Bianco interview with Dunn.

12. Hackborn email to Dunn, "Thank you," September 24, 2006, provided to the author by Dunn.

13. Bianco interview with Dunn.

14. Pui-Wing Tam and Joann S. Lublin, "H-P Gave Fiorina $1.57 Million in Bonus Payments Last Year," *Wall Street Journal*, February 14, 2005.

15. Dunn email to Babbio, Hackborn, Knowling, et al., "Leaks," February 14, 2005, HP0014146.

16. Bianco interview with Dunn.

17. Hackborn email to Dunn, "Leaks," February 14, 2005, HP0014146.

18. Perkins email to Dunn and Keyworth, no subject, February 14, 2005, PDHM00008787.

19. Sonsini email to Dunn, Keyworth, and Perkins, "WSJ Earnings & RRA," February 17, 2005, HP0014136.

20. Carol J. Loomis, "How the HP Board KO'd Carly," *Fortune*, March 7, 2005.

21. Dunn email to Sonsini, "Lisa—could you get this to Larry?" February 22, 2005, HP0015468.

22. Ibid.

23. Bianco interview with Dunn.

24. Anthony Bianco interview with Rick Belluzzo.

25. Bianco interview with Perkins.

26. Ben Elgin, Cliff Edwards, and Peter Burrows, "Handicapping the HP Hopefuls," *Business Week*, March 8, 2005.

27. Bianco interview with Belluzzo.

28. Perkins email to Dunn and Keyworth, no subject, March 9, 2005, HP0014125.

29. Dunn email to Perkins and Keyworth, "Business Week Leak," March 9, 2005, HP0014125.

30. Anthony Bianco interview with Andrea Redmond.

31. Ibid.

32. Quentin Hardy, "The UnCarly," *Forbes*, March 12, 2007.

33. Therese Poletti, "HP's Boss Gets to Work," San Jose *Mercury News*, April 2, 2005.

34. Ashlee Vance, "Does H.P. Need a Dose of Anarchy?" *New York Times*, April 26, 2009.

35. Tom Perkins, *Valley Boy*, p. 9.

36. Sherbin email to Dunn, cc Baskins, "Leak re timing of ceo announcement," March 20, 2005, provided to the author by Dunn.

37. Bianco interview with Dunn.

38. Ibid.

39. Ben Elgin and Peter Burrows, "HP's Next Chief: One Tough Call," *Business Week*, March 28, 2005.

40. Pui-Wing Tam, "H-P Picks NCR Chief Hurd to Take Over Struggling Giant," *Wall Street Journal*, March 30, 2005.

41. Sherbin email to Dunn, Baskins, and Winkler, "WSJ Leak," March 31, 2005, HP0014123.

42. Ben Elgin and Peter Burrows, "Memo to Mark Hurd," *Business Week*, April 1, 2005.

43. Interview of Mark Hurd by Bahram Seyedin-Noor and Bryan Ketroser (Wilson Sonsini Goodrich & Rosati), memo to HP Securities Litigation Team, August 25, 2006.

44. Peter Waldman, Don Clark, and Steve Stecklow, "H-P CEO Might Have Had Bigger Probe Role," *Wall Street Journal*, September 21, 2006.

CHAPTER SEVEN

1. Dunn email to Perkins and Keyworth, "Piper," February 15, 2005, PDHM 00008841.

2. Anthony Bianco interview with Pattie Dunn.

3. Interview of Kevin Huska by Bahram Seyedin-Noor and Bryan Ketroser (Wilson Sonsini Goodrich & Rosati), memo to HP Securities Litigation Team, August 25, 2006.

4. Menz email to O'Neill and Huska, "Call Detail Search for Dialed Number," February 15, 2005, HP0013254.

5. Huska email to Menz, "Request for Assistance—Mobile Phone Number," February 18, 2005, HP0015491.

6. Menz email to Huska, "Request for Assistance—Mobile Phone Number," February 18, 2005, HP0015491.

7. Dunn email to Hackborn, "Leaks," February 17, 2005, HP0023314.

8. DeLia email to Dunn, "Operation Robin," March 14, 2005, PDHM 0009081.

9. Dunn email to Hackborn, Babbio, et al., "Board Update, February 20, 2005, provided to the author by Dunn.

10. Bianco interview with Dunn.

11. Huska draft email, "WSJ Article dated 2/10/05," May 19, 2005, HP0015494.

12. Action Assignment Form 05–01–396, March 7, 2005.

13. Dunn email to DeLia, "Important on HP," April 20, 2005, SOS 0004.

14. DeLia email to Dunn, "Proposal," April 19, 2005, HP0010496.

15. Bianco interview with Dunn.

16. Interview of Ann Baskins by Bahram Seyedin-Noor and Bryan Ketroser (Wilson Sonsini Goodrich & Rosati), memo to HP Securities Litigation Team, August 21, 2006.

17. Patricia Dunn, "My Role in the Hewlett-Packard Leak Investigation," Submission to the Sub-Committee on Investigations, House Energy and Commerce Committee, September, 2006.

18. Dunn email to DeLia, "Project Kona," April 19, 2005, HP4723.

19. Dunn email to DeLia, "Project Kona," April 19, 2005, SOS 0001.

20. Anthony Bianco interview with Bob Sherbin.

21. DeLia email to Gentilucci, "Special projects," May 5, 2006, HP0012402.

22. Peter Burrows and Ben Elgin, "An SEC Query for HP," *Business Week*, June 13, 2005.

23. Dunn email to Babbio, Hurd, Keyworth, et al., "Brief update," June 11, 2005, HP0009517.

24. Perkins email to Dunn, no subject, June 12, 2005, PDHM00006241.

25. Interview of Baskins by Noor and Ketroser, August 21, 2006.

26. "Project Kona et al.: Preliminary Draft Findings," June 14, 2005, HO03559.

27. Thomas email to Lynch, no subject, November 11, 2005, HP0016503.

28. Gentilucci HP Investigative Memo, "Meeting with Dr. Jay Keyworth," November 17, 2005, HP0017791.

29. Peter Burrows, "Can This Really Be Hewlett-Packard?" *Business Week*, December 19, 2005.

30. Bianco interview with Dunn.

31. Email exchange between Dunn and Sherbin, "Keyworth quote in Business Week," December 8, 2005, HP0018564.

CHAPTER EIGHT

1. Perkins email to Dunn and Keyworth, "The News from Corvallis," April 20, 2005, provided to the author by Dunn.

2. Anthony Bianco interview with Tom Perkins.

3. Baskins email to Hurd and Dunn, "Meeting notes," April 20, 2005, PDHM0006218.

4. Quentin Hardy, "The UnCarly," *Forbes*, March 12, 2007.

5. Anthony Bianco interview with Pattie Dunn.

6. Hurd email to Dunn, no subject, June 6, 2006, provided to the author by Dunn.

7. Bianco interview with Dunn.

8. Tom Perkins, *Valley Boy*, p. 10.

9. Bianco interview with Perkins.

10. Bianco interview with Dunn.

11. Ibid.

12. Bianco interview with Perkins.

13. Anthony Bianco interview with David Nygren.

14. Nygren email to Dunn, cc Behan, "Board Compensation," June 29, 2005, provided to the author by Dunn.

15. Bianco interview with Perkins.

16. Bianco interview with Dunn.

17. Ibid.

18. Ibid.

19. Bianco interviews with Perkins and Dunn.

20. Ibid.

21. Ibid.

22. Bianco interview with Perkins.

23. Ibid.

24. Bianco interview with Dunn.

25. Ibid.

26. Michael S. Malone, "The Un-Carly," *Wall Street Journal*, April 14, 2007.

27. Gary Rivlin, "Hewlett-Packard to Lay Off 14,500 in Turnaround Effort," *New York Times*, July 20, 2005.

28. Baskins, "Meeting notes," April 20, 2005, PDHM0006218

29. Bianco interview with Dunn.

30. Bianco interview with Perkins.

31. Perkins email to Dunn, no subject, June 21, 2005, provided to the author by Dunn.

32. Keyworth email to Dunn, "John Hammergren," July 30, 2005, provided to the author by Dunn.

33. Dunn email to Perkins, "Sari Baldauf," December 2, 2005, provided to the author by Dunn.

34. Perkins email to Dunn, Redmond, Hurd, et al., no subject, December 9, 2005, provided to the author by Dunn.

35. James B. Stewart, "The Kona Files," *The New Yorker*, February 19, 2007.

36. Bianco interview with Perkins.

37. Perkins email to Dunn, cc Salhany, Babbio, and Hurd, no subject, November 22, 2005, provided to the author by Dunn.

38. Hurd email to Perkins and Dunn, no subject, December 2, 2005, provided to the author by Dunn.

39. Bianco interview with Perkins.

40. Anthony Bianco interview with Ray Lane.

41. Dunn email to Sonsini, "SV CEO," October 26, 2005, provided to the author by Dunn.

42. Perkins email to Hurd, no subject, February 3, 2006, provided to the author by Dunn.

43. Perkins email to Hurd, cc Dunn and Redmond, no subject, March 2, 2006, provided to the author by Dunn.

44. Hurd email to Perkins, cc Redmond and Dunn, no subject, March 3, 2006, provided to the author by Dunn.

45. Dunn and Perkins email exchange, no subject, March 2, 2006, provided to the author by Dunn.

46. Dunn, Perkins, and Hurd email exchange, "Wilf Corrigan," March 23, 2006, provided to the author by Dunn.

47. Hurd email to Perkins, cc Dunn, no subject, May 9, 2006.

48. Perkins email to Dunn, no subject, May 10, 2006, provided to the author by Dunn.

49. Dunn and Hurd email exchange, no subject, May 10, 2006, provided to the author by Dunn.

50. Perkins email to Dunn, cc Hurd, "Wilf," May 11, 2006, provided to the author by Dunn.

51. Baskins email to Dunn, "Wilf," May 18, 2006, provided to the author by Dunn.

52. Bianco interview with Perkins.

53. Interview of Ann Baskins by Bahram Seyedin-Noor and Bryan Ketroser (Wilson Sonsini Goodrich & Rosati), memo to HP Securities Litigation Team, August 21, 2006.

54. Bianco interview with Dunn.

55. Bianco interview with Perkins.

56. Bianco interview with Nygren.

57. Bianco interview with Dunn.

58. Ibid.

59. Bianco interview with Nygren.

60. Perkins email to Dunn, "3 Things," January 15, 2006, HP0009530.

61. Perkins email to Hurd, "The Off-Site/The Board," January 18, 2006, PDHMM00006344.

62. Dunn email exchange with Perkins, "The Off-Site/The Board," January 18, 2006, provided to the author by Dunn.

63. Dunn email exchange with Hurd, "Lessons learned," January 30, 2006, provided to the author by Dunn.

64. Salhany handwritten note, undated, provided to the author by Dunn.

65. Bianco interview with Dunn.

66. Dunn email to Hurd, no subject, January 30, 2006, provided to the author by Dunn.

67. Bianco interview with Perkins.

68. Bianco interview with Dunn.

69. Perkins, *Valley Boy*, p. 14.

70. Anthony Bianco interview with Jay Keyworth.

71. Bianco interview with Dunn.

CHAPTER NINE

1. Anthony Bianco interview with Jay Keyworth.

2. Dawn Kawamoto and Tom Krazit, "HP outlines long-term strategy," CNET, January 23, 2006.

3. Bianco interview with Keyworth.

4. Hurd email to Dunn, "CNET story re Board offsite," January 24, 2006, provided the author by Dunn.

5. Sherbin email to Fairbaugh, cc Gentilucci, "CONFIDENTIAL," January 20, 2006, HP0012461.

6. Sherbin email to Dunn, "Fresh board leak," January 20, 2006, HP0015603.

7. Dunn email to Perkins, "CNET story re Board offsite," January 23, 2006, HP0023223.

8. Perkins email to Dunn, "CNET story re Board offsite," January 23, 2006, HP0023223

9. Gentilucci email to Nye, McCauley, Clarence, and O'Neill, July 6, 2005, HP0015600.

10. Gentilucci email to Nye, McCauley, Clarence, and O'Neill, "Unauthorized Disclosure Task Force Concept/Ideas-Food for Thought for Call," July 6, 2005, HP0007115.

11. Anthony Bianco interview with Pattie Dunn.

12. Hunsaker email to Huska, Gentilucci, and Lynch, "Urgent FYI Confidential," January 21, 2006. This email was attached to a four-page formal memorandum that spelled out the criteria for conducting an attorney-client privileged investigation, HP0009571.

13. Baskins email exchange with Dunn, no subject, January 21, 2006, provided to the author by Dunn.

14. Dunn email to Hunsaker, "Investigation," January 27, 2006, HP 0009936.

15. Hunsaker email to Baskins, "EC cell phones," January 27, 2006, HP 00378.

16. Hunsaker email to Fimbres, "Investigation—privileged communication," January 28, 2006, HP0020911.

17. Gentilucci email to Nye, "Like to Hold a Brain Storming Session," January 24, 2006, HP0009555.

18. Nye email to Gentilucci, "On the Fly," January 25, 2006, HP0016407.

19. Security Outsourcing Solutions, "Kona II: Investigate Activity in Progress," Case #06–01–490, June 30, 2006.

20. Sherbin email to Dunn, "Three items," January 27, 2006, provided to the author by Dunn.

21. Sherbin email to Dunn, "Dawn Kawamoto CNET coverage," January 30, 2006, HP 03399.

22. Pui-Wing Tam, "Hewlett Packard's Wayman to Retire," *Wall Street Journal*, January 31, 2006.

23. Hunsaker email to DeLia, Gentilucci, Nye, and Adler, "Privileged Communication," January 31, 2006, HP00583.

24. Dunn email to Babbio, Hackborn, Hammergren, et al., "Wall Street Journal Story," January 31, 2006, HP0009417.

25. Perkins email to Dunn, "Confidential," January 31, 2006, HP0009420.

26. Dunn email to Hurd, "Confidential," January 31, 2006, HP0009420.

27. Hunsaker email to Gentilucci, "Investigation," January 28, 2006, HP 03364.

28. Hunsaker email to Adler and O'Neill, "Tracer," February 3, 2006, HP0017150.

29. Hunsaker email to DeLia, cc Gentilucci, "Directors," February 3, 2006, HP00734.

30. Hunsaker email to Baskins and Dunn, "Phase 2," February 26, 2006, HP03528.

31. Nye email to Adler, no subject, February 9, 2006, HP0007189.

32. Dunn email to Baskins and Hunsaker, "Kona," February 9, 2006, HP0021300.

33. DeLia email to Hunsaker, Gentilucci, Nye, and Adler, no subject, February 9, 2006, HP0007266.

34. Gentilucci email to DeLia, Hunsaker, Nye, and Adler, no subject, February 10, 2006, HP0007319.

35. "Jacob Goldfarb" and Kawamoto email exchange, February 15, 2006, HP 00909.

36. Hunsaker email to Baskins and Dunn, "Phase 2," February 22, 2006, HP 03528 and Hunsaker email to Nye, Adler, Gentilucci, and DeLia, "Phase 2," February 21, 2006, HP 000624.

37. Dunn email to Hunsaker and Baskins, "Phase 2," February 22, 2006, HP 03528.

38. Hunsaker email to Gentilucci, "Phase 2," February 22, 2006, HP 03813.

39. Anthony Bianco interview with Bob Sherbin.

40. DeLia email to Hunsaker, Gentilucci, Nye, and Adler, no subject, February 11, 2006, HP0007094.

41. Bianco interview with Keyworth.

42. Hunsaker email to Gentilucci, cc DeLia, no subject, April 21, 2006, HP0018734.

43. Security Outsourcing Solutions, "(Kona II)," investigative report, March 17, 2006, HP0009191.

44. Bianco interview with Keyworth.

45. Damon Darlin and Matt Richtel, "Zeroing In On Sources H.P. Used," *New York Times*, September 16, 2006.

46. Federal Trade Commission v. Action Research Group, Inc., Joseph Depante, Matthew Depante, Bryan Wagner, Cassandra Selvage, and Eye in the Sky Investigations Inc., United States District Court for the Middle District of Florida Orlando Division, Civil Action No.: 6:07-CV-0227-ORL-22JGG.

47. Action Research (Matt) email to DeLia, "Update—privileged case totals," March 11, 2006, HP4262.

48. Gentilucci email to Hunsaker, no subject, January 26, 2006, HP03334.

49. Hunsaker email exchange with Gentilucci, "phone records," January 30, 2006, HP00054.

50. Hunsaker email to DeLia, Gentilucci, Nye, and Adler, no subject, February 6, 2006, HP00321.

51. Gentilucci email to Hunsaker, DeLia, Nye, and Adler, no subject, February 6, 2006, HP0016866.

52. Nye email exchange with Adler, no subject, February 7, 2006, HP0009897.

53. DeLia email to Hunsaker, no subject, February 7, 2006, HP00058.

54. Hunsaker email to Gentilucci, "GK cell calls," March 5, 2006, HP 00436.

55. Hunsaker email exchange with Gentilucci, "Leak case," March 21, 2006, HP0007646.

56. Bianco interview with Dunn.

57. Action Research email to DeLia, no subject, April 4, 2006, HP 5663.

58. Mark Hurd, "Congressional Written Testimony," Hewlett-Packard's Pretexting Scandal hearing, Subcommittee on Oversight and Investigations, September 28, 2006, http://archives.energycommerce.house.gov/reparchives/108/Hearings/09282006hearing2042/Hurd.pdf.

59. Hunsaker email to Dunn and Baskins, "Draft Report," March 12, 2006.

60. Bianco interview with Perkins.

61. James B. Stewart, "The Kona Files," *The New Yorker*, February 19, 2007.

62. Dunn handwritten note to Sonsini, no subject, March 15, 2006, provided to the author by Dunn.

63. Lynch email to Gentilucci, "Privileged Information," March 16, 2006, HP0023994.

64. Stewart, "The Kona Files."

65. Bianco interview with Dunn.

66. Dunn email to Babbio, Hammergren, Keyworth, et al., "Board Update," May 3, 2006, provided to the author by Dunn.

67. Bianco interview with Keyworth.

68. Ibid.

69. Perkins, *Valley Boy*, p. 15.

70. Bianco interviews with Perkins, Dunn, and another director.

71. Bianco interview with Perkins.

72. Bianco interview with Dunn.

73. Stewart, "The Kona Files."

CHAPTER TEN

1. Anthony Bianco interview with Pattie Dunn.

2. Anthony Bianco interview with Tom Perkins.

3. The quote is from Stewart, "The Kona Files," *The New Yorker*. The lyric is from "Tears of a Clown."

4. Perkins email to Dunn, cc Hurd, no subject, May 21, 2006, HP0009554.

5. Dunn email to Perkins, cc Hurd and Baskins, no subject, May 21, 2006, provide to the author by Dunn.

6. Quoted in Stewart, "The Kona Files."

7. Bianco interview with Perkins.

8. Perkins email to Knight, Devoe, Wyndoe, Murdoch, et al., "Hewlett-Packard—Tom Perkins," May 29, 2006, PD 00027.

9. Perkins email to Redmond, "Hewlett-Packard—Tom Perkins," May 31, 2006, PD0027.

10. Anthony Bianco interview with Andrea Redmond.

11. Bianco interview with Perkins.

12. Ryan's talking points are attached to a Baskins email to Dunn, no subject, May 22, 2006, PD0070.

13. Bianco interview with Dunn.

14. Baskins email to Dunn, "Hewlett Packard—Tom Perkins," June 7, 2006, provided to the author by Dunn.

15. Sonsini email to Dunn, Hurd, and Baskins, "Hewlett Packard—Tom Perkins," June 7, 2006, provided to the author by Dunn.

16. Maria Bartiromo, "Inside the HP Case," *Business Week*, October 9, 2006.

17. Peter Lattman, "Issue Spotting: Larry Sonsini's Email Exchange," *Wall Street Journal* law blog, September 8, 2006.

18. Ibid.

19. Hunsaker memorandum to Baskins and Sonsini, "Response of Claims of Former BoD Member Tom Perkins," June 21, 2006. Released by the House Subcommittee on Oversight and Investigations on October 2, 2006.

20. Hunsaker email to Baskins, "KONA II," May 1, 2006, HP0019676.

21. Nye email to Crawford, "Cell Phone Information (Call Data)," March 17, 2006, HP0014011.

22. Bianco interview with Perkins.

23. Undated Perkins letter to all HP directors, cc Sonsini, Wayman, and Baskins.

24. David Kaplan, *Mine's Bigger*, p. 3.

25. Ibid., p. 4.

26. Ibid., pp. 3–4.

27. Bianco interview with Perkins.

28. Kaplan, *Mine's Bigger*, p. 240.

29. Anthony Bianco interview with Bob Sherbin.

30. Carly Fiorina, *Tough Choices* (2007 paperback edition), p. 319.

31. Anthony Bianco interview with Jay Keyworth.

32. Bianco interview with Perkins.

33. Perkins email to Baskins, cc Sonsini and Hurd, "Minutes," July 18, 2006. Released by the House Subcommittee on Oversight and Investigations on October 2, 2006.

34. Viet Dinh, "Dunn and Dusted," *Wall Street Journal*, September 26, 2006.

35. Bianco interview with Dunn.

36. Ibid.

37. Minutes of a Regular Meeting of the Board of Directors of Hewlett-Packard Company, July 19–20, 2006.

38. Perkins email to Baskins, Babbio, Baldauf, et al., "May 18th HP Board of Directors Meeting," July 28, 2006, PD00023.

39. Dunn email to Baskins, Sonsini, and Hurd, "May 18th HP Board of Directors Meeting," July 31, 2006, provided to the author by Dunn.

40. Hurd email to Dunn, Baskins, and Sonsini, "May 18th HP Board of Directors Meeting," August 1, 2006, provided to the author by Dunn.

41. Dunn email exchange with Hurd, no subject, August 1–2, 2006, provided to the author by Dunn.

42. Bianco interview with Dunn.

43. Perkins letter to HP directors, August 14, 2006, posted on www.thesmokinggun.com on September 5, 2006.

44. Bianco interview with Dunn.

45. Dunn to Babbio, Baldauf, Hackborn, et al., "Confidential Memo," August 17, 2006, PD 00079.

46. Anthony Bianco interview with Dr. Bethan Powell.

47. Baskins email to Hurd, Dunn, and Sonsini, cc Sherbin, "Alan Murray/ WSJ," August 18, 2006, provided to the author by Dunn.

48. Alan Murray, *Revolt in the Boardroom* (HarperCollins, New York, 2007).

49. Murray email to Sherbin, no subject, August 21, 2006, provided to the author by Dunn.

50. Bianco interview with Perkins.

51. Dinh letter to Morgester, August 21, 2006, released by the California Office of the Attorney General, October 4, 2006.

52. Baskins email to Hurd, Dunn, and Sonsini, no subject, August 24, 2006, provided to the author by Dunn.

53. Dunn email to Hurd, Sonsini, Baskins, and Sherbin, cc Hammergren, Salhany, and Babbio, "Action Planning," August 24, 2006, provided to the author by Dunn.

54. Anthony Bianco interview with Bob Sherbin.

55. Ibid.

56. Stewart, "The Kona Files."

57. Wilson Sonsini Goodrich & Rosati, "Report Regarding Kona Investigations," 8/30/06, WSGR-HP 1470, pp. 5, 11.

58. Ibid., p. 10.

59. Ibid.

60. Dunn email to Babbio, Baldauf, Hackborn, et al., "Wrapping up on last board meeting," September 2, 2006, PD 00083.

61. Hurd, Sonsini, and Baskins, cc Dunn, "Murray update," September 1, 2006, provided to the author by Dunn.

62. Dunn email to Charnas, Hurd, Sherbin, Baskins, and Sonsini, "Draft 8K," September 1, 2006, PDHM00001229.

63. Dunn email exchange with Sherbin, "Draft 8K," August'31, 2006, PDHM0000939.

64. Taaffe email to Sherbin, "8K," September 4, 2006, provided to the author by Dunn.

65. Sherbin email to Dunn, cc Taaffe, "8K," September 4, 2006, provided to the author by Dunn.

66. Sonsini email to Dunn, no subject, September 5, 2006, PDHM00001302.

67. Dunn email exchange with Hammergren, "Revised Draft #9B of 8K, September 5, 2006, PDHM00001302.

68. Bianco interview with Dunn.

69. Ibid.

70. Sherbin email exchange with Dunn, "Q&A," September 5, 2006, PD 00013.

CHAPTER ELEVEN

1. Murray email exchange with Sherbin, "pattie quotes," September 3, 2006, provided to the author by Dunn.

2. Anthony Bianco interview with Alan Murray.

3. David A. Kaplan, "Intrigue in High Places," Newsweek.com, September 5, 2006.

4. Hunt email exchange with Gentilucci, "Phone records scandal at HP," September 6, 2006, HP0006684.

5. Paul Kedrosky, "Patricia Dunn Should Resign," paulkedrosky,com, September 5, 2006.

6. Alan Murray, "Directors Cut: H-P Board Clash Over Leaks Triggers Angry Resignation," *Wall Street Journal*, September 6, 2006.

7. Taaffe email to Sherbin, "WSJ: H-P Board Clash Over Leaks Triggers Angry Resignation," September 5, 2006, provided to the author by Dunn.

8. Anthony Bianco interview with Bob Sherbin.

9. Rachel Konrad, "HP chairwoman under scrutiny after investigation into media leak," Associated Press Newswire, September 6, 2006.

10. Michelle Quinn, "A Valley icon is catalyst to storm," San Jose *Mercury News*, September 7, 2006.

11. Dunn email to Babbio, Baldauf, Hurd, et al., "Day 2," September 7, 2006, provided to the author by Dunn.

12. Dunn memo to Sherbin and Taaffe, cc Hurd, "My thoughts," September 6, 2006, PDHM00011487.

13. Kaplan email to Dunn and Hurd, "Newsweek Coverage," September 6, 2006, provided to the author by Dunn.

14. Kaplan email to Hurd, "Newsweek Coverage, September 6, 2006, provided to the author by Dunn.

15. Sherbin email to Hurd, cc Dunn, "Newsweek coverage," September 6, 2006, provided to the author by Dunn.

16. Sherbin email to Hurd, cc Dunn, no subject, September 6, 2006, provided to the author by Dunn.

17. Dunn email to Sherbin and Hurd, "Newsweek coverage," September 6, 2006, provided to the author by Dunn.

18. Pete Carry and Nicole C. Wong, "Attorney General: Charges likely over HP snooping," San Jose *Mercury News*, September 6, 2006.

19. Damon Darlin, "H.P.'s Chief Defends Efforts to Stop Leaks," *New York Times*, September 8, 2006.

20. Bianco interview with Dunn.

21. Sherbin email to Dunn, "Tomorrow's battle," September 6, 2006, provided to the author by Dunn.

22. Taaffe email to Sherbin, cc Dunn, "HP Media Statement," September 7, 2006, PD 00008.

23. Ibid.

24. Taaffe email to Dunn, cc Sherbin, "Meeting tonight," September 7, 2006, provided to the author by Dunn.

25. Bianco interview with Dunn.

26. Dunn email to Babbio, Baldauf, Hurd, et al., "Day 2," September 7, 2006, provided to the author by Dunn.

27. Redmond email exchange with Dunn, no subject, September 7, 2006, provided to the author by Dunn.

28. Bianco interview with Dunn.

29. Ibid.

30. Sherbin email to Dunn, Hurd, Fimbres, et al., "Apology to pretexted reporters," September 8, 2006, provided to the author by Dunn.

31. David A. Kaplan, "HP Scandal: The Boss Who Spied on Her Board," *Newsweek*, September 18, 2006.

32. Bianco interview with Sherbin.

33. Kaplan, "HP Scandal: The Boss Who Spied on Her Board."

34. Anthony Bianco interview with William Jahnke.

35. Damon Darlin, "E-Mail Offers Peek into Debate," *New York Times*, September 11, 2006.

36. Baldauf email to Hackborn, Salhany, Hurd, et al., "A message with wide distribution by Tom and his lawyer," September 13, 2006, provided to the author by Dunn.

37. Hackborn email to Salhnay, Hurd, Babbio, et al., "A message with wide distribution by Tom and his lawyer," September 13, 2006, provided to the author by Dunn.

38. Bianco interview with Dunn.

39. Steve Oney, "Call Mike Sitrick," *Los Angeles*, July, 2006.

40. Anthony Bianco interviews with Mike Sitrick and Dunn.

41. Bianco interview with Sherbin.

42. Stewart, "The Kona Files."

43. Dunn email to Babbio, Baldauf, et al., no subject, September 11, 2006, provided to the author by Dunn.

44. Nell Minow, "Coverage of H-P 'pretexting scandal misses point," Market watch.com, September 11, 2006.

45. Ina Fried, "Lawmakers, U.S. attorney join leak probe," CNET, September 11, 2006.

46. Ibid.

47. Bianco interview with Dunn.

48. Ibid.

49. Ibid.

50. Ibid.

51. Stewart, "The Kona Files."

52. HP press release, "George Keyworth Resigns as HP Director," September 12, 2006, http://www.hp.com/hpinfo/newsroom/press/2006/060912b.html.

53. Ibid.

54. Ibid.

55. Bianco interview with Perkins.

56. Ibid.

57. Ibid.

58. David A. Kaplan, "HP Scandal: Is It Clear Sailing?" *Newsweek*, September 25, 2006.

59. Rachel Lane and Greg Miles, "Hewlett-Packard Shows 'Crazy, Dysfunctional' Board, Welch Says," Bloomberg, September 12, 2006.

60. Anthony Bianco interview with Jay Keyworth.

CHAPTER TWELVE

1. "Mark Hurd Press Conference Remarks, September 22, 2006, http://news.cnet.com/pdf/ne/2006/Hurd_Press_Remarks.pdf.

2. Anthony Bianco interview with Pattie Dunn.

3. Damon Darlin, "Focus Turns to the Chief of H.P.," *New York Times*, September 22, 2006.

4. Philip Gollner, "California official says has enough to indict in HP case," Reuters, September 12, 2006.

5. "Lockyer's 'Crimes,'" *Wall Street Journal*, September 13, 2006.

6. Stewart, "The Kona Files."

7. Anthony Bianco interview with Tom Perkins.

8. Anthony Bianco interview with Bill Lockyer.

9. Rachel Konrad, "State investigating legality of HP media leak probe tactics," Associated Press, September 7, 2006.

10. Anthony Bianco interview with Robert Sherbin.

11. Brosnahan email to Dunn, no subject, September 21, 2006, provided to the author by Dunn.

12. Peter Burrows, "Exclusive: Mark Hurd on the HP Scandal," Business Week.com, September 26, 2006.

13. Bianco interview with Dunn.

14. Baldauf email to Dunn, no subject, September 22, 2006, provided to the author by Dunn.

15. Bianco interview with Dunn.

16. Ibid.

17. Hackborn email to Dunn, "Thank you," September 24, 2006, provided to the author by Dunn.

18. Bianco interview with Dunn.

19. Anthony Bianco interview with James Brosnahan.

20. Ibid.

21. Bianco interview with Dunn.

22. HP press release, "Patricia Dunn Resigns from HP Board," September 22, 2006, www.hp.com/hpinfo/newsroom/press/2006/060922a.html.

23. Ibid.

24. "Transcript: Mark Hurd's Sept. 22 press briefing remarks," www.hp.com/hpinfo/newsroom/press_kits/2006/boardconf/transcript_hurd.pdf.

25. "Transcript: Michael Holston's Sept. 22 press briefing remarks," www.hp.com/hpinfo/newsroom/press_kits/2006/boardconf/transcript_holston.pdf.

26. Maria Bartiromo, anchor, CNBC broadcast transcript from Video Monitoring Services of America, 4:00 to 5:00, September 22, 2006. The other panelists who appeared with Dinh were Harvey Pitt, Rob Enderle, and Tom Dewey.

27. Paul Kedrosky, "HP Live!: Dunn is Officially Gone," paul.kedrosky.com, September 22, 2006.

28. Damon Darlin, "At Hewlett-Packard, a Chief Wounded by Divided Attention," *New York Times*, September 25, 2006.

29. Mark Curriden, "Lions of the Trial Bar: James Brosnahan," *ABA Journal*, March 2009.

30. Ibid.

31. Bianco interview with Dunn.

32. Bianco interview with Brosnahan.

33. Jessica Guynn, "HP's Dunn looks toward future," *San Francisco Chronicle*, September 21, 2006.

34. Dunn email to Hurd, no subject, September 24, 2006, provided to author by Dunn.

35. Bianco interview with Dunn.

36. Bianco interview with Brosnahan.

37. Chatterjee email to Brosnahan and Dunn, cc Keaton and Batoyan, "Conversation with John Hemann," September 24, 2006, provided to the author by Dunn.

38. Bianco interview with Brosnahan.

39. Viet D. Dinh, "Dunn and Dusted," *Wall Street Journal*, September 26, 2006.

40. Patrick Hosking, "Snooping on HP board a pretext for disaster," *The Times* of London, September 9, 2006.

41. Teri Thompson, Nathaniel Vinton, and Michael O'Keefe, *American Icon: The Fall of Roger Clemens and the Rise of Steroids in America's Pastime* (New York: Alfred A, Knopf, 2009), p. 268.

42. David Brock, *Blinded by the Right: The Conscience of an Ex-Conservative* (New York: Three Rivers Press, 2002), p. 264.

43. Damon Darlin and Miguel Helft, "H.P. Before a Skeptical Congress," *New York Times*, September 29, 2006.

44. HP news release, "HP General Counsel Resigns," September 28, 2006, www.hp.com/hpinfo/newsroom/press/2006/060928a.html.

45. Peter Lattman, "The Mysterious, Strapping Stranger," *Wall Street Journal* law blog, September 26, 2006.

46. Bianco interview with Brosnahan.

47. Subcommitee on Oversight and Investigations, "Hewlett-Packard Prex-texting Scandal Hearing," Webcast, http://archives.energycommerce.house.gov/reparchives/108/Hearings/09282006hearing2042/hearing.htm.

48. Bianco interview with Sherbin.

49. Mark Hurd, "Congressional Written Testimony," Hewlett-Packard's Pretexting Scandal hearing, Subcommittee on Oversight and Investigations, September 28, 2006, http://archives.energycommerce.house.gov/reparchives/108/Hearings/09282006hearing2042/Hurd.pdf.

50. Bianco interview with Dunn.

51. Damon Darlin, "Ex-Leader Among 5 Charged in Hewlett Case," *New York Times*, October 5, 2006.

52. Anthony Bianco interview with Dr. Bethan Powell.

53. Damon Darlin, "Journalists Intend to Sue Hewlett-Packard Over Surveillance," *New York Times*, May 7, 2007; and Matt Richtel, "Hewlett-Packard Settles Spying Case," *New York Times*, February 14, 2008.

54. Greg Sandoval, "CNET reporters sue HP for invasion of privacy," CNET, August 15, 2007.

55. Damon Darlin, "H.P. Will Pay $14.5 Million to Settle Suit," *New York Times*, December 8, 2006.

56. Don Clark and Christopher Lawton, "SEC Says H-P Should Have Disclosed Why Director Quit," *Wall Street Journal*, May 28, 2007.

57. "'Bullying' Attack on Patricia Dunn by Author of Book on Hewlett Packard Responded to by Attorney James J. Brosnahan," LawFuel.com, March 1, 2007.

58. Scott Duke Harris and Therese Poletti, "State offers deal in HP case," San Jose *Mercury News*, January 18, 2007. Curiously, the state's settlement offer came days after the other Action Research defendant, Bryan Wagner, cut a deal with federal prosecutors to plead guilt to two felony counts of theft and conspiracy. Wagner admitted to illegally obtaining the Social Security numbers of pretexted HP directors and journalists. Wagner still has not been sentenced.

59. Bianco interview with Brosnahan.

60. Ibid.

61. Dunn letter to Hurd, Ryan, et al., no subject, undated, provided to the author by Dunn.

62. Perkins, *Valley Boy*, p. 14.

63. Scott Duke Harris, "The Tom Perkins Way," San Jose *Mercury News*, October 21, 2007.

64. Iain Thomson and Shaun Nichols, "Top 10 Worst Chief Executives," *PC Authority*, November 24, 2008.

65. Bianco interview with Perkins.

66. Bianco interview with Dunn.

67. Ibid.

68. "HP Chief Joins Whistle Blower on News Corp Board," Reuters, February 12, 2008.

69. Anthony Bianco interview with Jeffrey Sonnenfeld.

70. Dunn email to Brosnahan et al., "Conversation with Mark Hurd," September 5, 2007, provided to the author by Dunn.

INDEX

ANTHONY BIANCO wrote for *Business Week* for twenty-seven years, authoring more than fifty *Business Week* cover stories. He is the author of four books, most recently *Ghosts of 42nd Street: A History of America's Most Infamous Block* and *Wal-Mart: The Bully of Bentonville*. He lives in Brooklyn, New York.

PublicAffairs is a publishing house founded in 1997. It is a tribute to the standards, values, and flair of three persons who have served as mentors to countless reporters, writers, editors, and book people of all kinds, including me.

I. F. Stone, proprietor of *I. F. Stone's Weekly*, combined a commitment to the First Amendment with entrepreneurial zeal and reporting skill and became one of the great independent journalists in American history. At the age of eighty, Izzy published *The Trial of Socrates*, which was a national bestseller. He wrote the book after he taught himself ancient Greek.

Benjamin C. Bradlee was for nearly thirty years the charismatic editorial leader of *The Washington Post*. It was Ben who gave the *Post* the range and courage to pursue such historic issues as Watergate. He supported his reporters with a tenacity that made them fearless and it is no accident that so many became authors of influential, best-selling books.

Robert L. Bernstein, the chief executive of Random House for more than a quarter century, guided one of the nation's premier publishing houses. Bob was personally responsible for many books of political dissent and argument that challenged tyranny around the globe. He is also the founder and longtime chair of Human Rights Watch, one of the most respected human rights organizations in the world.

•   •   •

For fifty years, the banner of Public Affairs Press was carried by its owner Morris B. Schnapper, who published Gandhi, Nasser, Toynbee, Truman, and about 1,500 other authors. In 1983, Schnapper was described by *The Washington Post* as "a redoubtable gadfly." His legacy will endure in the books to come.

Peter Osnos, *Founder and Editor-at-Large*